The Complete Idiot's Te

CW00594615

The Most Common Office 95 Too

The Office 95 programs share quite a few common toolba
of commonly used buttons: what they look like and what

ICON	FUNCTION
	Opens a new file
	Opens an existing file
	Saves the file you're working on
	Prints the file
	Previews the file before printing
	Checks spelling
	Cuts selected item and moves it to the Clipboard
	Copies selected item and places copy in the Clipboard
	Pastes selected item from Clipboard
	Undoes the last action you performed
	Repeats a previous action
Times New Roman	Font
10	Font size
B	Bold
I	Italic
U	Underline
	Aligns left
	Centers
	Aligns right
100%	Zoom control
	TipWizard
	Help

Use Your Office Shortcut Bar

One of the easiest ways to get around your Office 95 programs is with the Office Shortcut bar. Here's a brief description of each Shortcut button I recommend placing on the bar.

ICON	FUNCTION
	Starts a new Office file
	Opens an existing Office file
	Starts Word
	Starts Excel
	Starts PowerPoint
	Starts Schedule+
	Opens Answer Wizard for online help

Things to Look For on Your Windows 95 Screen

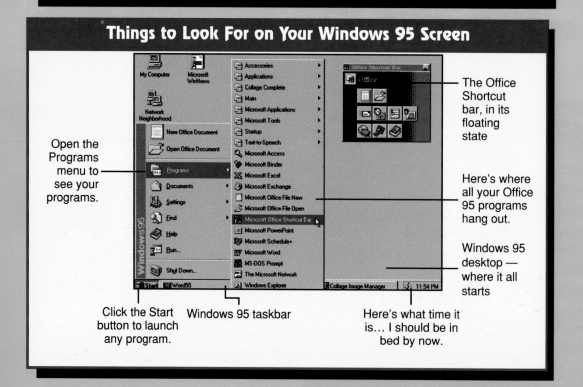

Open the Programs menu to see your programs.

The Office Shortcut bar, in its floating state

Here's where all your Office 95 programs hang out.

Windows 95 desktop — where it all starts

Click the Start button to launch any program.

Windows 95 taskbar

Here's what time it is… I should be in bed by now.

The COMPLETE IDIOT'S GUIDE TO

Microsoft Office 95

by Sherry Kinkoph

A Division of Macmillan Computer Publishing
A Prentice Hall Macmillan Company
201 West 103rd Street, Indianapolis, Indiana 46290 USA

To my dear friend, Stacey Federhart, who, to the best of my knowledge, has never even touched a stupid old computer, unless you count ATM machines.

©1995 by Que® Corporation

International Standard Book Number: 0-7897-0453-6

Library of Congress Catalog Card Number: 94-79168

98 97 96 95   8 7 6 5 4 3 2 1

Interpretation of the printing code: the rightmost double-digit number is the year of the book's first printing; the rightmost single-digit number is the number of the book's printing. For example, a printing code of 95-1 shows that this copy of the book was printed during the first printing of the book in 1995.

Screen reproductions in this book were created by means of the program Collage Plus from Inner Media, Inc., Hollis, NH.

Printed in the United States of America

Publisher
Roland Elgey

Vice President and Publisher
Marie Butler-Knight

Editorial Services Director
Elizabeth Keaffaber

Publishing Manager
Barry Pruett

Managing Editor
Michael Cunningham

Product Development Specialist
Seta Frantz

Production Editor
Kelly Oliver

Manuscript Editor
San Dee Phillips

Technical Edit by
Discovery Computing

Book Designers
Barbara Kordesh
Kim Scott

Cover Designer
Karen Ruggles

Illustrator
Judd Winick

Indexer
Ginny Bess

Production Team
*Steve Adams, Angela Calvert, Kim Cofer, Chad Dressler,
Jennifer Eberhardt, Kevin Foltz, Dave Garratt, George Hanlin,
Aleata Howard, Barry Jordan, Damon Jordan, Bob LaRoche, Joe Millay,
Erika Millen, Regina Rexrode, Erich J. Richter, Mike Thomas,
Suzanne Tully, Christine Tyner, Karen Walsh, Paul Wilson, Robert Wolf*

Contents at a Glance

Contents

4 Windows 95 Guerilla Training   31

5 Covering All the Office 95 Basics   51

18 Put Your PowerPoint Presentation in Order   239

Introduction

What's Going On?

What's the deal with this computer software stuff? Every time you turn around, companies come out with a newer version of this or that and then expect you to run out and buy it. Meanwhile, your head's still spinning from trying to figure out the old version you were working with. Not only that, but they tell you how much they've improved the new program, and without it, you'll never succeed in this world. Naturally, you want to be successful, or at least look like you are, so you run out and upgrade or purchase the latest and greatest version. Then you have to start over and learn all the new features and figure out how to make them work. This puts you in a constant pattern of buying and relearning, buying and relearning—all to keep pace with the technology.

What about those guys (we won't name names) who package four or five different programs into one box to make you think you're getting a really good deal? When you buy one of those boxes, you're not just wrestling with one new program version, but four or five of them, all at the same time. What a pain! I don't know about you, but who has time these days to wade through relearning four or five programs every year or two just to keep up with technology? This isn't technological progress, it's technological torture.

They've Changed Everything!

Welcome to computer software reality, you weary consumer, you. This time around, they've changed all of your precious Microsoft Office programs. Why did they do that? Just to make your computing life miserable, that's why. Actually, the real reason why is that there's a new and improved version of Microsoft Windows called *Microsoft Windows 95*.

Microsoft Windows 95 is a greatly enhanced way for you to run your computer system. Because it's so different from the old Windows, everybody's creating new software programs or versions to run on it—"everybody" includes the Microsoft Office creators. In the natural order of computer evolution, there is but one governing law. It goes something like this: With every new operating system comes new software to use on it. It's a tough but fair law, and every software company in this savage technology jungle follows it. That's where Microsoft Office 95 enters the picture.

Microsoft Office 95 (Office 95, for short) is a whole new set of Office applications created to run on the new Windows 95 interface. Of course, there's nothing wrong with the previous version of Office. All of its applications work on Windows 95, but when you're shopping for a new car, why settle for last year's model? Most of us want to use the latest and the greatest stuff on our computers, so that's why there's a new and improved Office 95. Plus, Windows 95 includes some pretty cool improvements, which is enough incentive for average always-looking-for-a-way-to-improve-my-computer consumers to buy a copy of it and install it on their systems.

So, Why Did You Pick Up This Book?

As you can imagine, there have been quite a few changes made to Office 95, as compared to the previous versions, so you'll definitely need a good book to help you figure them all out. That's why you picked this up, right? Maybe you picked up this book because you're a new convert to the Office applications. Someone in your company may have bought you Office 95 and now you have to learn how to use it—and fast! Don't worry, this book will help you make the most of each application, regardless of whether you're a first-time user or an old Office pro.

Come to think of it, you might have picked up this book because you like the color orange. I know it's a long shot, but it's still a good reason.

What's in This Book?

Now that you're holding the book, I probably should tell you what's in it. *The Complete Idiot's Guide to Microsoft Office 95* explains all about the new versions of the Microsoft Office programs: Word, Excel, PowerPoint, and Schedule+—including how they work and all the spiffy things you can do with them. This book covers everything from word processing, to creating graphics, to using an electronic appointment book. You'll learn how to build spreadsheets and presentations and how to put them to work for you. That's not all—for a limited time only, we'll tell you how to make the programs work together so you can tackle even bigger tasks.

Not that I have to tell you this, but when it comes to software programs, things can get a little intimidating. There's a lot to know about them. Things such as files, formulas, fields, formatting, and words that start with other letters of the alphabet. Yes, there's an ever-evolving lingo to deal with. But that's also why this book will come in handy. You'll learn this lingo and master your Office programs all at the same time. Plus, you'll have fun doing it. That's right—I said *fun*. Have you got a problem with that? Learning about the Office programs doesn't have to be so technical and boring, you know. Lighten up and laugh a little.

So, if you're ready to master Microsoft Office 95 and overcome your new-version headaches, then this book is for you.

How Is This Book Going to Help?

Basically, this book will help you:

➤ Grasp all the basics you need to know about the Office 95 programs clearly and simply. (Don't for a minute think you have to know "everything" to use a program. You don't want to be a computer geek, do you?)

➤ Learn the necessary steps for performing the various tasks associated with each program.

➤ Master the ins and outs of using Office 95 to create documents of all kinds, design graphic presentations with pizzazz, make complex figures simple with spreadsheets, keep an electronic calendar, and much more.

➤ Enter a world where you learn to use all of the products together. For some of you, this may mean a vice-presidency, full-market domination, and global power and prestige... or it could just mean you finally learn to make a slide presentation out of your Word report.

How Do You Use This Book?

Well, I suggest you read the parts that interest you or that you need help with, or the parts about new features. There's no need to read this from cover to cover, unless you have some major free time on your hands, or can't find anything else to entertain you (like when your cable goes out). The book has four sections:

Part 1 is all about Office 95 basics and covers the nitty-gritty, what-are-all-of-these-programs-anyway stuff. It includes information about using Windows 95, installing the programs, and even a crash course that goes over all of the common elements found in each Office program.

Part 2 will help you with the various Office 95 programs. You'll find chapters detailing how to use Word, Excel, PowerPoint, and Schedule+. You'll learn how to make your documents, spreadsheets, and presentations look good, which in turn makes you look good. Not that you aren't already good-looking enough.

Part 3 takes you through the various features for connecting the Office 95 programs, including a look at the mysterious object linking and embedding concept, called OLE.

Part 4 gives you steps for using all of the programs together. You'll explore ways for combining program capabilities such as using an Excel worksheet in a Word document and more.

At the end of the book, you'll find a glossary of all the crazy terms you'll need to know in order to use the programs.

Wait, There's More

In explaining all of this Office 95 stuff, there are times you'll need to type something into your computer. Anything you need to type or click on appears in bold, like this:

> **Type this in**

If there's any variable information to be typed in, such as your own name or a file name, it appears in italics, like this:

> **Type this *number* in**

In addition, there's a special font used for dialog box elements to help you quickly find what you're looking for. If you need to know the name of a certain check box, for example, it will look like this: Show Tool Tips.

You'll find extra boxed information scattered throughout the book to help you with terminology, boring technical background, shortcuts, and other tips. You certainly don't have to read these little boxes, although I did work hard putting them together for you. If you want to understand more about a topic, you'll find these boxes helpful or perhaps vaguely interesting.

Techno Talk

These boxes contain technical twaddle that will make you drowsy. Only read them if you're planning to appear on *Jeopardy!*, the game show for people who wish they'd been born computers. Just kidding. Look to these boxes when you want to find definitions and explanations of technical words and operations.

Check This Out!

Hey, you'll like reading these boxes. They contain tips, tricks, shortcuts, and other ways to cheat your computer out of a long, boring procedure. Plus, I'll throw in fascinating tidbits for you, just to keep things exciting.

It Has Changed!

To quickly discover the differences between the old version of Office and the new Office 95 programs, read these boxes. Skim through the book looking at these boxes to learn the changes in every new Office 95 program.

Okay. That's everything about this book. If you bought it already, you're all set to begin. If you haven't bought the book but are one of those people who reads the introduction before making a purchase, then stop wasting time and go pay for it before the store clerk starts giving you the evil eye.

Acknowledgments

Now for the obligatory author-thanks-everyone part of the introduction. Special thanks to Barry Pruett for being so creative, and to Martha O'Sullivan for doing all of Barry's dirty work and being so nice about it. Thanks go to Seta Frantz for putting her development expertise to good use. Even more special thanks to San Dee Phillips, who had to read every single word, and to Kelly Oliver, who had to make sure the book made it to the printer on time. Also, extra thanks to our tech editor at Discovery Computing for double-checking all the geeky stuff. Finally, big thanks to everyone in production who worked on this book to make it look nice.

Trademarks

All terms mentioned in this book that are known to be or are suspected of being trademarks or service marks have been appropriately capitalized. Que Corporation cannot attest to the accuracy of this information. Use of a term in this book should not be regarded as affecting the validity of any trademark or service mark.

Part 1
Just What Is
Microsoft Office 95?

Time to unlock the mysteries of Microsoft Office 95. In this part of the book, you'll learn what each Microsoft Office 95 program does and how to install it. You'll also be given a thorough grounding in the common elements found in all of the Office programs and Windows 95. And you know what they say, a journey of a thousand files begins with the first mouse click, or something like that. So, journey with me and unravel the reasons for combining several computer programs into one big package that takes up a whole lot of space on your hard drive. (I hope you remembered to pack a lunch.)

The Top Ten Things You Need to Know About Microsoft Office 95

Welcome to Chapter 1. Sit down and relax. There's nothing more conducive to learning than being in a comfortable environment and having something chocolate alongside you (I read that somewhere and adhere to it religiously).

Before you jump in and learn how to use Office 95, here's a sneak peek at the ten most important things you should know about Office 95 and its many features. Each of these ten topics will whet your appetite and make you drool in anticipation for more information about the subject matter. Of course, I won't leave you drooling for long (because that would be incredibly gross, and it will get this new book all wet)—we'll go over each of these topics in great detail throughout the chapters to come.

10. You Don't Have to Buy Each Program Separately

What a relief, eh? Whether you bought the Standard or Professional edition of Office, you got several great products for one great price. Because all of the products are designed to work together, they promote efficiency—and that ultimately means you get more work done. And you know what happens then, don't you? You'll get a raise or a promotion for all your hard work. Hey, it could happen.

The software costs less when you buy it in the integrated Microsoft Office 95 package. If you need these products now or know you're going to need them eventually, save yourself (or your company) some money and headaches by buying them all at once. (And keep thinking "raise, raise.")

You'll learn more about each of the individual programs in your Office package in Chapter 2 and throughout the rest of this book.

9. All the Programs Work with Windows 95

Now that Windows 95 is out and about, what better way to put it to work than with applications designed specifically for use on it? Each of the Office 95 programs utilize Windows 95's new look and feel. You'll find improvements in how the programs work as well as their speed in carrying out tasks—all because of Windows 95.

8. It's Better Than the Previous Version of Office

Anytime you tamper with an already-great product, be it laundry detergent or software, the tampering should result in marked improvements in the product's performance. This is not always the case—take the great New Coke versus Coke Classic fiasco of the '80s. Sometimes, you can take a good thing too far and really mess it up.

However, when most folks set out to improve something, they generally succeed. Office 95 *is* better than the previous Office packages, so you can rest easy now. I thoroughly endorse the new versions. Sure, I'll still let you know a few of my gripes along the way, but it's basically an improved package. A welcome edition is the Schedule+ program, an electronic calendar for tracking appointments and tasks. You'll find it covered in Part 2 of this book.

7. They All Look Alike

Each program in Office 95 looks very similar. There's a reason for this. You'll find common menus, commands, and toolbars in every application. Once you learn to use these features in one program, you can use them in all the programs. What simplicity! This makes these programs a lot more pleasurable to navigate. Because everything looks similar and is displayed the same way, the chances of getting lost or confused rapidly diminish. You'll learn more about common office features in Chapter 5.

6. They're Easy to Use

If these programs weren't easy to use, nobody would buy them. So, just what makes Office 95 so easy? You don't have to type any fancy command strings at a scary-looking command prompt; you don't have to remember any mumbo-jumbo technical terms; and you don't have to follow any complex algebraic instructions to make the computer do what you want. All you have to do is point and click your mouse to make things happen.

That's pretty efficient! You can practically use the programs in your sleep—which you may find yourself doing if you continue consuming large pasta dishes for lunch like I do.

You'll discover how easy it really is to use the Office programs in Parts 2 through 4 of this book.

5. They're All in One Location

You don't have to go in and out of a dozen different Windows menus or boxes to use the Office 95 programs. They're all conveniently located in a single toolbar that you can place on your screen. This handy toolbar makes it extremely simple to zip in and out of the Office applications. In fact, you can easily run one program while you're in the middle of another. And you can open documents, set up an appointment, or quickly find help—all you do is click the Microsoft Office Shortcut bar. You can learn more about this gadget in Chapter 6.

4. There's No Limit to the Things You Can Do with Office

If you're looking for a package that lets you do everything, then Office 95 is a perfect choice. You can handle all of your word processing tasks with Word, your spreadsheet tasks with Excel, juggle your personal appointments and dates with Schedule+, and whip up a classy slide show with PowerPoint. That covers just about everything you'd want to do with a computer. It also covers everything you'd want to do in an office.

3. You're on the Cutting Edge of Technology

By being one of the first million to purchase Office 95, you've proven yourself to be on the forefront of computer advancements, scaling new heights of software wonders, and boldly venturing where only over-worked, deadline-dashed programmers have dared to go. You should pat yourself on the back for possessing such prescient vision into the future of computer office operations.

2. You'll Have a Better Understanding of How Your Computer Works

Most of us don't set out to do this when we learn a new program, but believe it or not, once you fully understand how Office 95 works, you will have pretty much grasped the whole concept of using computer software to get things done. As you learn how to accomplish various tasks, you'll also learn how your computer software functions. It will happen without you knowing it—kind of like osmosis or something.

1. Darn It, It's Just Plain Fun

Finally, the number one reason for using Office 95—*it's fun, darn it, fun!* You really don't need any other reason than this. It's really cool to have all of these great programs at your fingertips. You don't have to use them for strictly serious stuff, you know. Want me to name a few things you can do? Well, you can whip out anonymous letters to your political opponents with Word, track your mate's spending habits with Excel, design a funky slide show for your kid's history report using PowerPoint, or keep track of your therapy appointments with Schedule+. It's up to you to be creative, so don't just sit there, turn the page and start.

Chapter 2

So, What Is Microsoft Office 95?

In This Chapter

➤ An explanation of what the Microsoft Office 95 programs are and what they do

➤ See what's different in Office 95 compared to the previous version of Office

➤ Answer the nagging question: "Can you still have fun with Microsoft Office?"

Let's start with a chapter that tells you all about each Microsoft Office 95 program. If you're already an old pro at using Microsoft programs, feel free to skip to the sections that you want to know more about or scan through to learn what features have been changed or added. If you're a novice computer user, you'd better stick around and find out what's going on.

Are You a Newbie?

Just how much of a computer novice, or newbie, are you? If you're confused by such terms as **file** and **hard drive**, you need to back up and read another book before trying this one. You need a comprehensive introduction to computers; I suggest you read *The Complete Idiot's Guide to PCs* by Joe Kraynak to get a thorough grounding in computer parts and theory, and how they work together. Plus, I personally know Joe and he wouldn't steer you wrong about anything.

One Big Software Package

So what exactly is Microsoft Office 95, other than a fancy name for throwing several programs together into one big marketing deal? Office 95 is several software applications sold as one complete package. The Standard edition of Microsoft Office 95 includes the programs Word, Excel, PowerPoint, and Schedule+. The Professional edition includes those four programs plus Access. All of the Microsoft Office 95 programs are specifically made to run under Microsoft Windows 95.

Is It a Program or Is It an Application?

It's both. You'll hear the words **program**, **software**, and **application** used interchangeably. They all mean the same thing: a special set of instructions written for the computer, telling it how to do something.

Most people would probably purchase each of the Office 95 programs separately as they needed them. They would probably start out with the word processing or spreadsheet program, and eventually buy the others when the time came (or when the tax refund arrived, whichever came first). However, in a seemingly brilliant marketing plan, Microsoft started offering these programs in one package at a bargain price. Now you can have all of the programs at once. Not only that, but Microsoft even added some special features for integrating the programs and making them work together. Office 95 provides virtually all the software programs needed for running an office or a small business. Many companies use Microsoft Office as the standard for getting their jobs done.

Are You Standard or Professional?

There are two editions of Office 95: a Professional edition and a Standard edition. The Professional edition comes with an additional program. For those of you who bought the Standard edition of Microsoft Office 95 and are starting to panic because you don't have as many programs as Professional edition owners, just calm down. That extra program that comes with the Professional edition is a database program called Access. Before you start worrying about whether you need a full-blown database program, you need to know that you can use Excel to create simple databases. So, don't think that you're missing out on anything.

What Do You Do with All These Programs?

Each of the Office 95 programs has a particular purpose, and each program is a valuable tool for getting work done. Although each of the programs can stand on its own, without actually having real legs, they become even more powerful when you begin linking them together to perform tasks. How about a run-down of the Office 95 programs and what you can do with each one? I thought you'd be excited about that. Here we go... .

Word

Even if you've never heard of Office 95 before, you can figure out what this particular application does based on its name. Word, now up to version 7.0, is a word processing program that enables you to create all kinds of text documents, such as letters, memos, business plans, and brochures and even complex documents, such as a book of your memoirs or your monthly grocery list. The best thing about Word is that, with it, you can add clip art, create tables, insert graphics, and make all kinds of changes to your text before you ever print anything out. You couldn't do that with the reigning office standard of yesteryear: the typewriter.

Not that you wanted to know this, but word processing programs are the most popular forms of software purchased today. I'll tell you more about Word in Chapters 7–11, but I'll give you a peek at its new 95 look now.

The lovely Word screen. Does it look new and improved to you?

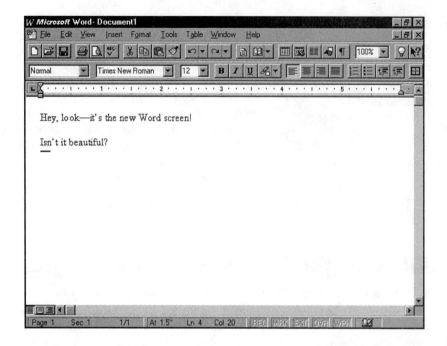

Excel

A spreadsheet program designed for working with numbers, Excel is an accountant's dream program. Just mentioning the name Excel can make most accountants' eyes sparkle. But you don't have to love numbers to get excited about Excel. Excel's a useful program for anybody, and you don't always have to crunch numbers with it—you can use it to organize all kinds of information.

Excel functions as an electronic ledger with rows and columns for entering all kinds of data. In addition to organizing data, Excel also performs mathematical functions on the data in a blink of an eye (or a sparkle, depending on whose eye it is). You can use Excel to generate numerous reports on financial information, create charts and graphs, and more. If you've never worked with a spreadsheet program before, you may be happy to know that Excel is one of the best programs available today. I'll tell you more about Excel in Chapters 12–15; in the meantime, here's what it looks like.

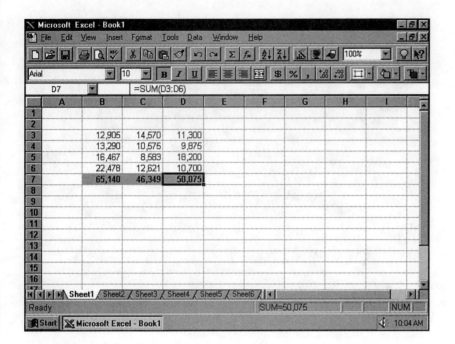

The exciting Excel program.

PowerPoint

PowerPoint is a graphics presentation program. What *is* a graphics presentation program? It's a program for turning computer data into visual presentations, such as slides and overhead transparencies. For example, a graphics presentation program can help you turn that great chart you made with Excel showing your department's quarterly sales increases into a visual presentation for your next management meeting. Get the picture? (No pun intended.) PowerPoint is a great communication tool, and you'll learn how versatile and important it is in Chapters 16–18.

The new PowerPoint 95, a graphics presentation machine.

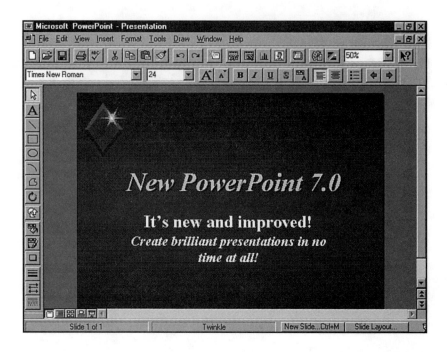

Schedule+

Schedule+ is an electronic calendar and scheduling program added to the Office 95 group. It's perfect for keeping track of meetings, special dates, tasks, contacts, and much more.

It Has Changed!
The old versions of Microsoft Office didn't come with Schedule+.

What's particularly appealing about Schedule+ is its versatility when networked with other computers. You can use it to set up group meetings with others on your network. If you're not networked, you'll still find the program valuable in helping you organize your daily, weekly, and monthly schedules. You'll learn about using Schedule+ in Chapters 19–21.

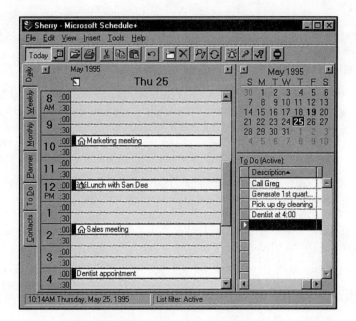

*Here's what
Schedule+ looks like.*

What's New in Office 95?

Time to find out what is new in Office 95 compared to the previous versions of Office. This may be of no interest to first-time Office 95 users, but you Office veterans will want to know what's different.

➤ **The Answer Wizard** Microsoft has added a new edition to their online Help system to assist you with every aspect of Office 95: the Answer Wizard. You just type in what you want to know; the Answer Wizard displays solutions and sometimes goes so far as to demonstrate how to perform a task. I have begun to notice that Microsoft seems to be obsessed with the name "wizard." They tend to call every whiz-bang feature a wizard. Strange, huh? Come to think of it, I did see a picture somewhere of Bill Gates wearing a pointy hat and a cape and waving a wand. So, maybe there's something to this wizardry stuff. Learn more about the Answer Wizard in Chapter 5.

➤ **Office Binders** This is a cool one; Microsoft has linked the Office 95 programs so that you can combine files from each application and put them into a binder (an electronic binder, of course). So? Well, you can then edit and print them as a single file. Pretty impressive. Now you can bind documents from Word, Excel, and PowerPoint to make a combined piece of work. Learn all about binders in Chapter 25.

➤ **Office Shortcut bar**   There's a new Microsoft Office manager bar in Office 95: a Shortcut bar. It lets you access documents and programs with a simple click, rather than having to open an application and find a file. It also contains a few new features, which you'll soon learn about in Chapter 6.

➤ **Find Fast technology**   This little feature keeps your files organized; you'll think there's a live librarian inside your computer. The Find Fast feature lets you manage and organize your files using indexing tools. When you're ready to look something up, just type in the word or sentence, and *kazam*—every file containing that text is located in seconds. (See Chapter 5 for more information.)

➤ **TipWizard**   It's another wizard—the TipWizard is designed strictly for giving you tips on how to best perform a task. Its entire name is the TipWizard Assistant, and it's kind of like having an instructor standing over your shoulder telling you how to do something. (You'll encounter the TipWizard concept yourself in the chapters about Word and PowerPoint.)

➤ **AutoCorrect**   Remember that great AutoCorrect feature Word 6 used to correct misspellings automatically when you typed them in? Well, now you can find AutoCorrect in every Office 95 program. No more excuses for misspelled words in your text, no matter what program you're using! (See Chapter 11.)

➤ **WordMail**   They've added an e-mail feature to Word to help you create e-mail messages with greater formatting controls and flexibility. You knew the world of e-mail messaging was going to get competitive soon, and here it is. You can now have snazzier-looking e-mail.

➤ **Template Wizard**   You can never have enough templates; Excel has a Template Wizard that lets you turn your own spreadsheets into templates to make more spreadsheets. Not only that, but there is an automated tracking system for storing template fields in a database of template components. (See Chapter 12.)

➤ **Internet Assistant**   For those of you who spend a lot of time exploring the Internet, you'll be happy to know about the Internet feature to Word that lets you create documents for the World Wide Web.

➤ **Data Map**   You can now place geographically based information (maps) into your Excel spreadsheets with this feature. (Microsoft's Setup program asks you during installation if you want to install this feature. If you said yes, it's installed. If you didn't, you can go back and install it at a later time.)

Those are just some of the many new features of Office 95. As you can see, some of them are advanced, or at least they make you a little woozy thinking about how you're going to use them. Besides these, each Office 95 program has its own new features and whiz-bang improvements to showcase; I'll explain those when we cover each program in detail in Part 2 of this book.

Is This Going to Be Any Fun?

Here's a profound statement for you: Office 95 is only as much fun as you are. Heavy, huh? Computers don't have to be the boring hunks of hardware that they appear to be. You can have a lot of fun with them, even in the office when you're working (however, they're even more fun when you're goofing off). But Office 95 isn't just for working at the office; there are many ways to use these products for your personal hobbies, interests, and financial planning. Like what, for instance?

➤ How about compiling a database of all your friends and relatives that you send Christmas cards to? You can do that and even create mailing labels.

➤ What about all those volunteer organizations you belong to that need, well, organizing? Get involved by helping them maintain their petty cash, creating flyers for the next event, or keeping track of the volunteers and the tasks they sign up for.

➤ Planning to buy a new house? Use an Excel worksheet to calculate mortgage rates, interest points, and other real estate information.

➤ Does your child have a science fair project due soon? Help him create a slide program using PowerPoint.

➤ Quit knocking yourself out trying to keep track of science fair projects, anniversaries, and power-lunches; use Schedule+ to stay ahead of your busy life.

➤ Have an urge to write the next great American novel or Hollywood's next trillion-dollar screenplay? Use Word to do it all.

➤ And what about those retirement and financial plans you've been thinking about, but are dreading to begin? Use Excel, Word, and even PowerPoint to help you with that very important planning.

Those are just a few serious suggestions, and I haven't yet begun to scratch the surface.

The Least You Need to Know

There are many things you can do with Office 95 that will make your life easier, so you'd better get started right away. Here's what you discovered in this chapter:

➤ The Standard edition includes Word, Excel, PowerPoint, and Schedule+. (The Professional edition includes Access, but don't worry about it.)

➤ Each of the programs has a specific purpose, but you can use them together for even greater power. Program integration is the key to getting the most out of Office 95.

➤ Using Office 95 is going to be a lot of fun; you're only limited by your imagination.

Chapter 3

Doing the Installation Dance

In This Chapter

➤ Quickly get Microsoft Office 95 up and running

➤ Learn the secrets to installing Office 95 from a CD-ROM

➤ Tips for uninstalling an Office program without blowing up your computer

Back in the olden days of computer software, installation was a tricky feat—a complicated dance of directories, files, and floppy-disk shuffling. But now, most programs come with a simple setup utility for installing software onto your computer's hard disk drive. (A utility program is a special computer program to help you manage things such as assisting with program installation.)

You can install Office 95 in a variety of ways, and you know what they say: variety is the spice of life. You can install Office 95 from floppy disks or a CD-ROM; if you're networked, you can install it from the network server or another shared network location. The first step to installing is figuring out which scenario applies to you and your situation.

Define File and Directory, Please!

A **file** is any computer data that you save on your computer. You can distinguish between files by their names. Your hard disk drive can store thousands of files. In order to keep your files organized so you can find them again, you used to store them in **directories**. A directory is like a filing cabinet drawer on your hard drive. In Windows 95, however, files are stored in **folders**—which are the same thing as directories.

The setup program takes care of most of the installation work. All you have to do is check on its default settings (initial settings chosen by the computer) when prompted and slip some disks in and out. What could be better than that? Well, if you happen to be the proud owner of a CD-ROM drive, and you bought Microsoft Office 95 on a CD-ROM, that could be better. Installing from a CD-ROM is a lot faster than installing from floppy disks, and it's just as simple to do. If you're installing Office 95 from a network, however, you'll need to ask your network administrator for assistance. Network installation works a little differently, depending on the type of network you have.

So let's start. In the remainder of this chapter, I'll show you the simple dance steps for installing the various Office 95 programs using the disks and the CD-ROM. Get ready to rumba.

Ye Olde System Requirements

Hold it, hold it, hold it. Before you can begin the installation process, you must have Microsoft Windows 95 loaded on your computer. This is crucial. You won't be able to install Microsoft Office 95 until you have Windows 95 up and running.

Windows 3.1 vs. Windows 95

If you're new to the Windows scene, you may be a little confused by my Windows banter. All Windows are not the same. You see, Windows 95 is a new and improved version of Windows 3.1. Windows 95 runs without relying on DOS, and it's faster, more intuitive, and tons more fun. Try not to confuse Windows 3.1 and Windows 95—they are two different animals.

You'll also need to make sure you have enough space (the computer's electronic storage area) on your hard drive if that's where you're installing Office 95. (This is pretty crucial.) For the typical installation, you'll need 55M of hard disk space. You'll need 89M if you pursue the custom installation.

If you're installing from a network setup, be sure to talk to your network administrator for tips on what to do.

IMPORTANT! If you have a virus-detection program running on your computer, be sure to disable it before you start the setup program. It could cause some problems during installation. Check your virus-detection program's manual for help in turning off the program.

Virus Detection? What's That?
A **virus** is a computer program written for the express purpose of vandal-izing your system or harming your data files. A **virus-detection program** can prevent a virus from infecting your computer. Lots of computer users have virus protection programs, such as Norton Anti-Virus, installed on their computers.

Any Other Requirements?

If you're wondering about other hardware requirements, you should have a 386 or greater microprocessor in your computer. You'll also need a VGA, or higher, monitor resolution. If you plan on using PowerPoint a lot, you'll need a 256-color video adapter. You'll also need a mouse. Have you got all that?

If you're getting nervous about any of these requirements, stop right now. Most computers sold today are 486 models, with VGA monitors and better. Besides, you can always crack open your Office 95 manual and consult it for hardware constraints that may be specific to your computer system or scenario.

Installation Dance Steps

As long as you've met the system requirements, have Windows 95 up and running, and are in possession of the Microsoft Office 95 package, you're ready to tango—I mean *install*. The following sections will focus on specific installation types.

Installing from Floppy Disks

If you're installing Office 95 from floppy disks, be prepared to spend some time inserting and removing a seemingly endless stream of floppy disks from your computer. But, don't dismay: the installation process, although long, is simple.

Check This Out...

What Start Button? If you're a new Windows 95 user, you might want to skip over to Chapter 4 for a run-through of how Windows 95 works with its new features.

These steps will take you through installing Office 95 from floppy disks. Make sure Windows 95 is running and that all other applications are closed before you start. Also, disable any virus-detection program you may be using.

1. Insert the first Office installation disk, labeled Disk 1, into the floppy drive.

2. Click the **Start** button on your Windows 95 taskbar; then select **Settings**, **Control Panel** (shown in the figure below) from the menus.

Find your way to the Windows 95 Control Panel.

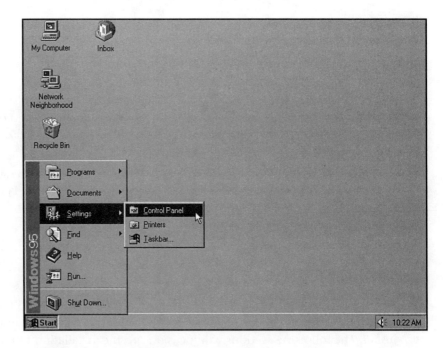

3. Locate the Add/Remove Programs icon in the Control Panel box. Double-click the icon to open the Add/Remove Program Properties dialog box.

Double-click this icon to
install a new program.

*You'll find a special
option for installing
programs in your
Windows 95 Control
Panel.*

4. The lovely Add/Remove Programs Properties dialog box displays three tabs. You'll
want to make sure the Install/Uninstall tab is at the front of the dialog box. You can
do this by clicking on its tab name. Then click the **Install** button.

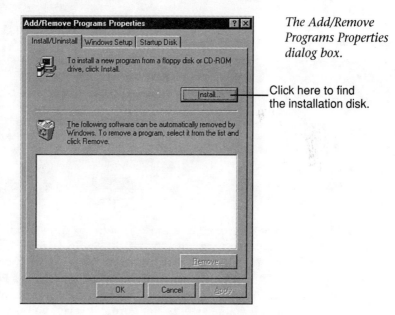

*The Add/Remove
Programs Properties
dialog box.*

Click here to find
the installation disk.

It Says It Can't Find the Installation Program

Don't panic. You can click the **Browse** button and then look for Setup among the directories and drives. Or you can type in the drive containing the disk and setup program's name (SETUP.EXE). Your text box might then look something like this: A:\SETUP.EXE; then click the **Finish** button.

5. This will open the Install dialog box, a rather vacant box that simply tells you to insert the installation disk and click the **Next** button. So do that, if you haven't already. When you do, Windows searches the disk for the setup program. When found, its name suddenly appears in a text box on your screen. Click the **Finish** button to start the Office Setup program.

6. As the Setup program begins (see the figure below), follow the on-screen instructions that lead you through the setup process. You'll be prompted to type your name and organization, type your product ID (or CD key), and you'll even see your product ID number. Be sure to write this number down and keep it somewhere safe; you'll need it if you ever have to call up the technical support people to ask a question.

You'll know you've successfully started the Setup program when you see this box on your screen.

7. You'll also be prompted to choose a folder, as shown in the next figure, where you want to install the programs. By default, Setup offers to install the programs to your C drive in a folder called MSOffice. Click **OK** to do so. If you don't like the default folder the Setup program suggests, just click the **Change Folder** button and type in a new folder. For most of us, the default folder is just fine; in fact, that's what I recommend. If you're a computer guru, however, you may have a different agenda in mind, in which case you can install the programs wherever you want.

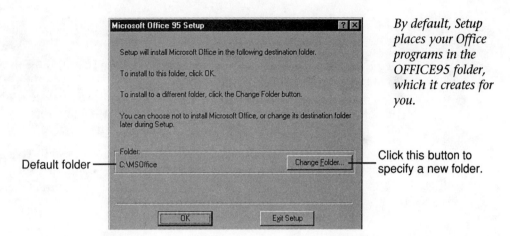

By default, Setup places your Office programs in the OFFICE95 folder, which it creates for you.

Default folder

Click this button to specify a new folder.

8. After all the introductory jazz (your name, organization, and so on), Setup displays the Microsoft Office 95 Setup dialog box, shown in the next figure. Here, you'll find four installation options to choose from: Typical, Compact, Custom, and Run from CD-ROM (if you are installing from a CD-ROM). There's a description beside each option telling you what it does. Select the option you want by clicking on the icon button next to the description. For most users, Typical is the best choice; it installs the most common features that the average computer user wants to have access to.

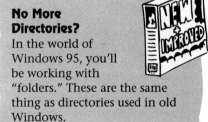

No More Directories?
In the world of Windows 95, you'll be working with "folders." These are the same thing as directories used in old Windows.

This option is your best bet.

Pick a setup option, any option.

What About the Other Installation Options?

Okay, hang on, I'll tell you about those. The Compact option is for those of you trying to squeeze the Office programs onto a laptop computer, or onto a hard drive with limited space. For most laptops, you'll only want to install the bare minimum of files needed to make the programs run. That's because a laptop's hard disk drive can only hold so much.

The Custom option lets you control exactly which Office files you install. This option is best used by experts who spend every waking moment studying such things. The Run from CD-ROM option is for people who plan on running Office from a CD.

9. Depending on the option you select, more on-screen prompts may appear. Simply read the instructions and make the appropriate choices for you and your computer. If you chose the Typical installation, you won't have to deal with these additional boxes.

10. Finally, the installation process begins in earnest. Just follow the on-screen prompts, inserting each disk as needed. A little installation-gauge box appears on-screen, indicating how much of the program is installed.

11. When everything's installed, **Setup** will tell you to restart Windows. Click **Restart Windows** and the computer restarts itself for you. (Or, if you're hooked up with a modem, you can click the **Online Registration** button and automatically register your software. If you're into messing with paperwork, you can also register by mail at a later time.)

Get used to seeing this gauge for a while. It'll appear for each installation disk you insert into the floppy drive.

Here's the last box you'll see in the installation dance.

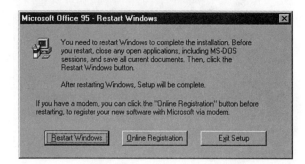

Only 11 installation steps—that doesn't sound so bad, does it? It's not. The worst part is whipping those floppy disks in and out of your drive in step 10. It seems to go on forever. Don't even think about getting up for a snack either, because as soon as you do, the computer is ready for another disk. So what are you supposed to do while you wait for the darn thing to install? I suggest you tidy your desk or count your ceiling tiles.

Pssst! Here's a tip for you. It's a good idea to make backup copies of your Microsoft Office program disks. Then keep the originals in a safe place in case something goes wrong later. Trust me on this one, it could save your life.

Restart Your Computer... Now

While installing, the Setup utility automatically adds the Office Manager feature to your Windows Startup group. This causes Office 95 to open automatically every time you start Windows 95. To see this happen, you'll have to restart your computer as prompted in step 11 in the previous section.

After your computer shuts down for a split second and comes back on, it automatically loads your Office 95 Shortcut bar, as shown in the next figure. (You'll learn all about the Shortcut bar in Chapter 6, so try to be patient.)

Your new Office Shortcut bar!

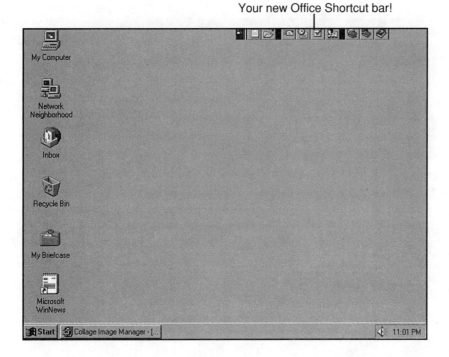

Office 95—loaded and ready to run.

Installing from a CD-ROM

Are you a lucky owner of a CD-ROM drive? You can install Microsoft Office 95 right from a CD-ROM. The best thing about installing from a CD-ROM is that it only takes a few minutes (as opposed to the countless time you could spend inserting and removing floppy disks).

Just follow the same steps I listed under "Installing from Floppy Disks." When you get to step 5, your computer looks for the installation program on your CD-ROM drive. When found, its name appears in a text box, as shown in the next figure.

If your computer is having trouble finding the installation program, you may have to type its name yourself. Type *D:\SETUP.EXE*, but substitute your own CD-ROM's drive letter. Click the **Finish** button, and away it goes. Continue following the preceding steps.

When you get to step 8, remember to choose the **Typical** installation option, which loads the best parts of the Office programs onto your hard disk drive. (If you prefer another type of installation, read the information about other options previously listed.)

From here on, the installation process proceeds smoothly. Compared to those floppy disk users, your installation takes just a few minutes. This only gives you time to count a few ceiling tiles or shuffle a few papers around on your desk, so move quickly.

The Office Setup program name appears in the text box.

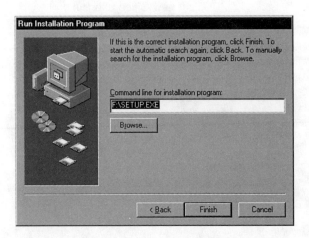

When the installation is complete, you should restart Windows. During the installation procedure, the Setup utility automatically adds the Office Manager feature to your Windows Startup program group. This causes Office 95 to open automatically every time you start Windows 95.

What If There's Trouble?

What could possibly go wrong, huh? Well, if you do encounter any trouble during the installation process, be sure to consult your user's manual for more information. I'd love to help you myself, but there's no way I can predict what kinds of installation trouble you and your computer are going to run into. Don't look so disappointed; I'm only a part-time psychic.

Somewhere among all of the manuals and paperwork that fell out of the Office 95 box, there should be a phone number for Microsoft's technical support people. You can call them for help. (If you can't find it, try 1-800-936-3500.)

Just remember a few things:

➤ You must have enough disk space on your computer to install Office 95; if not, you'll have trouble. This issue alone will probably cause people the most trouble. Why? Because Office 95 eats up a lot of space on your computer.

➤ If you don't have enough room for all of the Office 95 programs, you can just install the ones you'll work with the most. Use the Compact or Custom installation options (step 8 in the installation dance).

➤ Be sure to turn off any virus protection programs you may have running. These types of programs have been known to cause problems with installations.

➤ Also make sure you close any open applications on Windows 95 before you start installing.

➤ Don't forget to back up your installation disks. You may need these backups someday.

Out, Out, Darn Spot... er, Program!

Hey, get a load of this, Shakespeare fans—you can use the Office 95 Setup utility anytime to add or delete Office 95 programs. Pretty cool, eh? You can even use Setup to uninstall the entire set of Office 95 applications. Why would you want to do that? Well, some of you may find you're not using every Office 95 program, so why keep a program on your hard disk drive if you never use it? Uninstalling one or more programs frees up more computer memory and hard disk space, and more space means the computer works more efficiently for you.

> **Check This Out...**
>
> **Wait** Before you try uninstalling with the Office Setup utility, you'll be prompted to close your Office Shortcut bar first. Move your mouse pointer over the bar, right click, and then select **Exit** from the menu.

To remove Office 95 components, follow these steps:

1. To access the Office 95 Setup utility: right-click the **Microsoft Office** icon on the **Shortcut** bar and select **Add/Remove Programs**. Another way is to open the **Control Panel**, select **Microsoft Office** from the **Install/Unistall** tab, and then click the **Add/Remove button**. Either of these paths will open the Setup Maintenance dialog box with four options.

The Setup utility also lets you remove programs as well as install them.

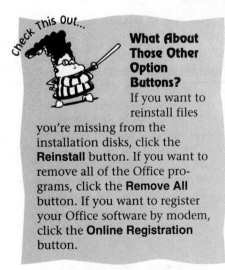

What About Those Other Option Buttons? If you want to reinstall files you're missing from the installation disks, click the **Reinstall** button. If you want to remove all of the Office programs, click the **Remove All** button. If you want to register your Office software by modem, click the **Online Registration** button.

2. Click the **Add/Remove** button to add or remove a specific program. A list of Office 95 applications appears. A check mark in the box next to the program name indicates that the program is installed. An empty check box means that the program (or component) is not installed.

3. To remove an application, click its check box to remove the check mark. Make sure the program name is highlighted, and then click **Continue** or press **Enter**.

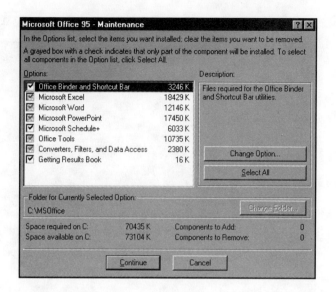

From the Setup Maintenance box, you can remove specific Office 95 programs.

4. Confirm your changes; then Setup begins removing the application you selected and restarts your computer when finished (if it needs to).

That's all there is to uninstalling. Now you can sit back and bask in its simplicity.

You'll Lose Your Data!

Always be careful about removing programs. When you do, you'll be removing your data files (files created using the programs). To prevent this, back up your data files before using the Setup feature.

Okay, I've Installed Everything, Now What?

This is it, the moment you've been waiting for. When you restart your computer after installing Office 95, you'll see the Office 95 Shortcut bar. To see where Setup placed your Office 95 programs, look for the Microsoft Office programs listed in your Programs menu. To open any program, simply click its icon. You can also use the buttons in the Shortcut toolbar to open things; you'll learn all about that in Chapter 6.

*Your Windows 95
Programs menu will
list Microsoft Office
as a folder.*

Office 95 Shortcut bar

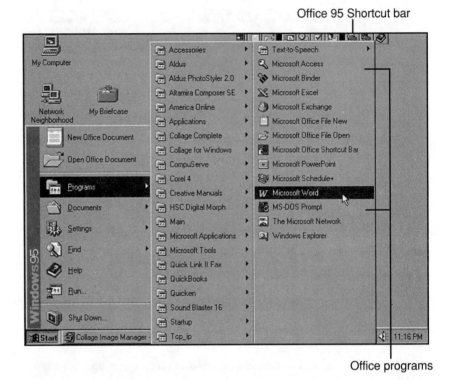

Office programs

The Least You Need to Know

After reading this chapter, you should have all of the Microsoft Office 95 programs
installed on your computer, and you should know these basics:

➤ All of the Office 95 programs are installed using the Microsoft Setup utility.

➤ You'll need plenty of space on your hard disk to install the Office programs.

➤ If you don't need a particular Office 95 program, you can uninstall it using the same
Setup utility, and your computer won't blow up in the process.

AAAAAAHH!!!

Windows 95 Guerilla Training

There's a big, new jungle out there, and it's called Windows 95. If you want to survive, then you need to learn new skills. You need to become familiar with the new terrain, learn where to find the secret foxholes, and equip yourself with the right weapons to hack your way through this jungle. What you need is Windows 95 guerilla training.

Why a chapter on Windows? Because, everybody's doing Windows these days, especially Windows 95. The Microsoft Office programs do Windows, too. So in order to use Microsoft Office 95, you need to know how to use Windows 95 (what astounding logic—I sound like Mr. Spock). In this chapter, I'll give you a quick run-down of how Windows 95 works and what to expect from it.

Check This Out...

Need More Info? Pick up a good book on the subject of Windows 95; try *The Complete Idiot's Guide to Windows 95,* by Paul McFedries. It covers detailed information about all the Windows 95 features.

This knowledge, in turn, will help you use the Office 95 programs. If you're new to Windows 95, read this chapter. If you're already an experienced Windows 95 user, you don't have to read this chapter; you can just wander off into the jungle on your own.

The History of Windows: Where Did It Come from and Why Am I Using It?

Let me tell you a little story. (Pay attention now, this will be on the test later.) Windows originated as a graphical user interface program, called GUI ("GOO-ey"). It was made by Microsoft Corporation, the same people who brought you Microsoft Office. To understand why Microsoft created the first Windows GUI, you first have to understand how gross-looking the underlying system was.

GUI Stands for graphical user interface. A GUI is a graphical program designed to help you interact with the computer that enables you to use icons, menus, and dialog boxes to control the computer tasks you want to perform.

First There Was DOS

Have you ever worked with DOS? Yuck! That's what I'm talking about. DOS is an operating system that tells your computer to act like a computer. DOS was around long before Windows. DOS is still around today, believe it or not. Unfortunately, DOS isn't very pretty to look at. It's command-driven, which means you have to type in cryptic words and abbreviations at a strange-looking prompt symbol to get it to do anything. Naturally, you have to memorize these commands and remember how to type them in correctly each time. In a nutshell, DOS is bland computing for the graphically impaired.

Before Windows...

The command prompt —

The eerie blackness of the DOS screen peering — into your very soul.

```
C:\>cd\msoffice
C:\MSOFFICE>cd\
C:\>
```

Techno Talk

Define These Visual Graphics

An **icon** is a small graphical picture that represents a program or file. All GUI programs use icons.

A **menu** is a list of commands. Menus appear as drop-down or pull-down lists. You select an item from the menu by highlighting it and pressing **Enter** or by clicking on it with the mouse.

A **dialog box** is a smaller window-box displaying more options from which you can choose. Dialog boxes usually appear when the program needs more information from you in order to carry out the task.

Then Came Windows

Thankfully, the Microsoft people designed a program to run on top of DOS that makes the computer easier to use and much nicer to look at. Instead of weird text commands, you control the computer using visual graphics—hence the name *graphical user interface*. All you have to do is click icons (little pictures), select commands from pull-down menus (lists), and open dialog boxes (mini-windows) to make the computer perform various tasks. There's nothing cryptic about any of it! The entire world rejoiced at such a clever program, and Windows quickly proliferated across the land and sea.

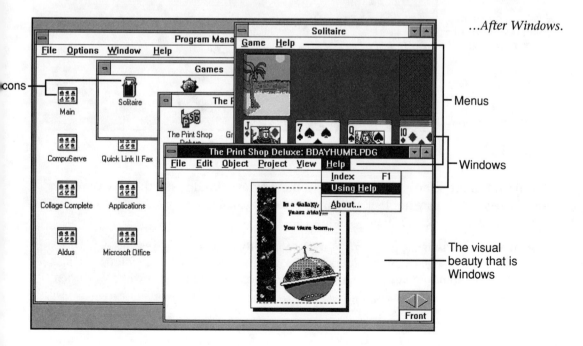

...After Windows.

Then They Made Windows 95

Eventually, the Microsoft people decided they could improve upon Windows, making it even better and easier to use—and eliminating its dependence on DOS. After a while, a seemingly long while, they came out with Windows 95. With Windows 95, you never have to deal with the DOS again (unless you really, *really* want to). Windows 95 is faster, more powerful, and gives you better performance when trying to do several computer things at the same time. Here's what it looks like:

The My Computer icon opens a box
for viewing your computer's contents.

The new and improved Windows 95. Is this a real GUI, or what?

When you press the Start button, you'll display this list.

Start button

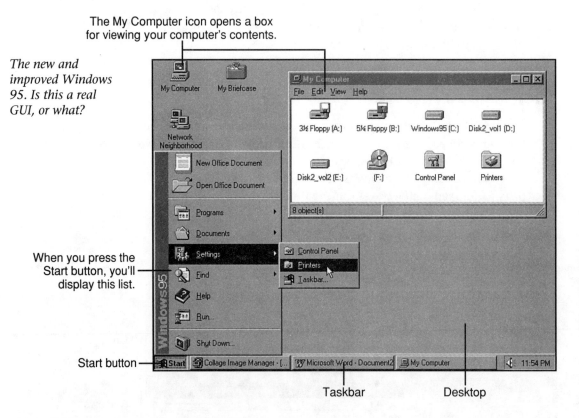

Taskbar   Desktop

You'll find all the same great features from the previous Windows in the new Windows 95. However, they may not look the same, so be prepared for some changes. Here are some new things to know about Windows 95:

➤ Instead of arranging programs and files into program group boxes and directories, you now arrange them in folders in a **Programs** menu. There isn't a Program Manager anymore, just a Programs menu. (You'll find this menu when you open the **Start** menu.)

➤ It's much easier to install hardware and software onto your Windows 95 system—and it's about time.

➤ Microsoft replaced File Manager with the **Windows Explorer**. You can use it to manage files, just like old File Manager, but you access it from the Windows 95 **Start** menu.

➤ You can easily view the contents of your computer's drives by opening the **My Computer** icon. You can also access your Windows 95 Control Panel and Printers folders using this icon.

➤ The Control Panel is still around; you can find it by opening the **Start** menu and choosing **Settings**.

➤ Print Manager's still around, too, using a new name. Access it through the **Start** menu by choosing **Settings**. You'll be happy to know that printing is a major area of improvement in Windows 95. It's easier to add new printers and change settings with the Add Printer Wizard feature.

➤ Networking is easier now with the Windows 95 **Network Neighborhood** icon. This is handy when you're hooked up to other computers in an office situation.

➤ You can dump files you no longer want by tossing them, electronically, into the **Recycle Bin**, a temporary storage place for items you're cleaning off your system.

➤ Have I mentioned the **Start** button yet? You can open any program or document by clicking the **Start** button, which is on a convenient taskbar at the bottom of your Windows 95 screen.

➤ There's a new hardware technology on Windows 95 called Plug and Play. It's infinitely easier to install new hardware devices, without all the headaches of hardware/software clashes.

➤ You'll enjoy the improved multimedia support and game capabilities. That's a hot field in the computer industry now, and it's growing by leaps and bounds.

That's just a brief overview of some of the changes in Windows 95.

Windows Navigation Tools—No Compass Required

If you're an absolute newbie to this Windows 95 thing, then you'll want to learn how to get around on it, right? The next two sections will show you the two main methods for moving around on your computer.

Careful Where You Point That Thing: A Word to New Mouse Users

One of the primary tools for navigating Windows 95 and Windows-based programs is the *mouse.* You can use your mouse to point at items on-screen and move them around. You can use your mouse buttons to select items and perform tasks.

Ever use a mouse before? Don't worry. It gets easier and easier each time you work with it. The mouse is a piece of hardware (so is your printer and keyboard). As you move the mouse around on your desktop, a little arrow appears on-screen and moves as well. That's your *mouse pointer.* It seems a little weird at first, but keep at it; using your mouse will become a natural part of your computer life.

There are four mouse actions to embrace. Learn 'em and love 'em:

Click   To quickly tap lightly on the mouse button, usually the left button unless otherwise specified.

Double-click   To lightly tap on the left mouse button twice in quick succession.

Right-click   To quickly tap lightly on the right mouse button.

Drag   To move the mouse while simultaneously holding down the left mouse button.

Keyboarding Tips

Although the vast majority of people use a mouse to work with Windows 95, I am legally obligated by a mandate from the technical editor to give equal time to the minority keyboard-lovers. Yes, you *can* use the keyboard to navigate the many windows, but it's a lot harder. Harder? Yes, that's what I said—you have to memorize keystrokes to perform certain tasks.

Here's what you need to know for keyboarding around:

➤ **Selection letters**   Underlined letters found on menu commands.

➤ **Shortcut keys or hot keys**   Keystroke combinations you use to perform tasks.

➤ **Arrow keys**   Use to move up, down, left, and right on your screen.

➤ **The helpful Ctrl and Alt keys**   Use to open menus and carry out commands.

Let me explain these. First of all, know your keys. The Ctrl key and the Alt key will become your faithful companions; you use them in conjunction with other keys to activate commands. All of the menu bars and most of the menu commands have under-lined letters in them, called *selection letters*. If you press the Alt key and one of these selection letters, it's the same as opening the menu or selecting the command with the mouse. For example, you can press **Alt+F** to open the File menu. Look for selection letters throughout the Microsoft Office 95 programs.

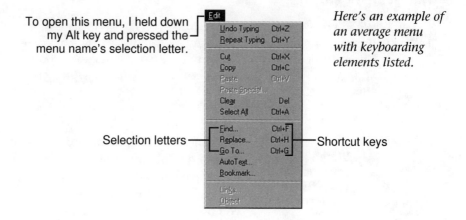

To open this menu, I held down my Alt key and pressed the menu name's selection letter.

Here's an example of an average menu with keyboarding elements listed.

Selection letters

Shortcut keys

Also on the menu lists, you'll find keypress combinations, called *shortcut keys*, for activat-ing commands. If available, these are located right next to the menu commands, and they will come in handy as you become more familiar with the programs. Because they're shortcuts, you can save time and effort in selecting commands.

You'll find yourself using the arrow keys quite a bit, too. They move you around the screen and up and down menu lists. (For more information about keyboard commands, check your Windows 95 or Microsoft Office 95 manuals.) Although the rest of this book focuses on mouse actions, if you prefer to use the keyboard, be my guest. You just won't see a whole lot of keyboard commands mentioned here.

Running (and Jogging) Windows 95

Now that you know what Windows 95 is and some ways to move around in it, you might as well start it up and look around. The next few paragraphs tell you how to run Win-dows 95 and how to exit it, and they take you on a visual tour of the opening screen.

The new Windows 95 starts immediately whenever you turn on your computer system. Mind you, *immediately* isn't necessarily a fast thing on a computer. Most computers, when started, hum and whir for a few seconds, and strange text appears on the screen. After that, the Windows 95 opening screen appears; then you're presented with a logon box.

It's Changed!

When you were using old Windows, you had to log on from a DOS prompt. Those days are over. Since Windows 95 is its own operating system, it doesn't need DOS anymore, so it starts up as soon as you turn your computer on. The logon box is a new feature you'll encounter every time you start Windows 95.

I Need Help with the Logon Box!

Be sure to consult your Windows 95 manual for help with setting up your own logon box with a password. If you set up a password the first time you used Windows 95, you'll have to type it in exactly as you designated it.

You can set up your logon box so that you have to use a password in order to use your computer. This feature is for people who are paranoid that others might use their computers and find all kinds of top secret information. If you have important files that you don't want tampered with, then it's a good idea to set up a password. If you're using a networked computer, you'll also have to use a password to access the network.

Anyway, to get past the logon box:

➤ You'll have to type in your password and click **OK**.

➤ If you haven't set up a password, just click **OK** to log on.

After you've made it past the logon box, Windows 95 opens up. Since you installed Office 95, you'll notice it starts up, too, placing the Office Shortcut bar on your screen. Take a look at the next figure. This is typically what you see after you start Windows 95.

Welcome to your Windows 95 desktop. From here, you can boldly go wherever your mouse pointer can take you. Think of this opening screen as your Windows 95 lobby. From this point, you can run other applications, use other Windows 95 features, and generally go about your own computer business. You'll always start from this opening screen.

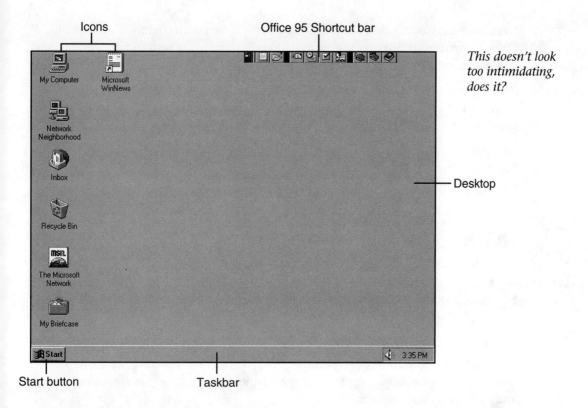

Icons

Office 95 Shortcut bar

This doesn't look too intimidating, does it?

Desktop

Start button

Taskbar

What's on My Screen?

One of the most-repeated descriptions you'll hear about Windows 95 is how *intuitive* the system is—meaning that you'll always be able to tell what everything does. In that case, it's time to play the exciting new game show, "What's on My Screen?" To play this game, you just point at an on-screen item with your mouse and guess at what it does. Are you ready? I'm setting the clock... okay, go. (I'm humming the theme song from *Jeopardy*.)

Give up? Okay, I'll tell you what each on-screen item does:

My Computer This icon opens to reveal all of the drives you have on your computer. You can use this feature to open each drive's contents and find out what folders and files you have. For example, to find out what's on your floppy disk, you can put the disk in your floppy drive, open the My Computer window, and select the floppy disk drive. It will list what's on the disk in the drive. It also lets you access the Control Panel and Printers folders.

Network Neighborhood   Use this icon when you're connected to a network of other computers. It displays the various elements found on your network and lets you use them.

Recycle Bin   This is where you toss things you no longer want on your system, such as old files. When you're ready to remove items, open this icon up and confirm the deletions.

Taskbar   Use the taskbar to open and use one or more programs at the same time. For every program you open, a button for it appears on the taskbar. You can easily click the buttons to switch to other programs.

What Happened to the Old Task List?

In Windows 3.1, you access a Task List for switching between programs you are working with. You press **Ctrl+Esc** to see the list because it isn't readily visible. But Windows 95 lets you do this with the taskbar, which is always on your screen (unless you choose to hide it).

Start button   To start any program, use this button. It displays a Start menu for launching programs, accessing the Control Panel, finding files, finding online help, and shutting down the computer.

Microsoft Network   An online service created by Microsoft. You can use it to communicate and exchange information with people all over the world.

Consult Your Manual
Remember to consult your Windows 95 manual for additional information about using any of the Windows 95 features. Or pick up a good Windows 95 book, like *The Complete Idiot's Guide to Windows 95.*

Locate the Exit Nearest You

Although I know you're not ready to quit Windows 95 yet, let me tell you how to exit it anyway, in case there's a fire or something. At least you'll be prepared. To exit Windows 95, follow these steps:

1. Open the **Start** menu and choose **Shut Down**.

2. In the Shut Down Windows dialog box, choose an appropriate exit option (typically the first one), and then click **Yes**.

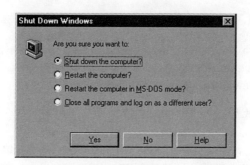

Turn it all off with the Shut Down Windows dialog box.

If you haven't saved your Windows work, Windows will ask you to do so before exiting. A little dialog box pops up with several choices about saving. Think of this as your friendly Windows 95 security guard. You'll be thankful for this feature the day you forget to save the presentation you've been working on for hours.

Looking at Windows a Little Closer

Quite obviously, the reason Microsoft named it Windows (95 or otherwise) is because of all the windows (also called boxes) that open up to reveal programs, tools, and other computer information. Each window has some common elements you'll need to know about. I suppose you're waiting for me to tell you about them, right? Okay, here goes.

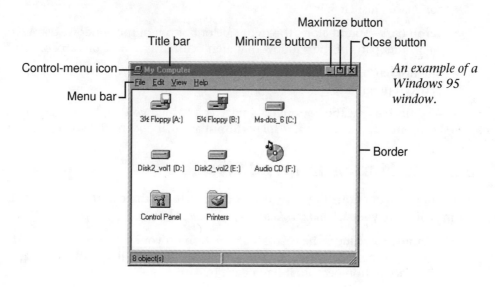

An example of a Windows 95 window.

41

Borders

Each window has a *border*, which you can use to resize the window. Just move your mouse pointer over a border; when the pointer becomes a directional arrow, you can click-and-drag a new border shape.

➤ You can drag any of the four sides of your window to change its size in that direction.

➤ You can drag any of the corners with the mouse to make the window bigger or smaller in two directions at the same time.

The Bars

The typical window can have several bars—but don't start ordering drinks; they aren't *those* kinds of bars. Here's a rundown of each type of bar:

➤ **Title bar**   At the very top portion of the window is a bar that displays the program or file name. If you're ever confused about which program or window you're in, look at the title bar for a clue. You can move a window by pointing at the title bar, holding down the left mouse button, and dragging the mouse.

➤ The **menu bar**   Located below the title bar, it displays a row of menu names. To open a menu, click the menu name, and a list of commands will appear. To select a command, just click it.

➤ **Scroll bars**   Found along the right side or bottom of the window. Use a scroll bar to view other parts of the window that aren't currently visible on-screen.

➤ The **taskbar**   At the bottom of your screen; use the taskbar to go back and forth between programs.

➤ A **status bar**   At the bottom of your screen (which you might encounter if you're in an opened application). It displays information about the file you're working on.

Minimizing, Maximizing, and Closing

In the upper right corner of your window box, there are three buttons with symbols in them. Those are your *Minimize*, *Maximize*, and *Close* buttons.

➤ **Minimizing** reduces the window to a button on your taskbar. (Click the Minimize button on the taskbar to open the window again.) You'll always recognize the Minimize button because it has a dash in it.

➤ **Maximizing** enlarges the window so that it takes up the entire screen. Just click the Maximize button for a full-size window. When a window is maximized, a Restore button appears. You can click it to restore the window to its original size. The Maximize button has an icon that looks like a window.

➤ The **Close** button stands out because it has a big X in its box. Click it to close the window.

They Changed These Buttons, Too?

Yes, back in Windows 3.1 you used a Minimize, Maximize, and Restore button to control the window's size. Those buttons are still around, they just look different. In Windows 95, you will find a Close button—a much-needed improvement to controlling your windows.

The Control-Menu Icon

In the upper left corner of most windows is a Control-menu icon. It sits to the left of the window title.

➤ If you click your mouse pointer on the **Control-menu** icon, it reveals a menu for controlling the window. You'll find commands listed for changing the window's size or closing the window.

➤ You can also double-click the **Control-menu** icon to close the window completely.

What About the Old Control-Menu Box?

Windows 3.1 uses Control-menu boxes, but in Windows 95, you will see Control-menu icons. It's a new look.

Windows Aerobics

You can open as many windows as you want. You can also move from window to window by clicking on each one. (You can use the taskbar to do this, too.) Multiple opened windows make it easier than ever to move items from one window and place them in another. However, there's a downside to multiple windows. The more you open, the more cluttered your desktop becomes. Each time you open a window, it will sit on top of the previous window. This makes things a little messy sometimes. If you're opening all kinds of folder windows, for example, a stack of opened windows piles up fast.

Check This Out...

Which Window Am I Using?
The active window's title bar is always a solid color so you always know which one you're currently using.

There are some options for tidying up these multiple windows. If you're working with multiple program windows, you can tidy them up using the program's Window menu commands. If you're working with windows from My Computer or Network Neighborhood, you can tidy up multiple windows with the Options dialog box:

1. Open your window's **View** menu, and then select **Options**. This opens the Options dialog box with tabs for controlling windows.

2. Click the **Folder** tab to bring it to the front of the box (see the figure on the next page). There are two options for viewing your windows. The first option opens a new window for every folder you view. The second option replaces the previous window with the new window's contents. In other words, when you select this option, only one window appears on-screen no matter how many you open—it's just the window's contents that change.

3. Choose an option, and then click **OK** to exit the box. You can open the Options dialog box at any time and change the selection for viewing your folder windows.

Another way to keep things tidy is with a shortcut menu on the taskbar. If you're working with multiple windows opened on your screen, you can arrange them neatly by *tiling* or *cascading* them on your desktop. To do so:

1. Move your mouse pointer down to the taskbar and right-click. This opens a shortcut menu for arranging windows.

Use the Options command on the View menu to change how your windows appear.

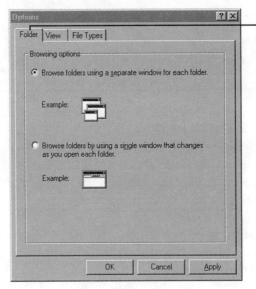

Click the Folder tab to bring its information to the front of the box.

2. Select a command from the menu, such as **Cascade** (stacks the windows nicely) or one of the **Tile** (displays the windows side-by-side) commands, and the windows will appear neatly on-screen for you.

Here's an example of multiple windows arranged neatly using the Cascade command from the taskbar's shortcut menu.

Open windows

Opened windows also appear on the taskbar.

What About Cutting, Copying, and Pasting?

Those functions are still around. You can use them to move or copy items from one window into another, whether its a program window or a folder window. The good, old Windows Clipboard (a temporary holding place for data) is fully functioning, same as before.

Other Windows Wonders

There's more to Windows 95 than just windows. Windows 95 comes with several applications of its own, although you can certainly add others such as the Microsoft Office 95 programs you installed in Chapter 3. Being the generous author that I am, I'll explain the Windows 95 wonders that you should know about before you use Microsoft Office 95.

The Accessories folder contains some fun Windows 95 features, such as a painting program and a calculator. You don't absolutely need to know about these accessories, but, in a working environment, they may come in handy. I'll describe these for you, and then you can explore them at your leisure. Note that you may not have all of these on your system.

Check out the Accessories folder.

WordPad is a simple word processing program that lets you work with text. It's not as sophisticated as Word for Windows 95, but it can handle basic word processing tasks. (WordPad is the replacement for the old Windows 3.1 Write program.)

Paint is a drawing and painting program for creating computer graphics. It has various tools for illustrating, making shapes, and using colors and patterns.

Calculator is an on-screen calculator for handling simple operations such as addition, subtraction, division, and multiplication.

Calendar can help you keep track of your schedule (kind of like a streamlined version of Schedule+, which comes with your Office 95 pack). You'll only have this accessory if you upgraded from Windows 3.1.

Cardfile is a very simple database program that resembles a card catalog or Rolodex. Use it to keep track of information such as addresses, phone numbers, and so on. You'll only have this accessory if you upgraded from Windows 3.1.

HyperTerminal can help you use your modem to dial online services. HyperTerminal is a new Windows Terminal (a feature from Windows 3.1).

Be sure to check your Windows 95 manual for more information about using each of these accessories.

What Happened to All My Old Windows Wonders?

It's hard to deal with change sometimes, especially when it's forced upon you. Windows 95 has many changes, and some things have seemingly disappeared from your system, replaced with new-fangled goodies. If you're a seasoned Windows 3.1 user and new to the Windows 95 environment, you may still be struggling with the change in your on-screen desktop. Where did everything go? Let me tell you.

No Program Manager

There's no Program Manager—it's gone. Instead of launching programs from a large window, you now launch programs by opening the **Start** menu and choosing **Programs**. The Programs menu lists all the applications you've installed on your system. The Programs menu is basically the same as the Program Manager window, except programs appear as folders on a menu rather than in a group window. And you aren't dealing with directories anymore, they're called folders now.

To use the Programs menu to open an application:

1. Click **Start** button (on the taskbar). This opens the Start menu.

2. Choose **Programs** (located near the top of the Start menu). A menu list appears listing all of your installed program folders.

3. Locate the program folder you want to open, and then choose its name. (For example, if you're looking for Microsoft Word, click the Microsoft Office folder.) An additional menu listing applications to launch will appear.

4. Choose the program name that you want to open. (If you opened the Microsoft Office folder, you can launch Word by clicking on its name.) That's all there is to it.

Programs menu

The Programs menu replaces old Program Manager.

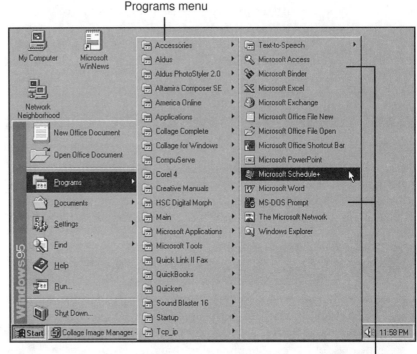

Office applications

File Manager's Gone

Windows 95 does not have a File Manager like in Windows 3.1—it has been replaced with Windows Explorer. You can do the same things with the Explorer that you did with File Manager, including moving and copying files to new locations, deleting files, printing files, and even launching programs. Actually, I think the Explorer looks pretty much like old File Manager, with a few stylish touches added.

To open the Windows Explorer:

1. Open the **Start** menu and choose **Programs**. The Programs menu appears.

2. Locate the Windows Explorer at the end of the Programs menu list, and then click it to select it. It opens into the Windows Explorer window, which looks very much like File Manager. From here you can use the menu bar to manage files and folders.

Check This Out...

Other Routes In case you were wondering, the Programs menu isn't the only way to launch programs. You can also use the My Computer window, the Run option, or the Windows Explorer to open applications.

The Windows Explorer replaces File Manager as the place you manage files.

What's My Computer?

The My Computer icon presents you with another way to look at your drives and the files they contain, but the name My Computer is way too goofy. My Computer lets you see your drives contents and find out how much space they have. It also provides quick access to the Control Panel (for controlling Windows 95 settings) and the Printers folders (for handling printers).

Isn't My Computer a Lot Like the Windows Explorer?

Well, I guess you can see some similarities, but you view your drives at a glance in My Computer, and you use the Windows Explorer for managing files and folders, and viewing the hierarchy of your file system.

My Computer has to be the worst-named new feature in all of Windows 95. Well, they didn't ask me to name it, so I have to go along with it like everybody else. I just want you to know I'm unhappy about it.

Here's how to use this feature:

1. Double-click the **My Computer** icon to open a window revealing the contents of your computer. You see an icon for each drive on your computer, plus the Control Panel and Printers folders.

So, Change It!
If you don't like the name of the My Computer icon, then you can change it. Consult your Windows 95 manual for tips on renaming your desktop items.

Check This Out...

49

2. To see what's in a drive, double-click the drive icon. This opens a window revealing the contents of the drive.

You can open as many drive windows as you want. You can even move and copy files and folders from window to window.

The My Computer window.

Drives ——

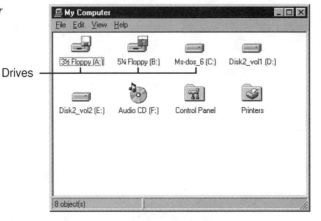

The Least You Need to Know

Hopefully, you're feeling a little more comfortable with your Windows 95 environment. The next chapter will make you feel even more relaxed. But before you continue, run through this checklist.

➤ Windows 95 is a GUI that just happens to be its own operating system, with powerful features for controlling how programs appear.

➤ Once you've learned the common elements and what they do, you've learned them for all the Windows 95 programs, including Microsoft Office 95.

➤ To start Windows 95, just turn on your computer. Windows 95 automatically loads without your help.

➤ To exit Windows 95, open the **Start** menu and choose **Shut Down**. Then choose **Shut down the computer**.

➤ To get around in Windows 95, you'll need your trusty mouse or keyboard.

➤ To open a program, open the **Start** menu and choose **Programs**; then choose the program from the list.

➤ To close a window, click the **Close** (X) button. This is true for any window, whether it's a program, a dialog box, or a folder.

Chapter 5

Covering All the Office 95 Basics

In This Chapter

➤ Common program elements in all their glory

➤ How to open and close an Office 95 program

➤ What it takes to save, open, and print files

This chapter is for anyone who hasn't worked with any of the Microsoft Office 95 programs before, or anyone who isn't very familiar with Windows-based programs in general. If you're already an experienced user with one or more of the Office 95 applications, you probably don't need a course in program fundamentals. However, the rest of you need to put on your warm-up suits and head out to the practice field. It's time for a chapter about Office 95 basics.

What Are the Basics?

Basically, the basics are the essential features found in every Microsoft Office 95 program. These include items you find on every screen, as well as commands common to all the programs. In the last chapter, you learned about the elements in a typical Windows 95 window; now you'll learn how to access the various program features and put them to work.

Ordering from Menus

Menus are where most of your Office 95 commands hang out. Because menus contain all of the necessary tools for making the computer do things, opening a menu is kind of like opening your desk drawer to grab your stapler or a paper clip. Your desk drawer probably holds most of the tools you need to get things done: pencils, erasers, scissors, tape, and much, much more. When you're not using your desk tools, they stay in your drawer. It's the same with your computer tools: the menu is shut until you need the necessary command.

You'll find Microsoft Office 95 menus organized in a tidy row on your screen's menu bar (below the title bar). Depending on the program you are using, you'll see menu group names such as File, Edit, and even Help. Those are all titles of menu groups. When you open a particular menu group, which you do by clicking on the menu name, a list appears revealing related menu commands. (These menus are said to *drop down* because the menu list literally drops down from the menu bar.) For example, the File menu contains commands such as Save, Open, Close, Exit, and Print that affect the file you're working on. To select a command from the menu list, click it with your mouse. After you choose a command, the menu disappears until you pull it down again.

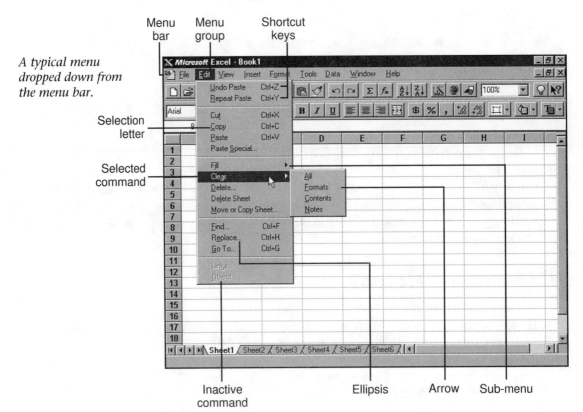

A typical menu dropped down from the menu bar.

Within Windows-based programs such as Office 95, you'll notice certain menu conventions and symbols. Here's what you'll encounter on your Office 95 menus:

Selection letters   The underlined letters you see in the menu commands. You can press the selection letter to choose a command with the keyboard (instead of clicking on the screen with the mouse).

Shortcut keys   Off to the right of some menu commands. (I told you about these in the last chapter, remember?) If you memorize them, you won't even have to open the menu; simply press the shortcut key to activate the command instead.

Ellipsis   The three dots following a menu command. The ellipsis indicates that a dialog box will appear when you select that command. (There's info on dialog boxes coming up.)

Arrow to the right of a menu command   Indicates there are more menus to view (a menu inside a menu). The additional menu appears after you select the menu command.

Inactive commands   Any faded-looking or grayish-colored commands on the menu. When a command appears gray, you can't use it for the moment. Don't even try; they won't work until they're ready to work.

Change Your Mind?

If you display a menu and then change your mind about making a selection, you can make the menu disappear by pressing the **Esc** key or clicking anywhere outside of the menu. Nothing is selected, and you escape without anything happening. The Escape key is the Houdini of keyboard keys.

All of the Office 95 programs use similar menus and commands. This gives each program a kind of déjà vu feeling. For example, most of the File menu groups throughout the various Office 95 applications contain the same command set. If you've seen one File menu, you've seen them all.

Talking with Dialog Boxes

On many occasions when you select a command, the computer needs additional information from you before it can carry out the task. When it does, a dialog box pops up on your screen. A dialog box is like a mini-window within your program window for making additional decisions. It presents you with a bunch of options from which to choose, places to type text, and buttons for activating the options.

A dialog box contains quite a variety of components. Naturally, I am supposed to tell you about them all. Hey, it's my job.

A typical dialog box and components.

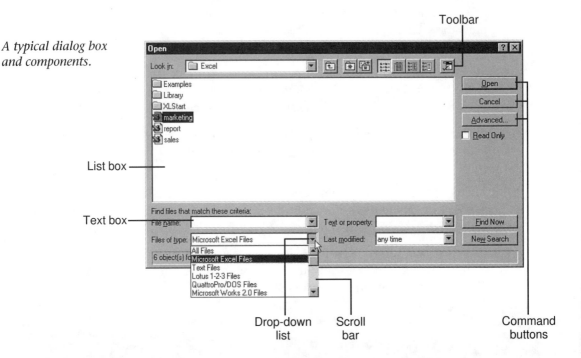

The **text box**   An area in which you type text, such as a file name. When you click inside the text box, the mouse pointer becomes a cursor for typing.

Yes, You Can Edit Text Boxes

You can edit, or make changes, to information you type into a text box. You can use the keyboard arrow keys to back up spaces, or the Delete key to remove mistyped characters.

Scroll bars   Use to move back and forth through a list. Click the arrows to move up or down.

List boxes   Exactly what their name implies: lists in a box. To select an item in a list, click it to highlight it. If the list is a long one, scroll bars may appear. You use them to move backward and forward in the displayed list.

Drop-down lists Have a downward-pointing arrow next to the first list item. When you click the arrow, a continuation of the list appears for you to view and choose from.

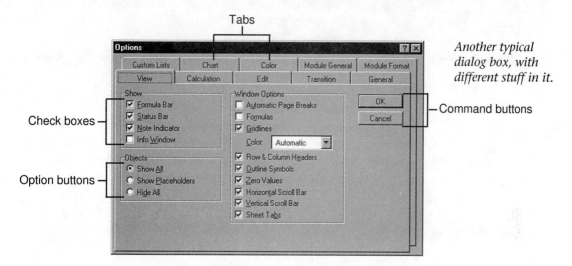

Another typical dialog box, with different stuff in it.

Toolbars May appear in some of the dialog boxes you use. Toolbars have icon buttons that act as shortcuts for performing tasks. Click the icon to activate the task.

Check boxes Tiny square boxes that turn a feature on or off. A check mark in a check box means the option is on; no check mark means it's off. You can turn on as many of these check boxes as you want. There's no limit.

Option buttons Little round buttons that turn a feature on or off. A black dot in the option button means the feature is turned on. Option buttons usually represent a group of choices from which you can choose only one at a time.

Command buttons Look like real buttons that you can click with the mouse to make things happen. Just about every dialog box has a command button that says OK. Click the **OK** button to have the computer carry out all of the dialog box selections you've made. Some command buttons even open additional dialog boxes.

Tabs Appear in some dialog boxes. You'll know them when you see them because they look like they have little folders tabs at the top of them. Each tab has a name on it describing its options. In order to select options from one of the hidden folders, you must click its tab name to move it to the front of the dialog box.

Quick Close
To quickly close a dialog box, click the **Close** button (if available) in the upper right corner of the dialog box or press **Esc**.

To make selections in a dialog box, click the various options with your mouse. In some cases, selecting something might open yet another dialog box. When you're through with the dialog box, click the **OK** button (or whichever activating button resides in the box), or press the **Enter** key to put your changes into action. If you change your mind about the dialog box selections, click the **Cancel** button (or press **Esc**).

Icons + Buttons = Toolbars

Icons are little pictures or symbols. *Buttons* are small squares that you click with your mouse. Combine icons and buttons, and you have a *toolbar*. Toolbars are a part of every Microsoft Office 95 program. So what's so hot about toolbars? Toolbars are collections of icon buttons that represent specific computer tasks, and they're the fastest way to select frequently used commands.

Icon button

Toolbars from Excel.

Toolbars

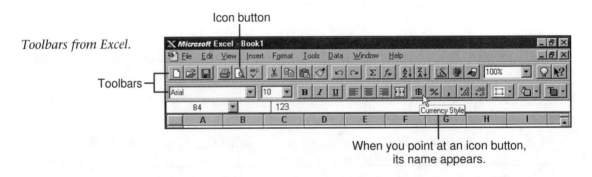

When you point at an icon button, its name appears.

The theory behind toolbars is this: instead of opening up menus and choosing commands, why not make the commands you use the most available as buttons that you just click to activate? So the people at Microsoft did just that. Take, for example, the Print command, which you use frequently. Instead of pulling down the File menu and choosing the Print command (or remembering what shortcut keys to press), you can just click the Print icon button on the toolbar. It's a lot faster. I guess they figured since we're so used to pressing buttons (like on the dishwasher, the microwave, and the remote control), we'd like to press them on our computer programs, too. Well, it's true (at least for me).

You'll find several toolbars available for every Office 95 application. For example, Word has nine toolbars to choose from. When any of the Office 95 programs first start up, the default toolbar will appear. With some of the Office 95 programs, such as Word and Excel, there are two or more default toolbars.

As you work with the program, you can change toolbars to access the icon buttons that meet your current needs. To change toolbars, move your mouse pointer over the toolbar and click the *right* mouse button. This displays a shortcut menu listing all of the available toolbars, with a check mark next to the one that's currently displayed. To change toolbars, click the one you want from the list, and your toolbar changes.

You can also change toolbars through the View menu, if it's available. Open the **View** menu and select the **Toolbar** command. A dialog box appears from which you can select the toolbars to show. You can select none at all, or you can display every toolbar available (but that would make the screen really, *really* crowded).

Get a Clue!
The pictures on the toolbar buttons are supposed to give you a visual clue as to what task the button performs. However, discerning what these artistic renderings mean isn't always easy. If you're ever in doubt about what task the button performs, move your mouse pointer over it, and the button's name appears. This is a ToolTip. (This won't work if the ToolTip feature is turned off. By default, it's on when you first use the Office 95 programs, so don't worry about it. If it is off, open the **View** menu, select **Toolbars**; and make sure to select the **Show ToolTips** check box.)

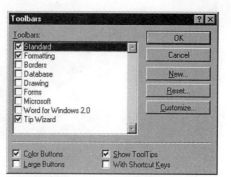

The Toolbars dialog box.

Microsoft has tried to come up with every possible toolbar combination you could want, but they've also made it easy for you to tailor the toolbars to fit your needs. You can edit the toolbars with the Customize button found in the Toolbars dialog box.

Scrolling Forth

Another common element in the Office 95 programs, and all Windows-based programs for that matter, is scroll bars. These are located on the right side and bottom of your screen. Believe it or not, a lot of times there's more to see in a file than just what fits in the window. To see other areas of the file, you have to move around with the scroll bars.

My, what lovely scroll bars.

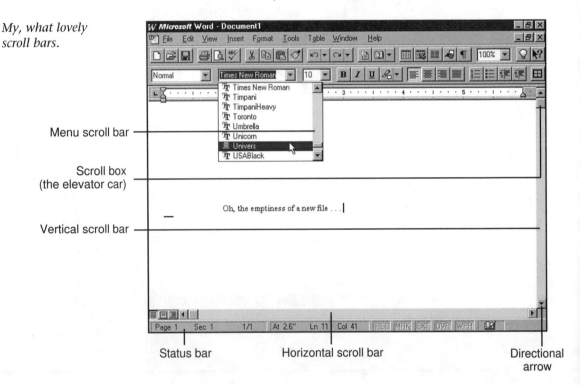

Menu scroll bar

Scroll box (the elevator car)

Vertical scroll bar

Status bar   Horizontal scroll bar   Directional arrow

Each scroll bar looks like a miniature elevator shaft. Click the arrows on the bar to move your view in the direction indicated. The box inside the bar is kind of like an elevator car, letting you know what "floor" you're on. You can also drag it along the bar to move your view. Scrolling is an ideal way to get around your window; remember that they don't move your cursor, only your view.

Status Quo

At the bottom of your Office 95 program screens is yet another bar. This one's called the *status bar*. Look back to the preceding figure to locate this bar. (It's only for important people, and, of course, you fit that description.) The status bar, also called the status line, displays information about the file you're working on. Depending on which Office 95 program you're using, the status bar reveals different kinds of information.

For example, in PowerPoint, you can click parts of the status bar to open dialog boxes or add new slides to your screen. In Word, the status bar reveals whether the Overstrike mode is turned on or not. So it's a good idea to look at your status bar from time to time.

Fundamental Operations: Start and Stop

Okay, okay, okay, everybody—listen up. We've gone over the basic elements found on all the Microsoft Office 95 program screens. Now let's talk about actual functions such as how to start an application.

How Do I Start a Program?

The most common way to open an Office 95 application is to use the Programs menu. (There's an even faster way using the Office Shortcut bar, which I'll tell you all about in the next chapter; but first things first.)

1. Click the **Start** button on your Windows 95 desktop. This opens the Start menu.

2. Select **Programs**. This will display a menu list of programs on your computer.

3. Click the Office 95 program you want to open, and away you go.

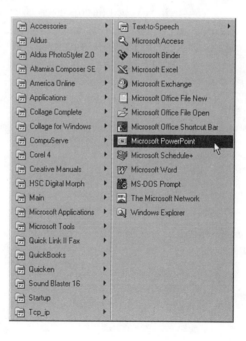

Use the Programs menu to open any Office 95 application.

How Do I Stop This Thing?

When you're ready to quit a program, you have several exit options. First, be sure to save any work you've completed. If you don't, the computer will ask you if you want to save your work as you're trying to quit (I'll tell you how to save in the next section). When you're ready to exit, use one of these quitting methods:

➤ Double-click the program window's **Control-menu** icon (that tiny icon in the upper left corner of the window on the title bar with a dash in it).

➤ Click the **Close** button (that tiny box with an X in it in the upper right corner of the window).

➤ Pull down the **File** menu and select **Exit**.

➤ Press **Alt+F4** on your keyboard.

We're not done with fundamentals yet. Keep reading the next section to learn more.

File Fiddling

Anytime you use the Microsoft Office 95 programs and save your work, you're creating a file. Files can be text files (such as Word documents), spreadsheet files (such as Excel worksheets), graphic files (such as PowerPoint presentations), and more. Once you've made a file, there are a number of things you can do to it.

Saving Files

When you make a file, you have to save it on the computer's hard disk (or onto a floppy disk if you want) so you can work on it again later. If you don't save it, it's lost forever. So one of the first things to learn about file fiddling is how to save a file.

➤ Pull down the **File** menu and select **Save**.

➤ If you've saved the file before and you select the **Save** button on the toolbar, the computer automatically saves it again using the same file name.

➤ If you're saving the file for the first time, the Save As dialog box pops up asking you to give the file a name. Type the name in the text box, and click **Save** or press **Enter**. Your file is now saved. If you want, you can also opt to save the file to a different drive or folder or as a different file type.

What Kinds of File Names Can I Use?

With Windows 95, you can name your files anything up to 255 characters long. In the previous version of Windows, you could only use 8 letters to name a file. For example, if you have a document you want to call LetterToMrSmith, you can do that now.

You can choose a new folder or drive to save the file to by clicking on this drop-down arrow and choosing a new location from the list.

Use the toolbar buttons to display detailed information in the List box.

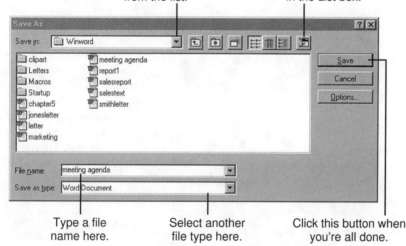

The Save As dialog box. Ooh-la-la.

Type a file name here.

Select another file type here.

Click this button when you're all done.

What About Extensions?

You old Windows 3.1 pros might remember using file extensions in previous versions of Office. A file extension provided a unique way of identifying which program you created the file in and the type of the file. Windows 95 file extensions are not displayed by default. Instead, files are now identified by icons next to the file name. For example, when you create a file in Word, a Word icon appears in front of the file name. Knowing the Office-related icons will help you recognize files and file types in the lists you may come across. However, if you do want to view file extensions again while in the Windows Explorer, open the **View** menu, select **Options**, and click the **View** tab. Deselect the **Hide MS-DOS file extensions** check box.

In the Save As dialog box, shown previously, there's an Options button you can press. If you click this button, you'll open the Options dialog box. In the Save tab, you can select from the many save options and even set up a password to protect your file.

Pay careful attention to the Automatic Save Every option. You can set up your Office application so that it automatically saves the file you're working on every few minutes. Why would you want to do that? Power failures, old chap. In case of a power failure or surge that occurs while you're in the middle of creating an important file, your computer will save the file contents automatically, without any instructions from you. This is a good safeguard to use for all of your Office programs.

Make sure to select the **Automatic Save Every** option, and set a minute increment from the **Minutes** box. I suggest **3** minutes as a good choice. To exit the Options box and return to the Save As box, click **OK**.

What Does the Save As Command Do?

That's a good question. You may have noticed the Save As command located under the Save command on the File menu. It works the same as the Save command with a slightly different spin. Perhaps you've typed up a letter in your Word program and saved it. Later you decide to send that same letter to someone else, but you also want to keep the original letter intact. So you open the original file and make a few changes. Then, instead of choosing the Save command, you select **Save As**. In the Save As dialog box, you can give the altered file a different name to distinguish it from the original one. When you've given the file a new name, you click **OK** or press **Enter**. Now you have two files that are almost alike, but they have slight differences in text and the names are different. What a nifty trick.

Saving is a crucial part of working with software, but how do you reopen a file you've already saved? It's easy. If you've saved a file previously and you want to open it again:

1. Pull down the **File** menu and select **Open**.

2. In the Open dialog box, highlight the name of the file you want in the list box, or type the file name in the text box.

3. Once you've located your file, click **Open** or press **Enter**. The file opens on your screen.

Opening a New File

If you want to start a new file, you use the New command.

1. Pull down the **File** menu and choose **New**, and the New dialog box appears.

2. Here you can select what kind of file to make (for example, in Word, **Normal** is the default choice) from the list of General files.

3. When you finish, click **OK** or press **Enter**. A new file opens on your screen.

You can use the **Close** command on the **File** menu to close a file without exiting the program. (Or another way is to click the **Close** button—the second one that appears below the title bar. Don't click the top right one; it closes your entire application.) When you close all of your program's files, you're left with the program's toolbars and a big empty screen.

Printing Files

Printing a file is a harmless procedure: all it takes is a quick click of the **Print** icon. However, before you activate the command, you might want to make sure your printer is turned on and ready to go. It's a little aggravating to tell your computer to print, only to turn around in a few minutes and find out that it's not online or it's out of paper.

When you're ready to print:

1. Pull down the **File** menu and select the **Print** command. The Print dialog box appears.

2. Click **OK**, and your file is sent to the printer.

Alternatively, you can click the **Print** icon button in the toolbar. Gosh, that was hard.

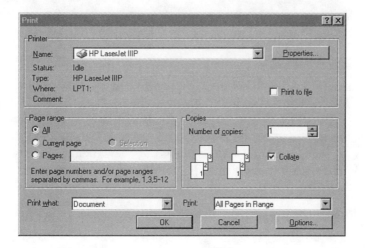

The Print dialog box.

The Print dialog box contains a number of printing options you can change. For instance, you can tell the printer how many copies of the file you want to print or even which page to print. If you select the **Options** button, you'll see more available printing features.

Sneak Preview

If you're worried about wasting paper (like a good environmentalist), you can preview how your file looks before you print it. To do so, open the **File** menu and select **Print Preview**. The entire page appears in preview mode. You can use the various preview commands to view the page, and when you're through, you can click the **Print** button to send the file to your printer.

A page in Word's preview mode.

Click here to print.

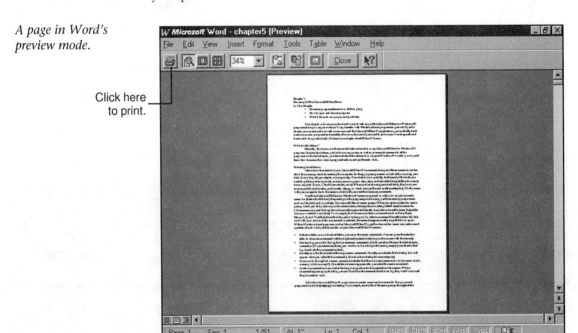

Hand Me That Magnifying Glass

While the Print Preview command certainly comes in handy, you can also utilize another command for looking at your file more objectively, even when you're in the middle of entering data. The Microsoft Office 95 programs have a Zoom feature that enables you to examine parts of your screen up close and personal or to view them from afar. Many toolbars have a Zoom icon button, and there is a Zoom command on the View menu.

With the Zoom command, you control the size at which your file is displayed on-screen. If you need to look at something that's been set in a tiny type size, you can zoom in and enlarge the screen so you can get a better look at the item. If you need to see your entire page at once, you can zoom out so the whole file fits on the screen.

When you select the **View, Zoom** command, the Zoom dialog box appears. In it, you can select what magnification percentage to use, or you can select options for fitting the file inside the window.

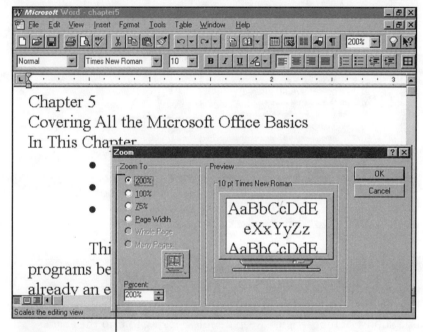

The Zoom dialog box.

In Word and PowerPoint, you can use the Zoom feature on the toolbar to display a list of magnification percentages.

Help Me!

In case you ever get in a jam, you can call for help without dialing 911: use the Help system. Help is an online system that assists you in times of trouble. Every Office 95 menu bar has a Help menu group. When displayed, the Help menu offers a topics table in which you can look up various topics you need assistance with, and an Answer Wizard with which you can find your way to the information you want.

For example, if you pull down your **Help** menu and select the **Microsoft Word Topics** command (or whatever Topics command appears based on the program you're using), an online Help Topics dialog box appears. From here, you can use the tabs and lists to look up a particular topic you'd like help with. (To close the box, click the **Close** (X) box.)

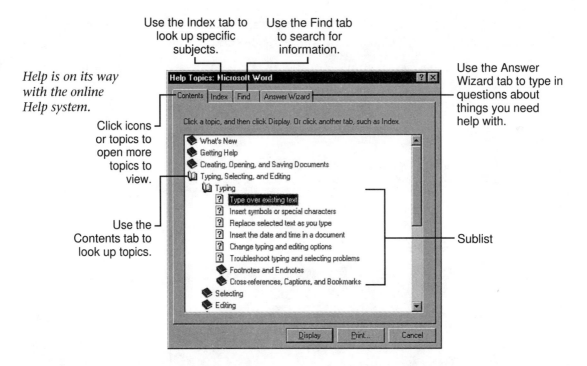

Use the Index tab to look up specific subjects.

Use the Find tab to search for information.

Help is on its way with the online Help system.

Use the Answer Wizard tab to type in questions about things you need help with.

Click icons or topics to open more topics to view.

Use the Contents tab to look up topics.

Sublist

Using the Contents Tab

Click the **Contents** tab in the Help Topics dialog box to view a list of topics (as shown in the preceding figure). To choose a topic, just double-click its name or icon. In many instances, this reveals a sublist of more topics. Keep double-clicking to find the exact topic you want to view information about. You'll note several different Help icons among the lists.

➤ A closed book icon next to a topic means there's a more-detailed list to view.

➤ An opened book icon next to a topic means the topic is selected.

➤ A question mark icon next to a topic means there's detailed text to view about the topic.

Using the Index Tab

Click the **Index** tab in the Help Topics dialog box to open another avenue for seeking help. The Index tab lets you look up topics from an exhaustive index list. Simply type in the word you're looking for and the index scrolls alphabetically to similar words. From there you can double-click to display topics.

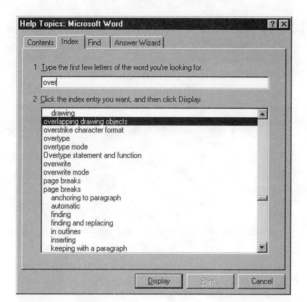

The Index tab.

Finding Things with Find

Yet another way to look up things is with the Find tab, which is also part of Microsoft's wizard collection. The Find feature can help you look up a specific topic based on words you type in. Everything's alphabetically arranged, as shown in the following figure. You type in a word and then look at the list boxes to see what's comparable.

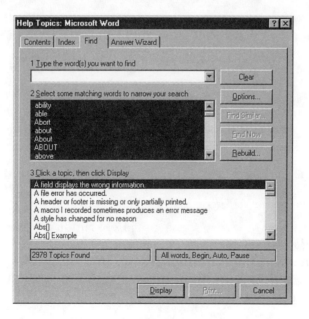

The Find tab.

The Answer Wizard

By far, the hippest help on the system comes from the Answer Wizard. To open the Answer Wizard, you can click its tab in the Help dialog box (which you opened from the Help menu), or choose it directly from the Help menu.

The Answer Wizard box.

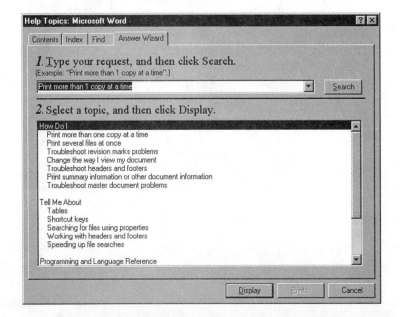

Inside the Answer Wizard tab, all you do is type in your request, click the **Search** button, and the list box displays the results. For example, let's say you're having trouble saving a file. You can type in a question such as "How do I save a file?" and Answer Wizard will answer you. I think that's pretty cool.

Answer Wizard may answer you with a list box of related topics, or it may even lead you through a tutorial on how to perform the requested task. If you see a list box appear after typing in your question, look through the topics. When you see something close to your request listed in the box, double-click it to see detailed information about the subject matter.

Other Help Routes

Another way to summon help is by pressing the **Help** button on your toolbar and then clicking on the area of the screen you need help with. For example, if you don't know what a toolbar button does, click the **Help** button, move the pointer (which then becomes a question mark icon) over the unknown button and click. This opens a window detailing how to use the feature.

One of the stranger sides of Office 95 is the TipWizard. In some of your programs such as Word, the TipWizard automatically appears as a toolbar located beneath your other program toolbars. Basically, it's there to offer you a friendly tip about using the program.

The TipWizard displayed.

If you don't want to look at these TipWizards after a while, you can easily make them disappear by clicking on the TipWizard toolbar button. When you get a burning desire to see a TipWizard again, simply click the toolbar button to bring it back onto your screen.

There's More Help on the Way!

Another way to get help is to press **F1** on the keyboard. This opens the Help dialog box directly. And speaking of dialog boxes, you can get help using them, too. Look for Help buttons in the dialog boxes you work with to offer more information about using the dialog box elements.

The Least You Need to Know

All right, troops, basic training is over. You now know what to expect as you face these Microsoft Office 95 screens and how to use the basic artillery. There's just one more feature to cover before we tackle each Office 95 application individually. Turn to the next chapter to find out what that is.

In the meantime, let's sum up what you learned:

➤ You use menus and dialog boxes to tell the Office 95 programs what to do.

➤ Toolbars offer you shortcuts to activating commonly used commands. You can customize your toolbars to show only the buttons you use the most.

➤ You can manipulate files with the commands on the File menu: Save, Open, New, Close, Print, Print Preview, and so on.

➤ Help is easy to find. You can click the Help menu to summon up an Answer Wizard or a table for looking up help topics.

➤ Click a **Close** box to close a file or program.

Office Shortcuts with the Shortcut Bar

As part of your final preparation before exploring Word, Excel, PowerPoint, and Schedule+ (it looks so important when you list them all out), I need to tell you about a special little tool that works behind the scenes to make your computing life easier. It came with your Microsoft Office 95 package, and I think you're really going to like it. (And for you pessimistic readers out there, if you don't like it, then that's just too bad.)

Looking for a Shortcut?

Who in their right mind isn't looking for a faster way to do work? I know I am. Time is precious, people. When Microsoft packaged all of the Microsoft Office 95 applications as one product, they added a special feature intended to link them and give them more power when used together. That feature is called the *Office Shortcut bar*, and it really is a shortcut to getting things done fast.

You saw the Shortcut bar for the first time back in Chapter 3. The Shortcut bar gives you the ability to combine various program features and accomplish tasks more efficiently. So, to get the most out of Microsoft Office 95, take this shortcut.

What Happened to MOM?

Users of the old Office package will remember the handy Microsoft Office Manager bar, also called MOM. It has been replaced in the 95 version with the Office Shortcut bar that can be customized just the way you like it. It's pretty much the same old bar as before, just a few new buttons and commands to use.

What Is the Shortcut Bar?

The Office Shortcut bar is a unique feature that connects all of the Office 95 applications and literally acts as a manager, delegating work and bossing the other programs around. You can open documents with it, set up appointments, quickly access online help, and even launch the various applications with it.

The Shortcut bar is that funny looking toolbar that appears in the top right corner of your Windows 95 desktop. As soon as you installed Microsoft Office 95 and restarted your computer, the Shortcut bar showed up. It's set up to start automatically whenever you start Windows 95.

The Office Shortcut bar appears as a toolbar on your screen.

The Office Shortcut Bar

Each of the icon buttons on the Shortcut bar represent certain tasks. You can customize the buttons to represent each Office application you've installed or other common tasks you'll use frequently. With some modifications, this toolbar will let you open any of the

Office 95 programs by simply clicking on the respective icon. You can also add other buttons to this toolbar, even buttons for other non-Microsoft programs that you use frequently.

What's on My Shortcut Bar?

By default, the Office Shortc ut bar starts out with a specific set of buttons. But don't for a minute think you're stuck with these. You can change them around at any time, which I'll tell you about later. For now, let's go over each default button and what it does.

Icon	Name	What It Does
	Start a New Document	Click this button when you're ready to start a new Office 95 document. It opens the New dialog box for choosing among Word, Excel, and PowerPoint documents.
	Open a Document	Use this button to open existing Office documents you've already created and saved.
	Send a Message	This button opens Microsoft Exchange to let you create e-mail fast.
	Make an Appointment	Use this button to set up appointments with your Schedule+ program. When you click this button, it takes you directly to the Appointment dialog box in your Schedule+ program.
	Add a Task	This opens Schedule+ and the Task dialog box and lets you add an item to your To Do list.
	Add a Contact	This opens Schedule+ and lets you add a contact name to your list with the Contact dialog box.

continues

73

Icon	Name	What it does
	Getting Results Book	Click this to access technical resources on your Office 95 CD-ROM.
	Office Compatible	Use this button to view demonstrations of programs that work with Office 95.
	Answer Wizard	This opens the online Help system and displays the Answer Wizard dialog box where you can get help fast.

Each of your Shortcut buttons provides you with a shortcut to starting a program or document. Some of the buttons open generalized dialog boxes that help you choose a particular file or task. Other buttons take you to familiar windows such as Schedule+ (more about this program in Part 2) or the Answer Wizard window (turn back to Chapter 5 for instructions on using this feature).

Starting a New Document

When you click the **Start a New Document** button, the New dialog box pops up on-screen, displaying oodles of tabs to choose from. Each tab contains templates and wizards from Word, PowerPoint, and Excel that you can use to build a new document from, depending on what programs you installed from your Office 95 package. As soon as you select a document style from any of the tabs in this box, you're whisked away to the appropriate program to create your own file.

Depending on what kind of document you want to make, you can choose from any of the tab categories:

General   Lets you choose a generalized document from PowerPoint, Excel, or the Binder Word.

Presentation Designs   Lists all the design styles for creating a PowerPoint presentation.

Spreadsheet Solutions   Use this tab to select an Excel spreadsheet type.

Letters & Faxes   If you're looking to whip up a letter or fax sheet fast, then this tab's for you. It lists the many Word templates for creating such documents.

There's a Shortcut Menu on the Short-cut Bar   Okay, now try this—move your mouse pointer to a blank area on your Office Shortcut bar (like the space between buttons) and right-click. This reveals a shortcut menu for dealing with the bar. You can use its commands to add buttons to the bar, customize, or even hide the bar completely.

74

Memos   Use this tab to create a memo in Word.

Reports   To make a report in Word, select this tab to see some possible ideas.

Presentations   Use this tab to choose from the six basic types of PowerPoint presentations.

Binders   Use this tab to open any Office 95 binder you've created. (Learn more about this in Chapter 25.)

Depending on what type of installation you chose, your New dialog box may show different kinds of tabs. Be sure to explore the possibilities in each tab before making a final selection from the New dialog box. Each tab lists several types of documents or wizards (custom-design documents); and you can even preview them in the **Preview** section of the tab window. Just click the document type you want to view, and then look at the **Preview** window to see what its structure looks like.

Here's a Little Trick If you move your mouse pointer over any of the Shortcut bar icons and right-click, a menu appears with four choices: **Open** (opens the program or dialog box associated with the button), **Create Shortcut** (unknown), **Properties** (reveals more information about the button), and **Hide Button** (hides the button). Use these commands to control the button, such as making it disappear from the Shortcut bar.

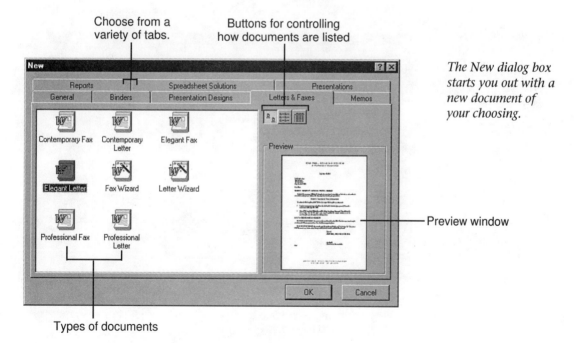

Choose from a variety of tabs.

Buttons for controlling how documents are listed

The New dialog box starts you out with a new document of your choosing.

Preview window

Types of documents

You'll also find buttons for controlling how the documents are listed in the dialog box:

Large Icons   When you select this button, the documents appear as icons in the list box.

List   To see the documents as a regular old list, select this button.

Details   Use this button to reveal details about the document file, such as size and when it was created.

As for the documents themselves, their icons will give you a clue as to which program they come from. For example, a **W** in the icon means the document is from Word.

So to use the New box, simply pick a document, and then either double-click its name or select it and click **OK**. The appropriate program, from which the document originally comes, will open up and you can begin making changes.

What's the Open a Document Button?

Select the **Open a Document** button when you want to open an existing file. An open dialog box appears, as shown in the next figure. From here you can look up your file, or perform a search to locate it. You can also preview what it looks like.

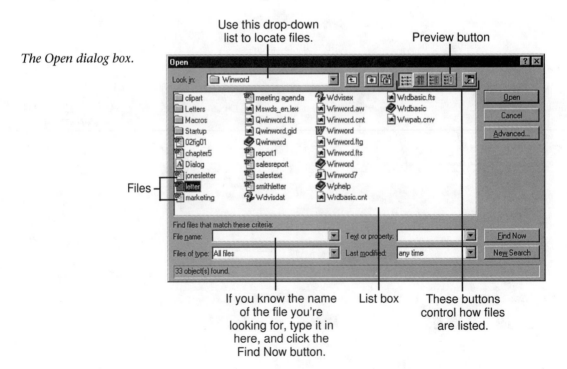

The Open dialog box.

Use this drop-down list to locate files.

Preview button

Files

If you know the name of the file you're looking for, type it in here, and click the Find Now button.

List box

These buttons control how files are listed.

➤ Use the **Look in** drop-down box to choose a specific folder that contains the file you're looking for.

➤ If you're not sure where the file's located, you can also type in the file name and click the **Find Now** button to perform a search for the document.

➤ Use the **Find files** criteria boxes to help you search for the document you're looking for.

➤ Use the **Advanced** button to perform a more exhaustive search for a file.

The various toolbar buttons in the Open dialog box control how the files are listed in the list box. Take a look at this table to see what each one does:

Button	Name	Description
	Up One Level	Moves the list back one level in the drive structure.
	Look in Favorites	Lists the documents saved in your Favorites folder.
	Add to Favorites	This puts the document into the Favorites folder.
	List	This displays the files as a list in the List box.
	Details	This button gives you details about each file in the list.
	Properties	Use this button to find out who made the file and how much is in it.
	Preview	This button lets you preview the file before selecting it, if applicable.
	Commands and Settings	This button opens a menu of commands for printing, searching, and sorting files.

You'll be using the Open dialog box quite frequently with all the Microsoft Office 95 programs, so you might as well get used to seeing it.

Ordering from the Office Menu

If you click the Microsoft Office Control-menu icon in the Shortcut bar (the little puzzle icon at the very left of the bar), a menu drops down. You can use this menu to perform a variety of tasks, including opening the Customize dialog box or turning off the Shortcut bar.

The Microsoft Office menu.

Here's what's on your menu:

Restore, **Move**, and **Minimize** Commands for controlling your Shortcut bar. For example, when you choose the Minimize command, your Shortcut bar becomes an icon button on the Windows 95 taskbar.

Auto Hide Instructs your computer to automatically conceal the Shortcut bar when you've opened a program.

Customize Opens a dialog box for retooling your Shortcut bar.

Add/Remove Office Programs Opens the Setup utility, where you can add and delete programs.

Microsoft Office Help Topics Hooks you up with the online Help system.

About Microsoft Office Displays some copyright information about the Office 95 product version and serial numbers.

Exit Removes the Shortcut bar from your screen.

Moving the Shortcut Bar Around

If you get tired of seeing the Shortcut bar in the same place all the time, then feel free to move it around. You can easily drag the bar to a new location. When you do, you might be surprised to see it change its shape.

Follow these steps to move the Office Shortcut bar:

1. Move your mouse pointer over a blank part of your Shortcut bar, such as between buttons.

2. Drag your Shortcut bar (hold down the left mouse button and move the mouse) to a new location on the screen.

3. Let go of the mouse button when the Shortcut bar is in place.

You can easily drag the bar back up to the top right corner again to keep it out of the way. When you drag it up there, it acts like a magnet and immediately reassumes its old location again. You can also double-click the Shorcut bar's title bar to move it back to the default position in the corner.

Microsoft Office icon

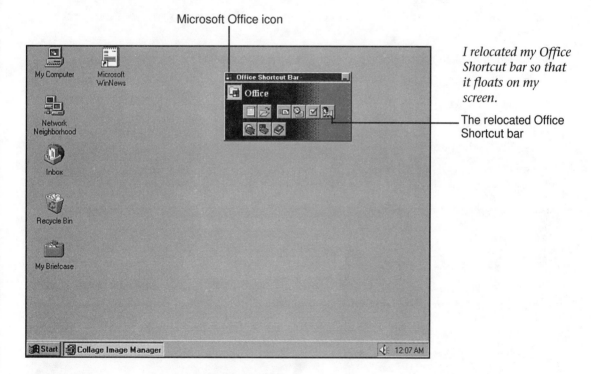

I relocated my Office Shortcut bar so that it floats on my screen.

The relocated Office Shortcut bar

Changing Your Button Size

By default, those Shortcut bar buttons are pretty small. The first time I used Office 95, I could hardly make out the pictures on my Shortcut bar (and I have reasonably good eyesight!). Thankfully, you can enlarge the buttons to make them more readable; here's how.

79

1. Click the **Microsoft Office** icon (it looks like a tiny puzzle shape at the far left of your bar) on the Shortcut bar (in its default location in the upper right corner). If your Shortcut bar is floating, you can right-click the title bar or right-click any empty space on the bar.

2. From the menu that appears, choose **Customize**.

3. When the Customize dialog box opens, click the **View** tab to bring the View options to the front of the box.

4. Click the **Large Buttons** check box under the Options heading in the tab.

5. When you finish with the View options, click **OK** to put them into effect.

Moving Your Buttons Around

If you don't like the arrangement of your Office Shortcut buttons, you can move them. Here's how:

1. Click the **Microsoft Office** icon to access the Microsoft Office menu.

2. Select the **Customize** command.

3. In the Customize dialog box, click the **Buttons** tab to bring the Button options to the front of the box.

4. Select the name of the button you want to move.

5. Click the up or down **Move** arrow to move the program to another place on the list. (Don't click the scroll bar arrows; that won't do the trick.)

6. When you're all done, click **OK**. The Shortcut bar reflects your icon changes.

The Least You Need to Know

Now that you know about the Office Shortcut bar, you're ready to learn about the individual Office 95 programs and how to make them work together.

For those of you who want a quick summary before you move on, check out this list:

➤ The Office Shortcut bar can be used to quickly open documents and run any of the Office 95 programs.

➤ The Office menu lists commands for customizing the Shortcut bar, hiding or exiting the bar, and accessing the Setup utility.

Part 2
Microsoft Office Ins and Outs

Hey—did you survive your crash course in basic operations, fundamentals training, and program installation in Part 1? Good, because boot camp is over. It's time for a real Office workout now. Get ready for a section of jam-packed information about using each of the Office 95 programs individually. I'll show you all the details needed to use Word, Excel, PowerPoint, and Schedule+ like a seasoned professional. You'll find important information about each program and how it works, which will come in handy later when you learn how to integrate them all. Grab your gear and let's move out.

Chapter 7

In a Word

In This Chapter

➤ Familiarize yourself with the Word screen

➤ Find out what's new in Word 7

➤ Create a document

➤ Learn how to use Word's ready-made templates

Who could live without a word processing program (a program made specifically for working with text) these days? I certainly couldn't. Just the thought of typing five pages (or five hundred!) on a clunky old typewriter gives me goose bumps. You do remember *typewriters*, don't you? I clearly remember the agony of yesteryear, having to retype high school term papers over and over because of spelling errors and rewrites. What torture! Thank goodness those days are long gone. (The typewriter days, that is... although I'm certainly glad I'm not in high school anymore either.)

Today's word processing programs simplify all of your document needs. You can use programs such as Word to create memos, letters, research papers, last-will-and-testaments, screenplays, grocery lists, and more. And you'll be happy to know that Microsoft's Word for Windows 95 is one of the finest word processing programs available. (No, I'm not getting paid to endorse their product, thank you very much.) In this chapter, we'll go over the essential features of Word and how to manipulate your words on-screen.

What's New with Word?

Okay, seasoned Office veterans, want a list of several of the new features in Word 7? Here it is:

➤ You can access a TipWizard box for instant hints by clicking the **Tip Wizard** button on your Standard toolbar (learn to use this feature later in this chapter).

➤ You can now use Word as an e-mail editor for your online or network correspondence. (This new aspect of Word is only useful to you if you're connected to a network or have a modem to go online.) See Chapter 25.

➤ While you're busy corresponding online or on your network, you can also use Word's Address Book to instantly drop address or contact information into your text.

➤ For those of you who like to whip up documents fast, you'll find plenty of new Word templates to choose from. (Learn more about those at the end of this chapter.)

➤ Microsoft completely revamped the Open dialog box, which makes it easier to locate, manage, and access documents. (You learned a little about the Open dialog box in Chapter 6.)

What Version Are We On? For those of you who keep track of such things, your new Office 95 Word program is now up to version 7.0.

➤ Word's Spell It feature automatically underlines misspelled words while you type. (More about this later in the chapter.)

➤ Microsoft improved Word's AutoCorrect and AutoFormat features to help you save time and energy setting up formatting, borders, and more (Chapter 11).

➤ Ever feel compelled to highlight portions of your text? Now you can with Word's Highlighter feature. You can use it to add color highlighting to words (see Chapter 8).

Those are some of the many improvements added to Word 7. You'll discover more as you keep reading.

Up and Running with Word for Windows

Before you can start working with Word, you have to start the program. (I realize you didn't need to buy a book to figure this one out.) There are several ways in which you can do this:

➤ Open on the **Start** menu; choose **Programs, Microsoft Word**.

➤ Click the **Start a New Document** button on your Office Shortcut bar at the top of your screen (if you haven't rearranged the default icons yet). Choose from one of the

Word document templates (the ones with giant **W**s on them) from among the many tabs, and click **OK** to open Word.

➤ If you set up your Office Shortcut bar to show a Word icon (see Chapter 6), click the **Word** icon.

First Glance

When you first open Word, it reveals a blank document page waiting for you to fill it with text. With a quick glance around the screen, you see most of the program elements that you were introduced to in the first part of this book. (The Office Shortcut bar may or may not appear on your Word screen, depending on what you decided to do with it back in Chapter 6.)

Other Routes to Word You can also launch Word from the **Windows Explorer** by double-clicking the Word executable file in the **Office** folder. Or open Word from the **My Computer** window by opening the drive and folder containing the program, and double-clicking the **Word** icon.

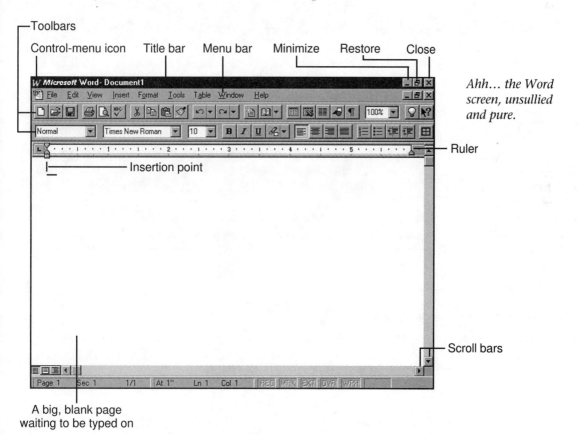

Toolbars

Control-menu icon Title bar Menu bar Minimize Restore Close

Ahh... the Word screen, unsullied and pure.

Ruler

Insertion point

Scroll bars

A big, blank page waiting to be typed on

By default, Word 7 is set up to start you out in Normal view. Word lets you view your documents in several different modes. Normal view lets you see a simplified version of your document without headers and footers, exact margins, and so on. There are several other ways to view your documents. Page Layout view shows you how your document will actually appear on paper. Outline view lets you see how your document looks in an outline format. I'll tell you more about view modes in Chapter 11.

Tip of the Day to You

If you're brand new to the world of Word, you may want to pull out the Tip of the Day box, alias TipWizard box. This box contains notes intended to help you get more out of your Word program. Depending on what you're trying to do on-screen, the TipWizard box may show you additional bits of information, such as instructions for editing text. It's a helpful feature that offers you a fast, easy way to further your Word education.

➤ To make the TipWizard box appear on your own screen, click the **TipWizard** button on the first toolbar. The icon looks like a little light bulb, so you can't miss it.

➤ To remove the TipWizard box from your screen, click the **TipWizard** button again.

There are two scroll arrows at the right end of the TipWizard box that let you scroll back and forth between tip information. There's also a Show Me icon (a light bulb with a question mark) that lets you point and click at on-screen items for more tips.

TipWizard button

Start each Word day with the Tip of the Day box for quick tips on using Word features.

The TipWizard box

86

Where Do I Go from Here?

If you become tired of staring at your blank Word screen after a while, feel free to start filling it in. The blinking vertical line inside your Word page is the *insertion point*. It marks the place where your text will appear when you type. To enter text, start tapping away at your keyboard. Go ahead and try it.

When you start typing, the insertion point moves to the right. When you reach the right edge of your screen, Word automatically moves to the start of the next text line. This snazzy little trick is called *word wrapping*. You don't press the Enter key to start a new line unless you want to begin a new paragraph. When you enter more lines than will fit on the screen, the lines of text automatically start scrolling upward so that your insertion point is always in view.

There's also a horizontal line on your Word screen, called the end of document line. Not that you have to be a brain surgeon to figure this one out, but I'm going to explain it anyway. The end of document line marks the end of your document, the point where you typed your last line of text. Both the insertion point and the end of document line start out at the same place on your screen, until you start typing text. The end of document line will always be under the last line of text in your document, but the insertion point can be anywhere.

Didn't There Used to Be a Tip of the Day Dialog Box?
Yes, in the previous version of Microsoft Office, a Tip of the Day dialog box popped up on your screen as a separate window every time you opened Word. It was very annoying, so I'm glad it's gone.

What's Word Wrap? As you type in a word processing program, the computer automatically "wraps" your text to a new line when you reach the right margin. There's no need to stop at the end of the line and issue a command to start a new line; the program takes care of that for you.

Spell as You Go

If you see any funny-looking, wavy red lines appear under any words that you type, don't be alarmed. That's the Word Spell It feature kicking in. It automatically checks your spelling while you type, and it's turned on by default. The wavy red line that you see under a word means one of two things:

> You've misspelled a word…

> Or the word you spelled isn't in Word's dictionary.

When you go back and correct the word, the wavy red line disappears. If you can't tell if the word is misspelled or not, move your mouse pointer over the word and right-click. Spell It recommends alternative spellings you can use. Select one from the list and the word is corrected.

Here's an example of how Word's Spell It feature works.

Wavy red line (if this book were in color, you'd see this clearly)

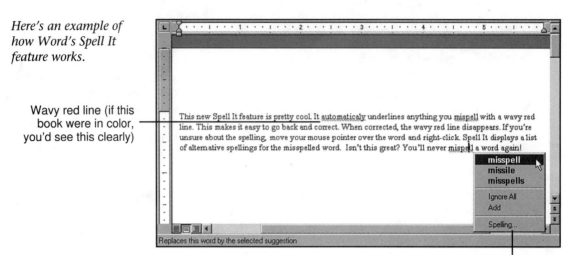

Right-click over a misspelled word to see a list of alternative spellings.

If you get tired of seeing the wavy red lines as you type, you can turn the feature off. Follow these steps:

1. Open the **Tools** menu and select **Options**.

2. Click on the **Spelling** tab to bring it to the front of the dialog box.

The Options dialog box.

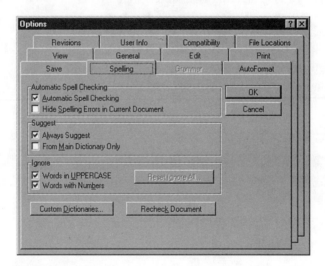

3. Deselect the **Automatic Spell Checking** check box.

4. Click **OK** to exit the box.

You'll learn more about the spelling correction features in Chapter 11, but I had to tell you about the wavy red line right away because you're going to notice it as you start typing text. I didn't want you to panic.

Shortcut Menus

Here's a great tip for you. Start clicking that seldom-used right mouse button in Word and you'll display a variety of shortcut menus. They call them shortcut menus, or context menus, because rather than opening a menu from the menu bar and choosing a command, the menu list appears immediately. Shortcut menus are only accessible with a click of the right mouse button. Keep your eye out for more shortcut menus throughout the Office 95 programs.

New Feature Alert!

The wavy red line feature is new to Word. Old-time Word users will remember a similar feature, called AutoCorrect, from the previous version of Word. You can use AutoCorrect to fix up common misspellings. It's still around, too, and you can learn more about it in Chapter 11.

Moving Your Mouse

In the previous paragraphs, you were supposed to be typing text into your Word document. Stop typing for a minute and move your mouse instead. As you move your mouse pointer around on-screen, you'll notice the pointer changes shape. Sometimes, it's the arrow pointer you've come to know and love, but other times, it's a strange-looking capital I symbol. I have an explanation for all of this (of course).

When the mouse pointer is inside the text area of your screen, it takes the shape of an I-beam. Among some nerdy technical-types, this I-beam thing is also known as the *cursor*. You can click the I-beam, or cursor, if you prefer (you little nerd, you), into place for editing between characters, before and after words, and so on. The I-beam's shape makes it easy to do this. Anytime you move the mouse pointer outside the text area, it becomes the old pointer arrow again.

Cavorting with the Keyboard

There are a lot of ways to maneuver around the Word screen. For starters, you can click where you want the insertion point to be, or you can use the scroll bars as described in Chapter 5. As in any program worth its salt, there are also some funky keyboard keys that can move you around. Here's a handy table to tell you how to use them.

Navigating the Word Screen with the Keyboard

Press	To Move
←	Left one character
→	Right one character
↑	Up one line
↓	Down one line
Ctrl+←	Left one word
Ctrl+→	Right one word
Crtl+↑	Up one paragraph
Ctrl+↓	Down one paragraph
Home	To the beginning of a line
End	To the end of a line
PgDn	Down one screen
PgUp	Up one screen
Ctrl+PgDn	To the bottom of screen
Ctrl+PgUp	To the top of screen
Ctrl+Home	To the start of the document
Ctrl+End	To the end of the document

Insert Versus Overstrike

Back to the subject of typing text again. You need to know that Word provides two modes for entering text: *Insert mode* and *Overstrike mode*. When you type using Insert mode, any existing text on your screen moves to the right to make room for the new text you're typing. (It's like a bulldozer, pushing your old text out of the way to make room for the new.) When you first start Word, you're in Insert mode (it's the default setting). Insert mode is ideal for inserting new words into the middle of existing sentences. In Insert mode, you can click the I-beam (alias *cursor*) into place and start typing.

When you type using Overstrike mode—called *Typeover* mode in some circles—the new text replaces the existing text you're typing. (Overstrike mode is like a tank that runs over all the characters that are in its way.)

To switch between Insert and Overstrike modes, press the **Ins** (or **Insert**) key on your keyboard. When the Overstrike mode is in effect, you'll see the bold letters **OVR** on the status bar (at the bottom of your screen). When you're ready to use Overstrike, switch to Overstrike mode, click the I-beam in place, and start pecking away at the keyboard. However, you should be careful when using Overstrike: although it works well when you want to replace text, you have to remember to turn it off when you're done so you don't accidentally replace more text than you intended. Don't say I didn't warn you.

| Page 1 | Sec 1 | 1/1 | At 1.7" | Ln 5 | Col 43 | REC | MRK | EXT | OVR | WPH | |

The letters OVR are bold when the Overstrike mode is on.

The status bar comes in handy on occasion, like when you need to know if you're in Insert mode or Overstrike mode.

Tons of Templates

If you're in a hurry to create a document, and you don't have time to design and format your own, use one of Word's *templates*. Templates are ready-made documents; all you have to do is add the text.

You may not know this, but every document you create in Word is actually based on a template—a model document with default settings for fonts, point sizes, and more. Word for Windows has a number of templates for you to use, or you can make your own. Each time you open Word, the default template, called Normal, is already in place and ready to go. It's a bare-bones template with only a few formatting features in place.

You'll find the rest of Word's templates in the New dialog box. To get there, open the **File** menu and select **New**. (Clicking the New button on the Standard toolbar won't open the New dialog box. You'll need to use the File menu to open it up.) The New dialog box displays a bunch of available templates to choose from. These steps will show you how to do it.

> **Template Tips** Your Office 95 suite comes with many templates, but not all of them will install with the Typical installation option. You can go back to the Microsoft Office 95 setup program and install additional templates as needed. Consult your manual for more information.

1. Open the **File** menu and choose **New** to open the New dialog box.

The New dialog box.

Tab categories

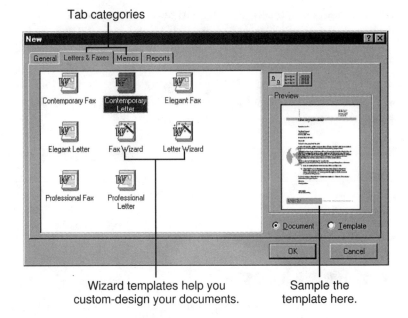

Wizard templates help you
custom-design your documents.

Sample the
template here.

2. Click the tab that matches the type of document you want to make.

3. Among the templates shown in the selected tab, click the one you want to use and view a sample of it in the Preview area (located on the right side of the box).

4. To actually select the template to create, double-click its icon, or highlight it and click **OK**. If you've chosen a wizard template, a series of dialog boxes will appear which help you create the document.

When the template finally appears in full form on your screen, you can start filling it in with your own text.

Techno Talk

Wizard Templates

As you look through the list of templates in the New dialog box, you'll notice that some of the templates have the name **Wizard**. If you select a wizard, a tiny bearded man wearing a pointy hat appears (hey—it could happen). A wizard template is a special do-it-yourself designer template. Word's wizard templates walk you through the steps for creating standard documents. When you select a wizard template, on-screen prompts appear asking you to choose from a variety of options for your template. Click the **Next** button to move to the next wizard prompt. When you're all finished designing the template, click **Finish**. Now you can fill in your new template.

I Want a New Template!

A hard to please Word customer, eh? If you don't see any templates or wizard templates that you like, you can design your own from scratch. Sound like fun? It can be, if you follow these steps:

1. Open the **File** menu and select **New** to reveal the New dialog box.

2. Click the **General** tab and highlight the **Normal** template.

3. Click the **Template** option button underneath the Preview area.

4. Click **OK** to continue. A blank document page appears on your screen with a default name, such as TEMPLATE1, in the title bar. Go ahead and build your template the way you want it, entering the basic text and any other items you want in the model. Add all the formatting that you want to include.

5. When you finish, open the **File** menu and click **Save As**.

6. In the Save As dialog box, type in a file name that will make your template unique from the others. Click **Save**, and Word saves your template under the specified name. Your new template appears in the New dialog box along with the other templates and is ready to go the next time you want to use it again.

The templates you create yourself
are saved in the Templates folder,
unless you designate otherwise.

The Save As dialog box.

Type your template name here.

93

The Least You Need to Know

For those of you who dozed off in this chapter, here's what you missed:

➤ Word is the Microsoft Office program designed to take care of your word processing needs. It enables you to create documents and edit them to perfection.

➤ When Word first starts, you're in Normal view mode.

➤ You don't have to do anything special to create a document; just start typing text.

➤ Word's Spell It feature underlines any words you misspell with a wavy red line.

➤ You can move around your Word screen with the mouse or the keyboard.

➤ If you want to create a document fast, use one of Word's many templates—predesigned documents that you simply add text to.

Chapter 8

Editing Etiquette and Formatting Frills

In This Chapter

➤ Learn to apply editing commands to your Word text

➤ Find out what it means to clone your text

➤ Start using the Word toolbars

➤ Simple formatting techniques to make your documents proud

In the previous chapter, I told you how to move around in your Word document and start typing in text. But a funny thing happens after you begin; text begins to accumulate and you inevitably have a need to make changes to it. Why? Because words and paragraphs can be messy things. You shouldn't be surprised to learn that Word offers a myriad of editing techniques and formatting attributes that you can apply to your text. Lucky for you, I happen to have a chapter ready to explain all of this.

Stop the Presses, I Need to Make a Few Changes

The primo, number-one reason word processing programs exist is this: *ease of editing*. Editing is the process of making changes to your work before you commit the document to paper. In the olden days of typewriters (good grief, why am I bringing those antiques up again?), you committed your text to paper as soon as you pressed a typewriter key. If you made a mistake, you had to start over with a clean sheet of paper, or try to apply a variety of messy fix-up solutions.

With a computer program, you can type the text, make changes to it, rewrite it, and rearrange it without wasting precious time, paper, and ink. You make all of these changes on-screen using a variety of techniques. Best of all, you can do these things over and over again until you've built the perfect document. (Just be sure to save everything.)

First of All, Know Your Toolbars

As you start editing and formatting your text, you'll want to use your toolbars. Why? Because they're there—and they're easy to use. (Besides, they're taking up prime real estate on your Word screen so they must be important, right?) Word starts up with two default toolbars displayed, the *Standard* toolbar (the top one) and the *Formatting* toolbar (underneath the Standard toolbar).

You'll learn how to use the Formatting toolbar later in this chapter. However, you might get some use out of the Standard toolbar when it comes to editing your Word text. In case you're curious, here's what each button on the Standard toolbar does.

Button	Name	Function
	New	Starts a new document
	Open	Opens an existing document
	Save	Saves a document
	Print	Prints a document
	Print Preview	Previews a document before printing
	Spelling	Starts the spell checker
	Cut	Cuts a selected item and places it in the Clipboard

Button	Name	Function
	Copy	Copies a selected item onto the Clipboard
	Paste	Pastes a cut or copied item from the Clipboard
	Format Painter	Copies and pastes formatting
	Undo	Undoes your last edit/action
	Redo	Redoes a previous undone action
	AutoFormat	Automatically formats your document
	Insert Address	Inserts network or online addresses/contacts
	Insert Table	Inserts a table
	Insert Microsoft Excel Worksheet	Inserts a specific worksheet from Excel
	Columns	Turns selected text into columns
	Drawing	Opens the drawing toolbar
	Show/Hide ¶	Reveals or hides nonprinting characters, such as paragraph or tab marks
	Zoom Control	Changes your viewing perspective
	TipWizard	Controls the TipWizard box
	Help	Opens online help

Use 'Em or Lose 'Em!

If you're not going to use your toolbars at all, you might as well remove them from your screen. This will give you more text area to type in. Open the **View** menu, select **Toolbars**, and deselect any selected toolbars you no longer want to see. Click **OK**, and they're gone. You can easily bring them back again following the same steps.

You can also right-click on a blank area inside a toolbar to display a toolbar menu for quick selecting and deselecting.

Oh yeah, don't forget—you can customize your toolbars to contain only the commands you use the most. Click the **Customize** button in the Toolbars dialog box (or on the right-click menu), and follow the directions shown.

Make Your Selection, Please

As you edit your documents, you will eventually find that you need to move, delete, or copy text. Why? Because that's what happens to your text—trust me on this one. To edit in this way, you have to learn how to select text. You have to grab it somehow to manipulate it, and there's only one way to do it—electronically.

Selected text appears highlighted on the screen in reverse: white type on a black background instead of black text on a white background. Selecting text—whether it's one character, one word, or several paragraphs—enables you to edit it quickly.

To select text with the mouse:

1. Move your mouse pointer (which is assuming the shape of a cursor) in front of the first character you want to select. Click the cursor in place.

2. Hold down the left mouse button and drag the mouse to the last character of the word or block you want to select.

3. Let go of the mouse button, and your text is selected. You can then use a variety of commands that affect the selected text, such as copy, move, or delete.

Can I Select Things Using the Keyboard?

Yes, there's a way for keyboard-lovers to select text, too. To select text with the keyboard, move the insertion point to the beginning of the text you want to select. Hold down the **Shift** key and use the arrow keys to move to the end of the text. Release the **Shift** key, and the text appears highlighted. To select the entire document at once, press **Ctrl+A**.

Click inside the selection bar to highlight portions of your text.

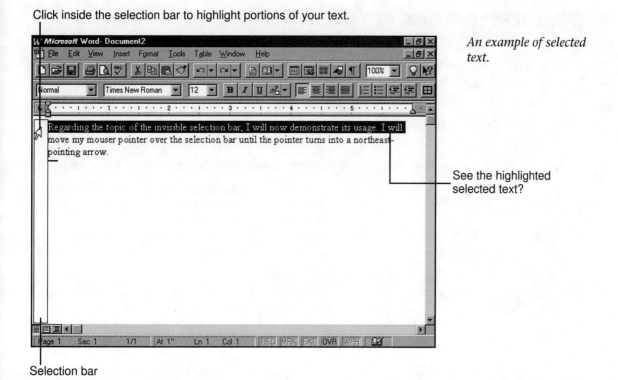

An example of selected text.

See the highlighted selected text?

Selection bar

Belly Up to the Selection Bar

Now, before you run off and start selecting text all over your screen, there's yet another method of text selection to learn about. There's an unmarked column, called the *selection bar*, in the left margin of the text area (see the preceding figure). You can use this bar to select portions of your text. When the mouse pointer moves from the document to the selection bar, it changes from an I-beam into a northeast-pointing arrow. When you see this arrow, you know your pointer is hovering over the selection bar.

Here's how to use the bar:

➤ To select a line of text, move your pointer to the left of the line into the selection bar area. Click the left mouse button, and the whole line is suddenly highlighted.

➤ If you want to select the entire paragraph, double-click the pointer in the selection bar.

➤ To select the entire document, hold down the **Ctrl** key and click anywhere in the selection bar.

Wipe It off the Face of Your Screen

Deleting text is a crucial part of the editing process. Being the innovative word processing program that it is, Word offers several different ways to delete text (besides typing over the text using Overstrike mode). You can delete single characters or large blocks of text; you can even delete entire *pages* of text.

➤ To delete a character to the right of your insertion point, press the **Del** (or **Delete**) key on your keyboard.

➤ To delete a character to the left of the insertion point, press the **Backspace** key.

➤ If you press and hold down the **Del** or **Backspace** key, you can delete even more letters. Be careful when you do this, however; the deletion really picks up speed fast. You're liable to fall off the page and hurt yourself if you go too quickly.

➤ Plus, there's the Cut command you can use to remove text. Select the text and click the **Cut** button on the Standard toolbar. I know this has nothing to do with the Del or Backspace keys—I'm throwing it in as an option, that's all.

Check This Out...

Uh-Oh! If you accidentally delete something you didn't mean to delete, you can undo the deletion. Open the **Edit** menu and select the **Undo** command, or click the **Undo** button on the Standard toolbar. The drop-down arrow next to the Undo button on the toolbar lists several of the previous edits you performed. You can choose to undo any from the list.

You can also delete large chunks of text with the Del key. To do so, select the text you want to erase, and press the **Del** key. Presto-chango, it's gone. You can use this method to get rid of single words, sentences, paragraphs, and even pages of text.

Cloning Your Text

The ability to copy text from one place to another in your document can really come in handy as you edit your Word documents. Windows has a great little feature, called a *Clipboard*, that can help. The Clipboard is a temporary storage area where you can store data before placing it in another application or file. (Clipboard saves only the last item that you copied or moved.) This method beats retyping text.

There are three commands you can use to manipulate data from one application or file into another: **Cut**, **Copy**, and **Paste**. The Cut command moves data to the Clipboard. When you open the file or application where you want to place the data, you use the Paste command. The Copy command follows a similar route, except the original piece of data stays where you found it. You'll find Cut, Copy, and Paste commands in the Edit menus of the various Office 95 programs.

The easiest way to copy text in Word is to first copy it to the Windows Clipboard.

1. Select the text you want to copy.

2. Pull down the **Edit** menu, and select **Copy**. Better yet, click the **Copy** button on the Standard toolbar; it's faster.

3. Now move the I-beam to the place where you want to put the copied text, and click the cursor in place.

4. Pull down the **Edit** menu again, and this time select the **Paste** command. (You can also click the **Paste** button on the toolbar.)

For an easier copy and paste job, select the text you want to copy, and point at the place where you want to copy it. Hold down the **Ctrl** key and the **Shift** key at the same time and click the right mouse button. Instant copy! Another fast trick is to right-click on selected text with the mouse to reveal a shortcut menu from which you can select the Cut, Copy, or Paste command.

Techno Talk

Spike It!

When most people think of the Windows Clipboard, they remember that it can hold only one stored item at a time. However, Microsoft Word's *Spike* feature lets you do more than that. You know those metal spike desk accessories, the pointy stick-things that let you spear pieces of paper (like notes and bills)? Okay, maybe you don't have one on your own desk; after all, they are pretty serious weapons and they're old-fashioned. However, the concept behind them was that they kept papers from getting moved around or lost on a desk. Well, that's sort of what the Spike feature is like. You use this feature to move different items from one place to another, in a set order.

To Spike your own text, select the text you want to move and press **Ctrl+F3**. Repeat this step for as many items as you're moving. When you're ready to paste them into a new location, position your cursor where you want them to appear and press **Ctrl+Shift+F3**. All the items are pasted in the order they were cut. Add that one to your repertoire of Word tricks.

Pack Up the Text, We're Moving

You can move your text in much the same way as you copy text. The only difference is that you use the Cut command instead of the Copy command. To move text:

Use the Toolbar Buttons Don't forget that the **Cut**, **Copy**, and **Paste** commands are always available as toolbar icon buttons. This is true in all of the Office programs you use. Be sure to look for them; they'll save you time when cutting, copying, and pasting data.

1. Select the text.

2. Pull down the **Edit** menu, and choose **Cut**. (You can also click the **Cut** button on the toolbar.)

3. Place the cursor where you want to move the text, and click it in place.

4. Pull down the **Edit** menu again and select **Paste**. (You can also click the **Paste** icon on the toolbar.) You have moved the selected text to the new position and deleted it from its original position.

What's the Difference Between Copying Text and Moving Text?

I'm glad you asked that. When you copy text, the original stays the same, and the duplicate text shows up in the newly designated place. When you move text, it is deleted from its original location and moved to a new place. Confusing the two commands can cause some headaches. You may accidentally move text you were supposed to copy. If this happens, you'll have to copy it back to its original location, assuming you can remember where that was.

For a faster move, select the text, and point at it with the mouse pointer. Hold down the left mouse button and drag the text to the new location. Let go of the mouse button when you reach the new destination, and the text is moved.

Seek and Ye Shall Find, Then Ye Can Replace

One of the things you'll encounter when editing is the old find-and-replace scenario. Let's say you've typed a long letter to the president of the Doohickey company, but then you find out that the name is supposed to be Doohackey, not Doohickey. Since you used the name incorrectly in about 30 places in your letter, you need a way to change them all fast. That's where the Find and Replace commands come in handy.

The Find command looks through the document for the text you specify. The Replace command replaces a word or words you designate with new text. You'll find both commands located on your Edit menu. In fact, they often work together. Here are steps for using both commands.

To search for text:

1. Pull down the **Edit** menu and select the **Find** command. The Find dialog box appears.

2. Type in the word you want to find, select any options you want to apply to the search, and click **Find Next**. Word finds your text.

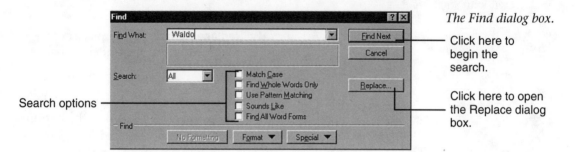

The Find dialog box.

Click here to begin the search.

Search options

Click here to open the Replace dialog box.

If you want to replace the specified word with a new word, click the **Replace** button in the Find box to open the Replace dialog box (this is where we start using the Replace command).

Click here to start the search.

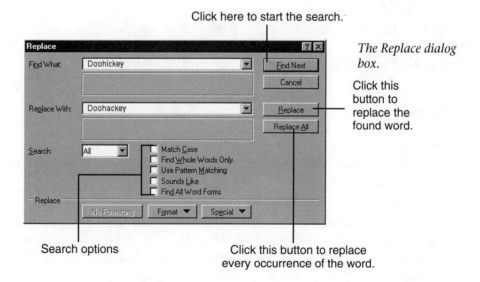

The Replace dialog box.

Click this button to replace the found word.

Search options

Click this button to replace every occurrence of the word.

Or better yet, select the **Edit** menu again, but choose **Replace** this time. When you have the Replace box on-screen, follow these instructions:

1. Enter the word you're looking for in the **Find What** box, and enter the replacement word or words in the **Replace With** box.

I Want to Delete It! If you want to delete the specified text instead of replacing it with something else, leave the Replace With box empty in the Replace dialog box.

I Goofed! If it turns out that you searched and replaced the wrong text, you can recover everything if you click the **Undo** icon or select **Edit Undo** using the menu route.

2. Select any appropriate search options.

3. To start the search and replace, click the **Replace** button.

4. When Word finds an occurrence of the specified text, the dialog box appears, and you have an opportunity to replace the word or skip to the next occurrence.

5. Click the **Replace All** button to replace every instance of the text in the remainder of the document.

Take a look at the Find and Replace dialog boxes again. You may have noticed two special buttons at the bottom of the boxes. Let me tell you what those do. The Format button lets you look through your file for text that has specific formatting, such as bold. When you click the **Format** button, a list appears with formatting options you can choose from. The Special button lets you search your file for specific characters or symbols. Both of these buttons can help you locate specific types of text items or characters in your documents.

Formatting Text for Fun and Profit

Did your mother ever tell you that you needed to build some character? Or did she tell you that you *were* a character? Well, your Word text works with character too, but we like to call it *character formatting*. Character formatting refers to the attributes that apply to individual characters in a document. Attributes include things such as bold letters, fonts, point sizes, italics, and more. In a nutshell, formatting is how your text looks.

You can change how your text looks to create different effects. For example, let's say you want a particular line in your memo document to stand out. You can italicize the entire line or even underline it using Word's formatting capabilities. Perhaps you want your report title to get noticed? Make it bold and set it in a larger size. With the various Word formatting features, you can add emphasis and give a professional look to all of your documents.

The Formatting Toolbar

The Word for Windows programmers put icons for all of the formatting commands on a separate toolbar: the Formatting toolbar. It's the second toolbar you see on your Word screen, and it's loaded with buttons for controlling how your text looks.

Click any of the following toolbar buttons to turn formatting features on or off, to open drop-down lists to select from, or to control how your text appears.

Button	Name
Normal ▼	Style
Times New Roman ▼	Font
10 ▼	Font size
B	Bold
I	Italic
U	Underline
🖊▼	Highlight
▤ ▥ ▦ ▧	Alignment
≔ ≔	Numbered and Bulleted Lists
⮐ ⮕	Indents
⊞	Borders

About Those Toolbars...

When you progress to an advanced stage of Word usage, you can change your toolbars. You have nine toolbars to choose from, or you can design your own. Open the **View** menu and choose the **Toolbars** command to display the Toolbars dialog box. There you'll find all the available toolbars, plus options for customizing your own toolbar.

A Fount of Fonts

One of the essential elements of formatting is fonts. A *font* is a particular style and size of type. Fonts come in families such as Times Roman or Courier, and each family has a set of point sizes that generally range from 6 points to 72 points, sometimes more. (There are 72 points in an inch, in case you wanted to know.)

The fonts and sizes available on your computer depend on your Windows 95 installation and your printer. If you've installed other programs that load all kinds of fonts onto your computer, you can use those in your Word documents as well. The formatting toolbar tells you which font is currently in use and its point size. You can change to another font or point size by clicking the drop-down arrow next to the font name or point size on the toolbar. The drop-down menus that appear list the fonts or sizes available to you. Select the one you want from the list to put it into effect. You can even type font names and sizes directly into the boxes.

A formatting drop-down menu.

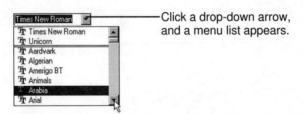

Click a drop-down arrow, and a menu list appears.

You can change the font before or after you start typing text. The choice is entirely up to you, since it's your program, your document, your text, your time, your money, and your book (assuming you bought this thing and didn't steal it). I made you a little list of ways to change fonts... .

➤ To change the font of existing text, select the text and use the formatting toolbar to change it to another font and point size.

➤ Alternatively, you can choose the **Font** command from the **Format** menu to access the Font dialog box, in which you can make the same kinds of changes.

➤ Point at a word and right-click to open a shortcut menu, choose the **Font** command, and open the Font dialog box.

Can I Change My Default Fonts?

Sure. To permanently change your default fonts, open the **Format** menu and select the **Font** command. Make changes to the font and style in the Font dialog box. Click the **Default** button. Another dialog box appears asking you to confirm your changes. If you select **Yes**, the default font for that document template will change and remain changed for all future documents built with that template (more on templates coming up).

Make Your Text Stand Out in a Crowd

To add emphasis to your Word text, use any of the formatting buttons on the toolbar to make your characters **bold**, *italic*, or <u>underlined</u>. Select the text you want to affect and click the corresponding buttons to change the appearance of your text. When selected, these buttons look like they're pressed in. This means they're in effect until you turn them off.

For example, if you're ready to type in some new text and you want it bold and italicized, click the **Bold** and **Italic** buttons on the toolbar before you start typing. Once you select these buttons, any text that you type will take on the appearance of bold and italicized letters. If you want to change the look of existing text, first select the text, and click the appropriate buttons.

A lot of people find it easier to set formatting in text by memorizing the keyboard shortcuts rather than clicking buttons and menus. For example, sometimes it's as fast to press **Ctrl+B** on the keyboard to set text bold than to click the **Bold** button on the formatting toolbar. You might be one of those people, too, so have at it.

What's the Format Painter Button For?

You can quickly copy the formatting on one word or a block of text to other selected text using the Format Painter button. Select the text with the formatting you want copied, and click the **Format Painter** button. Drag your pointer over the new text you want formatted, and the formatting is applied!

Hand Me That Highlighter, Please

If bold or italic text doesn't stand out enough to you, try highlighting your text. The Highlight button on your toolbar lets you highlight your text in a variety of colors. This spiffy feature will do you good only if you have a color printer or you invite everyone over to see your monitor screen. If you're sending the document to someone electronically (e-mail) and the recipient has a color monitor, the highlighting feature may dazzle him. Even if you aren't able to utilize the highlighting in another way, it's still looks snazzy on your own screen.

The Highlight options.

Highlight button

Highlighted text (sorry this book's not in color, or you could really see this)

Click the drop-down arrow to choose from other highlight colors or cancel text that you have already highlighted.

This Highlighting Feature Is Kinda Neat! The Highlight feature is new to Word 7. Someone must have thought it would be a good idea to give users the ability to take an electronic highlighter to their text. Don't let the kids get hold of it.

I personally enjoy using the Highlight feature when creating complaint letters or when answering my hate mail. Here's some more things to know about Highlight:

➤ To highlight your text, select it and click the **Highlight** button.

➤ To change your highlight color, click the drop-down arrow and choose another color.

➤ To see more colors, move your mouse to the right of the list.

108

➤ To unhighlight text, select the text, click the drop-down arrow and choose **Cancel**.

➤ Yellow is the default color.

Try the Amazing AutoFormat Feature!

If you don't know what kind of formatting you want to apply to your document, use Word's AutoFormat feature. It looks through your document and suggests formatting, which you can agree or disagree with. For example, maybe your boss just handed you a file of straight text, completely unformatted. Rather than sweat your way through the file trying to make it look nice, apply the AutoFormat feature to do it for you.

The AutoFormat can help you make your documents look nicer. For those of you who can't ever seem to make up your minds about things, such as whether to make a word bold or italics, you'll like using this feature. Isn't this primarily why you bought a computer anyway, so it would do all your work for you? On the other hand, every time I use AutoFormat, I feel like there's a teacher grading my work. I'm probably paranoid, huh?

Use the Toolbar
You can also click the **AutoFormat** icon button on the toolbar, but you won't see any of the swell dialog boxes. Instead, AutoFormat goes right to work, without any prompting by you.

To apply AutoFormatting, follow these steps:

1. Open the **Format** menu and choose the **AutoFormat** command.

2. An alert box will appear telling you Word is about to apply AutoFormat. Click **OK**, and it's off and running.

3. When the AutoFormat dialog box appears, click the **Review Changes** button to see what Word recommends you do to your document. If you review the changes, you can decide what formatting commands to keep or reject. And remember, you're not under any obligation to agree with your hundred-dollar word processing program's recommendations, okay?

4. As you review the recommended changes, click the **Find** buttons to go back and forth between recommendations. To reject a change, click the **Reject** button. When you're through reviewing, click **Cancel**.

5. Back in the original AutoFormat box (from step 3), you can accept the AutoFormat changes by clicking the **Accept** button, or reject them all by clicking the **Reject All** button.

6. Click **OK** to exit the dialog box and execute any formatting recommendations.

109

The Least You Need to Know

Everything you ever wanted to know about editing and simple formatting packed into a single chapter! But wait—that's not all there is to formatting. In the next chapter, I'll show you even more tricks for controlling how your document looks, including how to position text in your document.

In the meantime, here's a summary of your editing etiquette and simple formatting frills:

➤ You can use a variety of editing techniques to make your document perfect, including moving, copying, and deleting text.

➤ Selecting text enables you to edit it quickly, whether it's one character, one word, or several paragraphs.

➤ There's an invisible selection bar on the left side of the text area of your Word screen. Use it to select text, too.

➤ To cut, copy, and paste your text, you'll need to use the Windows Clipboard, a temporary holding area.

➤ The commands on the Formatting toolbar and the Format menu make it easy for you to apply character formatting to make your text look good.

➤ If you don't know what formatting you want to use on your document, try out the AutoFormat command and let Word make some suggestions.

Jockeying for Position with Your Text

Another way to control the look of your Word documents is to use positioning techniques, such as changing margins, tabs, indents, and alignment (also considered to be *formatting commands*). All of these changes can affect the spacing of your text on the document page and can make the difference between an easy-to-read document that is pleasing to the eye, or one that just makes you gag from the sight of it.

If you've never worked with a word processing program before, you may be surprised at the dizzying array of commands that you can apply to your page's layout. There are literally oodles (however many that is) of ways you can place your text on the page and manipulate it—it's enough to give you a headache. In this chapter, you learn how to deal with margins, indents, spacing between lines of text, tabs, horizontal alignment, vertical alignment, and columns. Whew!

Hey! Mine Came with a Ruler!

Before we start talking about positioning and spacing your text, I need to introduce you to your free Word for Windows ruler. That's right, there's a ruler on your screen that you can use to help place your text on the document page.

Hopefully, your ruler appeared by default when Word started. If not, open the **View** menu and select the **Ruler** command.

➤ If the word **Ruler** has a check mark in front of it, the ruler will appear.

➤ If there's no check mark in front of the word, the ruler will not appear. It doesn't get any easier than this.

If you're viewing your document in Page Layout mode, your screen may display two rulers, a horizontal one that appears below the Formatting toolbar (or below the TipWizard bar, if it's turned on), and a vertical one at the left side of your text area. (If you're viewing in Normal mode, you won't see the vertical ruler. Don't worry about the vertical ruler for now. Just concentrate on the horizontal ruler. You'll learn more about viewing modes in Chapter 11.)

There are two triangle shapes at each end of your horizontal ruler that represent the position of the margin settings and indents. Drag these shapes left or right across the ruler to reset your document's margins and indents.

Tabs appear on your ruler as funky little symbols, too. (You won't see any tabs yet because we haven't set any, so don't get excited.) The number markings on the ruler show inches from the left margin of the page.

Pay attention in the upcoming sections for tips on how to use your ruler to set up your document's spacing.

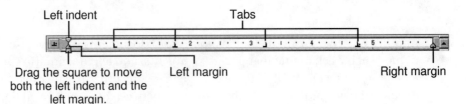

Left indent   Tabs

Use Word's ruler to adjust the spacing within your document.

Drag the square to move   Left margin   Right margin
both the left indent and the
left margin.

Marginal Margins

The margin is the space between your text and the edge of your page. There are four margins on each page: left, right, top, and bottom. (I guess you probably could have figured that out on your own, unless you're using round paper to print your documents on.) There's a 1.0-inch margin at the top and bottom of your page, and a 1.25-inch margin on the right and left sides. For most of us, the default margins work just fine. However, you can change any of the margins to suit your own needs. For example, if you've written a letter that just barely runs over onto the second page, you may be able to make it fit perfectly on one page by adjusting the margins ever so slightly.

I adjusted the left margin to move this paragraph over.

Right margin marker

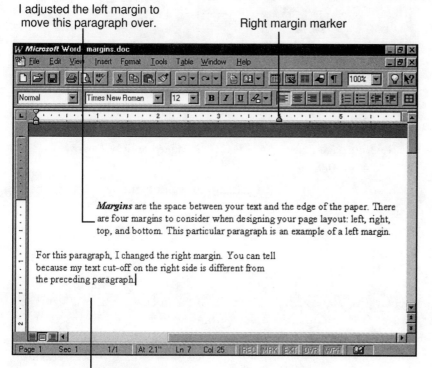

Examples of margins.

This paragraph shows a different right margin.

You can control the left and right margins using your ruler. To change these margins, simply drag the appropriate margin symbol to a new position on the ruler. The ruler's margin markers only apply to the paragraph where the insertion marker is parked. In the preceding figure, the insertion point is at the end of the second paragraph, so the margin marker that appears on the ruler pertains to that paragraph only.

Alternatively, you can use the Page Setup dialog box to set margins. To access this box, open the **File** menu and choose **Page Setup**. You will find the page margin settings in the Margins tab. Click the **Margins** tab to bring it to the front.

113

The Margins tab of the Page Setup dialog box.

Control your margins by adjusting these settings.

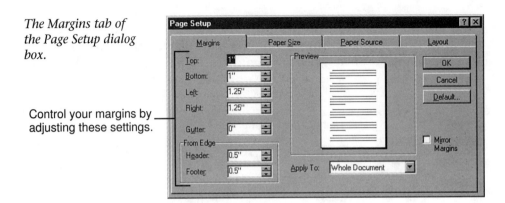

Here's what you can do in the Margins tab:

➤ To change any of the four page margin settings, click the up or down arrows to increase or decrease the settings.

➤ Look in the Preview box to the right of the settings to see how the settings affect text.

➤ If you prefer, you can type a specific margin measurement into the appropriate box next to the arrow buttons.

➤ Click **OK** or press **Enter** to exit the Page Setup dialog box.

When you change the margins, you control how much of the document they affect. You can apply the new settings to your entire document, from the location of the insertion point on, or to a block of selected text. It's up to you. Just select the text to be affected by a margin change and modify the margins, or place your cursor directly in the paragraph or block of text where you want the margin change to occur and then modify the margins.

Identifying Indents

If you weren't too excited about margins, then perhaps indents will give you a thrill. Indents are just margins that affect individual paragraphs or lines. For example, when you start a paragraph and press the **Tab** key to scoot the first line over slightly, you're creating an indent. When you set a bulleted text list in the middle of a page, you have created an indent.

Sure, pressing the **Tab** key is an easy way to indent; it's rather mindless, but there are other methods you can use to indent as well—real computer-savvy methods that only smart Word users use.

To indent a block of text in the midst of your page, highlight the text, and then summon the Paragraph dialog box by opening the **Format** menu and choosing the **Paragraph** command. (Or right-click to open a shortcut menu, and then select **Paragraph**.) You control indent options with the settings on the Indents and Spacing tab of the Paragraph dialog box.

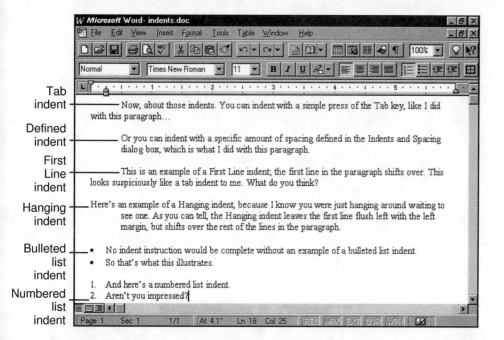

Take a look at these examples of indents.

Tab indent

Defined indent

First Line indent

Hanging indent

Bulleted list indent

Numbered list indent

Click the **Indents and Spacing** tab to bring it to the front of the dialog box; then try some of these options:

➤ In the **Indentation** section, you can set the left and right indents. Click the arrows to increase or decrease the measurement.

➤ Or type a precise measurement into the text box next to the appropriate indent.

➤ In the **Special** drop-down list box, you can set a First Line indent or a Hanging indent. A First Line indent moves the first line of the paragraph over but leaves the remaining text lined up flush with the left margin. A Hanging indent leaves the first line flush at the left margin but shifts the remaining lines in the paragraph over to the right.

➤ When you finish setting indents in the Paragraph dialog box, click the **OK** button, and the changes will appear in your text.

Change these settings
to control indents.

Line spacing
controls

*The Indents and
Spacing tab of the
Paragraph dialog
box.*

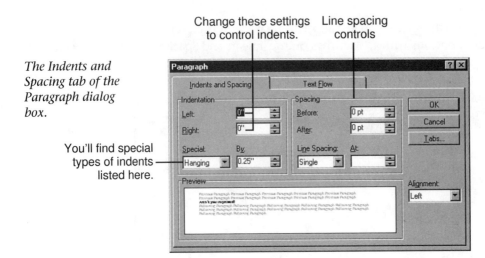

You'll find special
types of indents
listed here.

Speedy Indents for Fast-Paced Word Users

For even faster indents, use the indent buttons on the Formatting toolbar. Click the **Increase Indent** button to indent text by one tab stop. Click the **Decrease Indent** button to undo an indent.

To create the indent for a bulleted list or numbered list, use the **Bullet** or **Number** buttons on the Formatting toolbar. Select the text that you want to change to a list, and click the appropriate button. (You can also choose Bullets and Numbering from the old right-click menu.) To establish a bulleted or numbered list indent before you enter new text, click the **Bullet** or **Number** button before you start typing. Every time you press **Enter** while composing your list, a new bullet or number will appear to create the new list item. To turn off bulleted and numbered indents, just deselect the **Bullet** or **Number** toolbar button.

Give Me More Space!

The Paragraph dialog box you just learned about also contains commands for controlling *pagination* (page numbering and layout) and the space between lines of text. Take a look at the Paragraph dialog box again (glance back at the preceding figure) and locate the Spacing section. Here's a rundown of what you can do with the spacing commands:

➤ The **Before** and **After** settings (which are measured in points) are used to control the amount of space before and after text lines.

➤ Pull down the **Line Spacing** drop-down list to find such standard line spacing designations as single-space, double-space, and the like.

➤ Click the **Text Flow** tab to access the text flow options, which you use to control the flow of text from one page to another.

➤ The **Widow/Orphan Control** option can help you keep single words or small bits of text from being abandoned on the last line of one page or the first line of another.

➤ The **Keep Lines Together** option prevents the occurrence of a page break in the middle of a selected paragraph.

➤ The **Keep with Next** option prevents the occurrence of a page break between two designated paragraphs.

➤ The **Page Break Before** option places a page break before a specified paragraph instead of in the middle of it or after it.

If used effectively, all of the pagination and spacing options can help you create better-looking documents that are easier to read, or at least very nicely spaced.

Picking Up the Tab

Tabs provide another way of strategically putting space in your document to make it look nice. Tabs come in handy when you're trying to line up columns of text in your document.

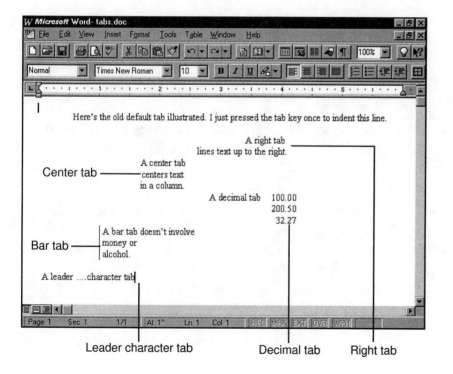

Tabs in action.

Leader character tab   Decimal tab   Right tab

More Ways to Open the Tabs Dialog Box
You can also access the Tabs dialog box via the Paragraph dialog box. Just click the **Tabs** button. Wait, there's more! You can also double-click any tab symbol set on your ruler to open the Tabs dialog box, too.

Whenever you press the **Tab** key on the keyboard, the Word for Windows cursor moves over one tab stop. By default, Word has tab stops set up at 1/2-inch intervals across the width of the document page. These default tab stops are left-aligned tabs, which means the text lines up on the left. But, hey, you don't have to use these default tabs. You can set your own tabs.

To set your own tabs, you'll need some help from the Tabs dialog box. Open the **Format** menu and choose **Tabs**; the Tabs dialog box appears.

The Tabs dialog box.

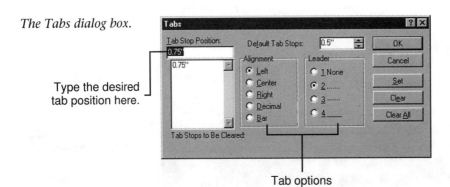

Type the desired tab position here.

Tab options

1. To set a tab stop, just type the desired position in inches in the **Tab Stop Position** text box.

2. Click the **Set** button to set the tab, and it appears in the **Tab Stop Position** list box.

3. Click **OK** to exit the dialog box.

To apply your newly set tab, just press the **Tab** key.

If you thought that was swell, let me tell you about the other tab options you can use. If you ever get tired of the 1/2-inch default tabs, you can change them with the Default Tab Stops option in the Tabs dialog box. Click the directional arrows to select a new default setting, or type one in the **Default Tab Stops** text box.

As I mentioned a second ago, the default tab is a left-aligned tab, which means the text lines up to the left. However, you can choose to align tabbed text other than to the left. In the Alignment section of the Tabs dialog box, you have five tab types to choose from. If you pick Left, Center, or Right, the text that you tab will line up at that respective

118

position. If you choose Decimal, your tab lines up the text at the decimal point. If you choose Bar, a vertical bar appears in your text, and your text is left-aligned to the bar (which is helpful when you're trying to separate tab columns).

The Leader section of the Tabs dialog box enables you to insert dots, dashes, or ruled lines to fill up the empty space between your tab stops. The default option is to have nothing between the stops (None).

Setting Tabs on the Ruler

By now, some of you may be wondering, "Hey, why aren't we learning to set tabs using that free ruler?" Well, I was just getting to that part, so hold your horses. It's really easy to set tabs using your ruler.

At the far left end of the ruler is a tab type symbol. Click it to determine what kind of tab you want to set (right, center, decimal, and so on). To set a new tab stop, click at the desired position on the lower half of the horizontal ruler. To move a tab stop, drag it to a new position. To delete a tab stop, drag it off the ruler. When you set tab stops, they apply to any paragraphs you've selected; if you don't select any paragraphs, they apply from the current insertion point onward.

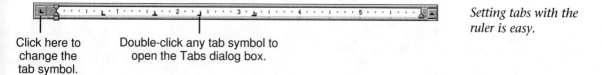

Setting tabs with the ruler is easy.

Click here to change the tab symbol.

Double-click any tab symbol to open the Tabs dialog box.

In case you're at all confused about which tab symbol means what, here's a table to define them all.

Tab Symbols Defined

Symbol	What It Does
⌊	Left-align tab
⊥	Center tab
⌋	Right-align tab
⊥	Decimal tab

119

When you're tired of all the tab stops you've created, get rid of them. You can drag each tab symbol off the ruler, or you can open up the Tabs dialog box and select **Clear** or **Clear All** to remove the tab stops (but not the default tab stops). Let's move on to rotating and aligning your text.

It Could Be Your Struts, But Let's Check Your Alignment

Yet another way to control how your text looks on the page is with the *alignment* (also called *justification*) commands. Alignment refers to how your text is positioned horizontally on the page, such as left, right, or centered. Alignment differs from tabs and indents because you typically use it on blocks of text. By default, Word lines up your text at the left margin. But if that's not good enough for you, Word offers you several other alignment options to choose from.

Alignment examples.

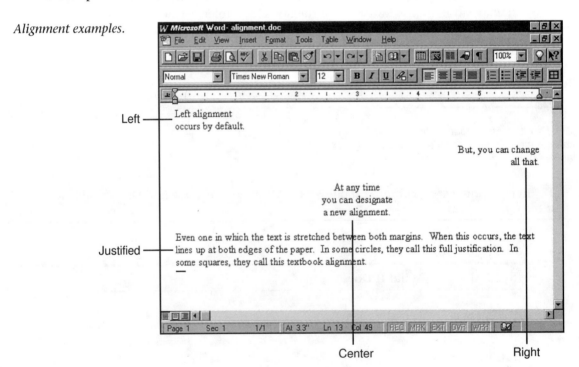

➤ Right alignment lines all your text up at the right margin.

➤ Center alignment centers your text between the left and right margins.

➤ Justified alignment lines up your text at both the left and right margins: the text stretches out between the two margins. You're probably used to seeing justified text all the time in newspapers and books.

120

You can set your text alignment before or after you start entering characters. The fastest way to choose alignment is to click the alignment buttons on the Formatting toolbar. The images on the four little icons show how the text will be aligned. Just click the one you want to turn on that type of alignment.

If you don't like clicking buttons on the toolbar, you can use the alignment controls in the Paragraph dialog box. Open the **Format** menu and select the **Paragraph** command to access the Paragraph dialog box. The alignment commands are in a drop-down box on the Indents and Spacing tab. (You can also get to the Paragraph dialog box with a right-click on your text; then select **Paragraph** from the menu that appears.)

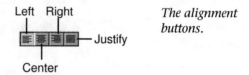

The alignment buttons.

What About Vertical Alignment?

Here's something interesting that you probably haven't thought about yet. The alignment controls affect the horizontal positioning of your text, right? So, how do you control the vertical positioning? Why, with the vertical alignment commands, of course. Occasions may arise when you need your page spaced out vertically as well as horizontally. For example, you may create a newsletter that requires you to make sure the top and bottom text are flush with the top and bottom margins, no extra white space allowed. In such instances, you can use the vertical alignment controls.

Vertical alignment commands are located in the Page Setup dialog box on the **Layout** tab. To find them:

1. Pull down the **File** menu and select **Page Setup**.

2. In the dialog box, click the **Layout** tab to bring the Layout options to the front of the dialog box.

3. Under **Vertical Alignment**, click the drop-down arrow to reveal a list of vertical alignment choices. By default, your text always aligns with the top margin of the page. However, you can change to a center alignment (which centers the text between the top and bottom margins) or a justified alignment (which stretches the text out between the top and bottom margins).

4. Click **OK** to exit the dialog box.

Creating Columns

Are you trying to use Word to make a newsletter or another kind of document that needs columns? Let me show you how to make columns with the Columns command.

1. First move your insertion point to the section of your document where you want columns to appear.

2. Open the **Format** menu and choose the **Columns** command. The Columns dialog box appears, displaying a variety of column types to choose from.

Choose a column style from these options.

The Columns dialog box.

Set an exact number of columns in this box.

Use these settings to control column width and spacing.

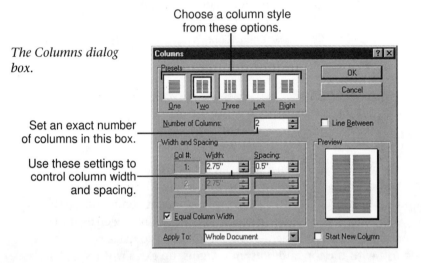

Use the Column Button

There's also a **Column** button on the Standard toolbar you can use to set up columns fast. Click it to reveal a table of columns. Highlight how many columns you want to use and release the mouse button to lay them out.

3. Under the **Presets** settings, click the column style you want to use.

4. If you don't like any of the Presets choices, then create your own column style using the **Number of Columns** setting.

5. You can control the column spacing with the **Width** and **Spacing** settings. By default, your columns will have equal width. If you don't want that, then deselect the **Equal Column Width** check box. To change any of the column widths, click the appropriate column and use the arrow keys to change the setting.

6. Open the **Apply To** drop-down list to choose how much of your document appears in columns.

7. When you finish with your column options, click **OK**.

Columns

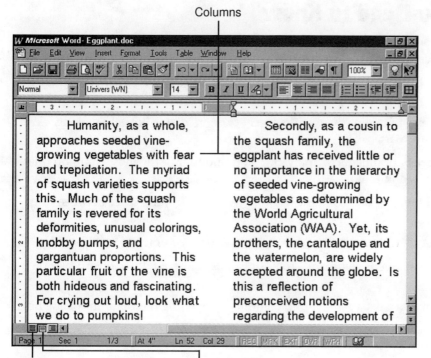

An example of columns.

Click this button to return to Normal view.

Click here to see your columns side-by-side on-screen.

Now if you want to see your columns side-by-side, you'll need to click the **Page Layout** view. See those little icon buttons next to your horizontal scroll bar? The second one is the Page Layout view (which you'll learn more about in Chapter 11). You can always go back to Normal view by clicking the first button down at the scroll bar.

How About a Little Column Trick? To insert a vertical line in between your columns to separate them, select the **Line Between** check box in the Columns dialog box.

Check This Out...

The Least You Need to Know

In this chapter, you learned a lot about making your Word documents look great by controlling your design and positioning. Let's go over everything one more time.

➤ By adjusting the margins, indents, and horizontal and vertical spacing, you can control how your text prints on the page.

➤ You can set exact margins by opening the Page Setup dialog box and making changes on the Margins tab.

➤ There is a variety of indents to apply, and you find four of the most common ones on your Formatting toolbar.

➤ The Paragraph dialog box contains commands for controlling space between lines and text flow.

➤ Tabs are a lot like indents, but you use them to set up columns of text instead.

➤ You can use alignment commands to position text horizontally and vertically on a page.

➤ You can easily turn existing text into columns by opening the Columns dialog box.

Chapter 10

Add Some Finishing Touches

In This Chapter

➤ Give your Word documents some style

➤ Learn how to insert headers and footers

➤ Steps for creating tables and sprucing them up

➤ Add some graphics to enhance your text

Are you ready for a real Word workout now? Good because in this chapter, we're going to run through all the tricks for jazzing up your documents, bench-press tables using only one hand, and do graphic calisthenics without even breathing hard. Are you sure you're ready? Okay, then, drop and give me 50.

What Kinds of Finishing Touches?

By now, your head may be spinning from all of the formatting information. Who would have thought that typing a few words onto a screen could involve so many things? As it turns out, communicating with words is a very exacting science, and a good word processing program must offer you every possible scenario for your text and how it looks. (Besides, you paid big bucks for it, so it had better be able to handle some special effects.)

Finishing touches are the key to making your Word documents communicate. Sure, every Tom, Dick, and Harry can type up a letter and apply bold to a few words, but it's not every Word user who knows how to apply formatting techniques skillfully. Take the time to learn to design a great-looking document, and you and your documents will be way ahead of those other word processing users.

For that reason, it's important to learn how to set styles, insert headers and footers, whip up some fancy tables, add some artwork, and create a few special effects to make your text stand out. While these options may sound a little intimidating, you'll find that you get a lot more out of Office 95 if you learn to do these things. And as fancy-sounding as a header or footer may be, the Microsoft people have made it relatively painless to create these things. Let's start with styles.

Keeping in Style

You could always use some more style, right? Word for Windows uses styles, too. A *style* is a group of formatting settings that you can use over and over again throughout your documents. For instance, say you create a document with headlines, subheads, or even special paragraphs for tables. Instead of highlighting each of these elements and formatting the characters every single time, you can set up specific styles to apply instead. That way, the only step you have to take to format your text is to select a particular style (as opposed to the many steps required to pull down multiple menus and open dialog boxes).

Check This Out...

What Are Those Funny Symbols? In the Style drop-down box, you may notice that the style names have different icons next to them. A paragraph icon (looks like a funny P) indicates a paragraph style, and a character icon (looks like an a) indicates the style is a character style.

Sound too good to be true? Well it is. There is a catch. *Styles can only apply to individual paragraphs.* You can define a style for any paragraph in a Word document. If you later change the style, all paragraphs to which that style was applied automatically change to reflect the new style. Keep in mind that in Word, you create a paragraph every time you press the Enter key. Even if you press Enter to make a blank line between two paragraphs, the blank line is considered a paragraph, too.

When the insertion point is in a paragraph, the name of the style assigned to that paragraph appears in the Style box located at the far left end of the Formatting toolbar. Normal is Word's default style. Word comes with some other styles, or you can create your own.

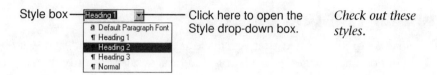

Style box ———— | Click here to open the | *Check out these*
Style drop-down box. | *styles.*

To assign a style:

1. Select the paragraph (or paragraphs) you want to format.

2. Click the **Style** drop-down box on the Formatting toolbar.

3. From the list of styles, select the one you want to apply.

If the drop-down list doesn't have enough to choose from, you can open the **Format** menu and select the **Style** command. This opens the Style dialog box, which contains even more ready-made Word styles to use.

More styles!

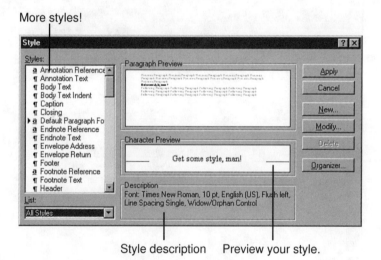

The Style dialog box.

Style description   Preview your style.

An easy way to create your own style is to use the Style drop-down box on the toolbar. First set up the paragraph on which you want to base your style; include any special formatting you want to use. Make sure your insertion point is somewhere in that paragraph, and then click the **Style** drop-down box in the Formatting toolbar. Enter a new style name, being careful not to duplicate an existing name. Click anywhere outside of the box or press **Enter**, and you have created a new style. You can now apply it by name to new paragraphs that you add to your document.

Header Hunters and Footers

A *header* or *footer* is text that you place at the very top (header) or very bottom (footer) of your document pages. A header or footer may consist of only the page number, or it can contain titles, author names, dates, cholesterol ratings, small recipes, or whatever information you want. You can place a header/footer on every page, or every other page, or with about any combination you want.

To add a header or footer to your document pages, you first have to display the Header and Footer toolbar on your screen. To do this, open the **View** menu and select **Header and Footer.** The Header and Footer toolbar appears, and you're ready to go. Type your header or footer text in the outlined text box. You can use the Formatting toolbar buttons to control how your header or footer text looks.

When you set headers and footers, a floating toolbar appears on your screen.

Type your header or footer in the outlined box.

Header and Footer floating toolbar

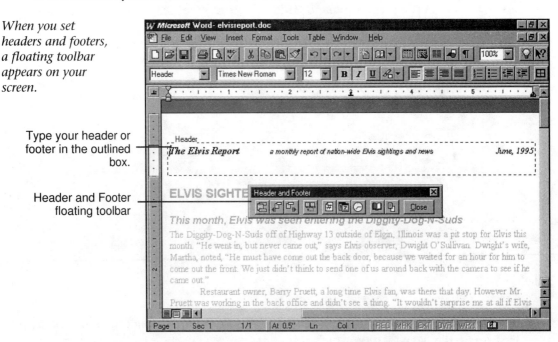

The following table describes each of the Header and Footer toolbar buttons.

Header and Footer Toolbar Buttons

Button	Description
	These buttons allow you to move back and forth between headers and footers and sections of your document.
	Use this button to make the current header or footer the same as the previous one.
	Use these buttons to add page numbers, the date, or the current time to your header or footer text.
	Opens the Page Setup dialog box where you can control which pages the header or footer falls on.
	Toggles between showing the text on the document page with the header/footer or just the header/footer by itself.
Close	Closes the Header and Footer dialog box and returns you to the document page.

When you finish setting your header or footer, click the **Close** button on the Header and Footer toolbar. If you ever need to go back and edit your header or footer, bring back the Header and Footer box and make your changes (open the **View** menu and select **Header and Footer**). To delete a header or footer, just delete all of the text in its outlined box.

Having Trouble Setting a Footer? When you first select the Headers and Footers command, it assumes you want a header. To set a footer instead, just click the very first button on the floating toolbar.

A Table for Two

Ever set a table on your computer? You will now. Word tables let you organize your text into a row and column format. You can use tables to list information, or as illustrative charts. For example, the tables in this book show icon buttons, button names, and descriptions of what they do. The information appears into columns and rows in a consistent fashion. You'll find a table of keyboard keys coming up in this section that list keypresses and what they accomplish. There's a myriad of things you can put into tables: facts, figures, graphics, paragraphs, and so on.

The key to Word tables is that you can organize the information in a systematic fashion. Each intersection of a row and column is called a *cell*. Each table cell can have any kind of text or formatting. In fact, a table cell can contain anything except another table.

An example of a Word table.

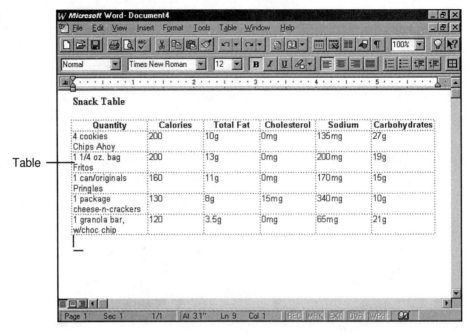

Table ⎯⎯

To build a table in your document:

1. Click your cursor where you want your table. (If you select any text, Word tries to make a table out of it, so be warned.)

2. Next, open the **Table** menu and choose **Insert Table**.

The Insert Table dialog box.

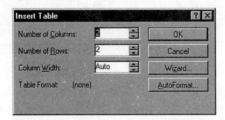

3. In the Insert Table dialog box, determine how many rows and columns your table will contain (you can always adjust these numbers again later).

4. In the **Column Width** box, select a width for your table columns. Select **Auto** if you want the page width divided evenly among your designated number of columns.

5. Click **OK**, and a blank table appears into your document.

To fill in a cell on your table, click inside the cell. Enter and edit text there just as you would in any other part of the document. If you enter a lot of text, it automatically wraps itself to fit inside of your column width. To help you move around your table, here's a chart of special key combinations.

Moving Around in a Table

Press	To
Tab	Move to the next cell in the row.
Shift+Tab	Move to the previous cell in the row.
Alt+Home	Move to the first cell in the row you're in.
Alt+PgUp	Move to the top cell in the column you're in.
Alt+End	Move to the last cell in the row you're in.
Alt+PgDn	Move to the last cell in the column you're in.

Here's what else you can do with tables:

➤ You can easily delete the contents of a cell by selecting it and pressing the **Del** key.

➤ You can also delete entire columns or rows. To do this, select any cell in the column or row you want to delete. Open the **Table** menu and choose **Delete Cells**. In the dialog box, select **Delete Entire Row** or **Delete Entire Column**. Click **OK**, and the row or column disappears. The other rows and columns move over to take its place.

➤ To insert a row or column into your table, move to the cell to the right of which you want to add a column or below which you want to add a row. Then open the **Table** menu and choose **Table Select Row** or **Table Select Column**. Then select the entire row or column, open the **Table** menu again, and choose **Insert Columns** or **Insert Rows** to instantly insert a new one. (You can insert a new row at the bottom of a table by just pressing **Tab** from the last cell.)

➤ If you need a wider column, you can use your mouse pointer to drag the column edge to a new size. Simply place the pointer on the right column border and drag it to the width you want.

Check This Out...

Get Seated at a Table Fast!
Just click the **Insert Table** button on your Standard toolbar. Drag your mouse over the exact number of columns and rows you want to create, (highlighting the squares which represent cells), let go of the mouse button, and your table is ready!

Check This Out...

Border Shortcut! Another way to select borders fast is to click the **Borders** button on the toolbar. When you click it, a Borders toolbar appears at the top of your screen with icons representing border styles. You can also make the Borders toolbar appear by clicking the **Show Toolbar** button in the Borders and Shading dialog box.

Techno Talk

What About the Shading Part of the Tables Borders and Shading Dialog Box? Borders and shading kind of go hand-in-hand, so to speak. The Shading tab lets you control colors and background shading in your Word table. Just click the **Shading** tab to bring it to the front of the box, and choose from among the many color options. You can also control your table border's line color with the Color drop-down list in the **Borders** tab.

➤ If you prefer a more meticulous method for widening columns, select the entire column by clicking at the top of the first cell in the column, open the **Table** menu, and choose **Cell Height and Width**. (You can also right-click on the column to bring up a shortcut menu; then select **Table**.) In the dialog box that appears, click the **Column** tab to bring it to the front of the box. Type in the width you want in the **Width of Column** text box, or use the up and down arrows to set the width. Click **OK** or press **Enter** when you finish.

Adding Table Borders

You can also add a border to your table. On-screen, Word shows your table cells separated by grid lines; however, those grid lines don't print out on paper. You can add your own lines or another kind of border. Want to try? Follow these steps:

1. Place the insertion point anywhere inside your table.

2. Open the **Table** menu and choose **Select Table**.

3. Open the **Format** menu and choose **Borders and Shading**.

4. In the Borders and Shading dialog box, click the **Borders** tab to bring those options to the front of the box.

5. In the Presets section, choose **None** to remove a grid or box, choose **Box** to add an outline around the outside of your table, or choose **Grid** to add a box around the outside and grid lines between cells.

6. In the Line section, choose a line thickness to use.

7. When you like your selections, click **OK** or press **Enter**. Your table prints with a border or grid!

It's a Work of Art!

With Word, you can add graphics in your documents to spruce things up. A *graphic* is usually a picture of some kind, and computer graphics are special graphics files. Word lets you work with graphic files from Lotus, AutoCAD, Windows Metafiles, Micrografx Designer, and more (see your Word manual for more information). Word also comes with its own set of graphics, called *clip art*. You'll find the Word clip art graphics in the CLIPART file in your WINWORD folder.

Explain Those Terms Again

A *graphic* is a picture. Computer graphics include images, lines, and shapes that are stored as computer files. *Clip art* is a collection of ready-made computer graphic images.

To add graphics to your Word document, do this:

1. Place the insertion point where you want to insert the picture.

2. Open the **Insert** menu and choose **Picture**. The Insert Picture dialog box appears.

3. A list of clip art files appears. (If it doesn't, then use the **Look in** drop-down box to choose the **CLIPART** folder.) Scroll through the list of files and click one to highlight it.

Filter This

Word uses *graphics filters* to convert graphic files from other programs into a format that it can use. Word comes with several default filters, but if you need other filers, you can add them with your Microsoft Office setup program. Be sure to consult your manual for more information.

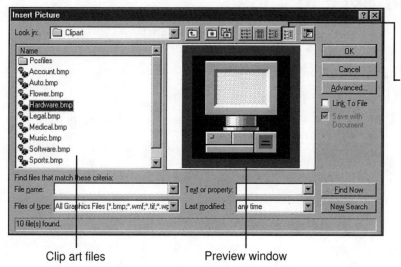

The Insert Picture dialog box.

Click here to open the Preview window.

Clip art files   Preview window

4. Click the **Preview** button (fourth toolbar button from the left) in your dialog box to open a Preview window and see what the graphic looks like. (You can continue scrolling through the list of files, viewing each one in the Preview window until you find one you like.)

5. When you're ready to select the art, highlight its file name in the list, and click **OK**. (Or for a faster route, double-click the file name.) The graphic now appears in your Word document.

Once you insert the graphic in your document, you can select it to resize or crop it. Click it, and eight little black squares, called *selection handles*, appear around it.

Draw It Yourself, Then! If you don't like any of the clip art you find in Word, draw your own art using Word's drawing feature. To open the Drawing toolbar, click the **Drawing** button on the Standard toolbar. Use the drawing tools to create your own shapes and images.

Use any of these methods to manipulate your graphic:

➤ Point at one of the selection handles, and your mouse pointer turns into a double-headed arrow.

➤ Drag the handle to resize the graphic.

➤ To crop the graphic (which means to show only a certain portion of it), hold down the **Shift** key and drag the handle inward.

➤ To get rid of a graphic, select it and press the **Del** key.

➤ To copy or move the graphic, select it and use the **Cut** and **Copy** commands from the **Edit** menu or the **Cut** and **Copy** toolbar buttons (as explained in Chapter 5).

The Least You Need to Know

Enough of this document design business. In the next chapter, I'll show you what to do with a document once you finish it. In the meantime, go over these design notes:

➤ Style can simplify your Word formatting chores.

➤ Headers and footers can help you organize your Word pages.

➤ With Word's Table feature, you can use columns and rows to logically organize and present information in your document.

➤ Use graphics to complement your Word documents.

Chapter 11

Printing, Proofing, and Previewing

In This Chapter

➤ Try out different viewing modes

➤ Learn how to proof your document using Word's many proofing features

➤ The real scoop on adding fields

Once your words are on-screen just the way you want them, and any other on-screen items are in place, you're ready to print. *But, wait!* Before you do, you might want to check out Word's proofing features to see how they can help you perfect your document. There's nothing worse than cranking out a 20-page document from your printer only to find out that it's filled with spelling errors.

In this chapter, I'll tell you how to switch perspectives and preview your file before printing. Plus, I'll also show you some cool things you can do with Word to make your word processing tasks even easier, such as turning on an AutoSave feature and using fields in your text. Don't worry, this is the very last chapter covering Word basics.

A Different Point of View

Sometimes, you need to view your document from another perspective to see if you like the way it looks. Word has several different views in which you can display your document.

Am I in Normal?

Trying to figure out what view mode you're in can be a little confusing. In Normal view, you can see on-screen all the special formatting you've applied to your text. However, Word simplifies certain aspects of the page layout to speed up your editing; for example, you do not see columns and headers and footers in Normal view.

Normal view.

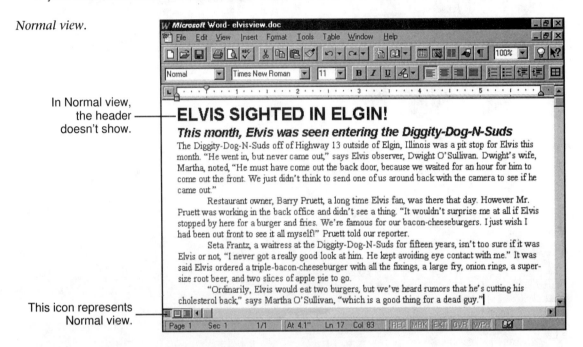

In Normal view, the header doesn't show.

This icon represents Normal view.

The Very Professional Page Layout View

To see your document page exactly as it will print, switch to Page Layout view. Page Layout view is ideal for fine-tuning the details of your page composition. You can per-form editing tasks just as you would in Normal view, yet you can see headers and footers and all the other page details you've incorporated.

Check This Out...

Use the Buttons! The views are also available as icons; but don't look for them on the top toolbars. Instead, you'll find them located at the far left end of the horizontal scroll bar (at the bottom of your screen).

To view your document in Page Layout view, first pull down the **View** menu. You'll notice that among the various display views listed here, one has a little dot in front of it; the little dot identifies the view currently in effect. To change views, just select another view from the list. In this case, select **Page Layout**.

A word of caution: Page Layout view may make your computer run a little more slowly because of the additional computer processing that's required to display every page detail—but since you're using lightning-fast Windows 95, you probably won't notice. However, it's a good idea to switch back to Normal view as soon as you finish with Page Layout view, just to speed things up again.

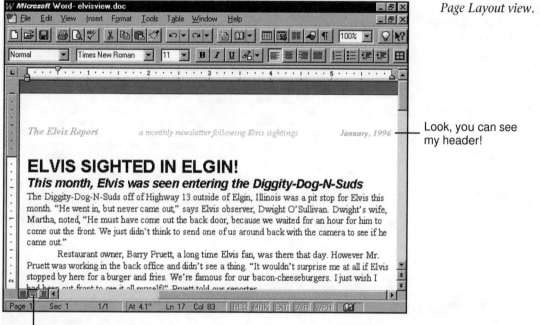

Page Layout view.

Look, you can see my header!

This icon represents Page Layout view.

Turn In Your Outline

If you ever want to examine the structure of your document, I highly recommend Outline view. If you've selected different styles (see Chapter 10 for more information) for headlines, subheadlines, and regular text, you can see the structure of your document come to life when you switch over to Outline view. In Outline view, Word displays only your document headings and subordinate text (see the next figure). This makes it easy for you to quickly rearrange headings, subheadings, and more. You can quickly attach new styles, too. To view a document in Outline view, open the **View** menu again and select **Outline**. You can choose to view all of your document's headings, include text, or a number of other structural views. You can even choose to view text with or without formatting applied.

Outline view.

Plus signs indicate heading styles.

Bullets indicate regular text.

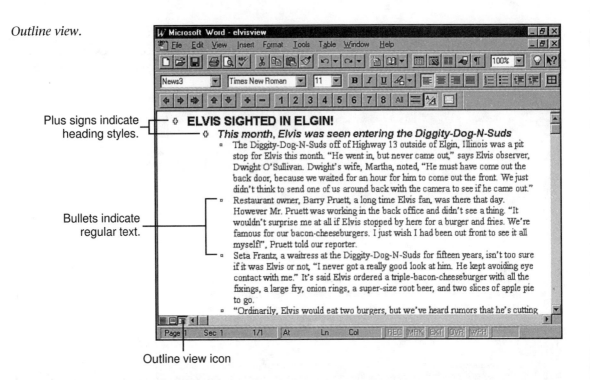

Outline view icon

What About the Master Document View?

If you're prone to working with exceptionally long documents, you can use Master Document to help keep things organized and manageable. When you click the **Master Document** view, you can work in an expanded outline view, and additional toolbar buttons appear to help out. Type in the outline for your document using the styles for making headings and subheadings. You can use the buttons on the toolbar to add headings, move up and down the outline, expand and collapse headings, create and remove subdocuments, and more. When you finish setting up your outline, save the master document with a unique name. Be sure to consult your Word manual for more information about using the Master Document view.

Zooming Around

If display view modes aren't your cup of tea, try Word's zooming feature. The Zoom command enables you to look at your document from various perspectives ranging from up-close (to get a close look at a font or a point size) to a bird's-eye-view (to get a preview of your overall page layout). Open the **View** menu and select the **Zoom** command to access the Zoom dialog box, in which you can control what magnification to view your screen. Alternatively, you can click the **Zoom** drop-down list on the toolbar and select a magnification setting from there.

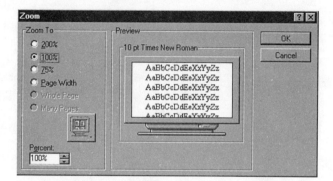

The Zoom dialog box.

Clear the Screen!

If you get tired of seeing all the toolbars, scroll bars, title bars, and borders on your Word screen, you can make them all go away and leave just a giant working area. To do this, open the **View** menu and choose the **Full Screen** command. (To return to your normal screen, click the floating **Full Screen** button.)

Proofing and Printing with Word

Word for Windows has made it easy to check your document with a fine-tooth comb before you let anyone see it. If you're into picking things apart like a vulture, Word includes a spell checker and even a new word count feature to help you. Once you've proofed your work, checked it out with Print Preview, and made sure you have everything in order, then you're ready to print.

Have Yourself a Spelling Bee

For some people, spelling is an agonizing part of communicating with words. This struggle starts from childhood and almost always results in the purchase of a 10-pound dictionary that you lug about throughout your college days and beyond. Thankfully, most of today's word processing programs come with a spell check program designed to help people overcome this struggle.

Word's spell checker program can help alleviate some of the pressure of spelling words correctly. Notice I said *some* of the pressure? It's not a fail-proof system. You still have to read what you write to know if you've said what you meant to say. But, hey, it can still help.

Check This Out...

What About Spell It?

Back in Chapter 7, I told you about Word's Spell It feature. It automatically checks your spelling as you type and if it finds anything unusual, it underlines your text with a wavy red line. (Go back to Chapter 7 for pointers on using Spell It.) But Spell It isn't the only way to proofread your document. Word will also let you spell check from the beginning of your document to the end. You just need to activate the command. (Keep reading this section.)

Techno Talk

Quick Check To check the spelling of a single word in your document, position the insertion point in or immediately to the right of the word and press **F7**.

The spell checker searches your document, checking it against a standard dictionary for misspelled words. It even helps you check each word the Spell It feature marked with a wavy red line. You just tell the spell checker where to start, and it immediately begins to scour your text. If the spell checker encounters anything unusual or unknown, the program flags it for you to fix. When Word finds something it doesn't like, you can choose to ignore the flag, change the alleged misspelling, or add the spelling to the internal dictionary's files. Want to see how it works?

1. First, select the text you want checked. If you want the program to check from the beginning of the document to the end, move your insertion point up to the top of the document (the first line of the first page).

2. Open the **Tools** menu and choose the **Spelling** command. (If you're looking for a quicker way, click the **Spelling** button on the toolbar.)

3. The spell check commences immediately. When Word finds a word that is not in its dictionary, it highlights the word in the text, and the Spelling dialog box appears.

4. The spell check offers suggestions for replacing the text in the Suggestions list box.

5. You can choose from the various command buttons to accept the Change To suggestion or move on by ignoring it. To accept Word's suggestion, click the **Change** button. To negate Word's suggestion, just click the **Ignore** button.

6. You can also choose to add the word to the dictionary by clicking the **Add** button.

7. Use the **AutoCorrect** option to have Word automatically correct any future misspellings of the word as you type.

The questionable word
highlighted in your text.

Spell check button

*The Spelling
dialog box.*

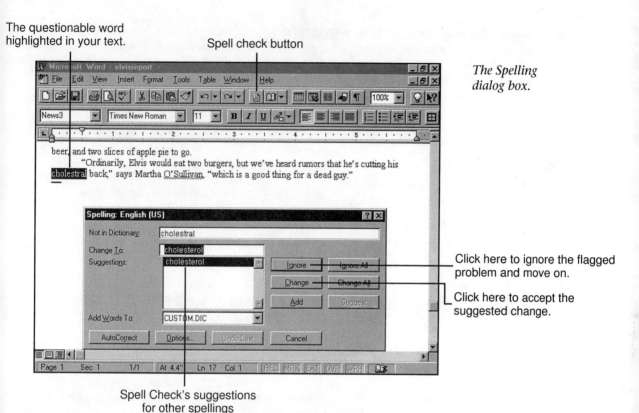

Click here to ignore the flagged
problem and move on.

Click here to accept the
suggested change.

Spell Check's suggestions
for other spellings

When Word finishes checking your entire document, a dialog box appears politely telling you so. You can also cancel the spell check at any time by clicking the **Cancel** or **Close** button in the Spelling dialog box or hitting the Esc button on your keyboard.

New Tool Menu Options

Aside from proofing options on your **Tool** menu, you'll also find new **Language** and **Word Count** options. The Language command lets you mark words as other languages. The Word Count command opens a dialog box that keeps track of the word count in your document. These features are new additions to Word 7.

The Amazing AutoCorrect Feature

I want you to stop reading this for a minute and type something on your Word screen. Type **teh**. That's right, type in the word "the," but spell it wrong. After you type the word, press the **Spacebar**, but keep your eyes on the screen. Did you see what happened? Word automatically corrected the misspelling! Isn't that cool? Microsoft calls this feature AutoCorrect. It's a part of Word's spell checking feature that corrects commonly misspelled words automatically.

Turn It On First! AutoCorrect won't work unless it's turned on. If your AutoCorrect is off, then you need to open the **Tools** menu, choose **AutoCorrect**, and check the **Replace Text as You Type** check box.

You can have AutoCorrect watch for the words you commonly misspell in addition to the words that are already part of AutoCorrect's library. That way, anytime you misspell one of those words on-screen, it will (magically) correct itself. To use this feature:

1. Open the **Tools** menu and choose **AutoCorrect**. The AutoCorrect dialog box opens to display a list of programmed misspellings, along with options for adding your own misspellings to the list.

2. Type a word you often misspell into the **Replace** box, type the correct spelling in the **With** box, and then click the **Add** button.

3. Keep repeating these steps to add other common misspellings that you struggle with. When you finish, click **OK** to exit the box.

Now, anytime you misspell this word as you're typing, Word fixes it for you. What a great idea, huh? You can even use AutoCorrect to automatically spell out company names whenever you type in initials, or any other kinds of words you want to abbreviate for fast typing, but make Word insert the full text.

The AutoCorrect dialog box.

Type your own common misspelling here.

Type the correct spelling here.

Don't forget to click the Add button to add a word to the list.

AutoCorrect will add the word to its list.

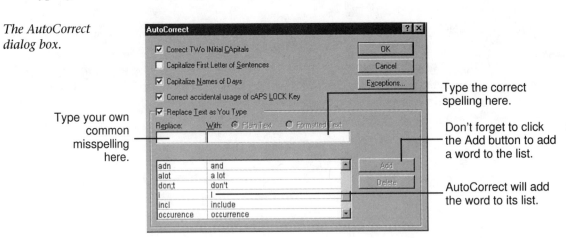

Previewing and Printing

Although I covered the topic of printing with the Office programs back in Chapter 5, that was quite a few pages back. Knowing how tired your little fingers are from turning all these pages, I'll fill you in on how to print again here, plus how to preview your document first. You can thank me later.

Even though you're probably in a hurry to see your work in print, don't forget about the Print Preview feature. Word enables you to preview how your document looks before you print it. To activate this feature, open the **File** menu and choose **Print Preview**. From Print Preview, you can magnify parts of your document for a closer look, or you can view all of your document pages at once. The toolbar buttons at the top of the Print Preview screen allow you to view your document from different perspectives. You can also send the document to your printer from here by clicking the **Print** button on the toolbar.

To print your document without previewing (assuming you turned your printer on and everything's in order), click the **Print** button on your toolbar. This tells Word to print your document right away. If you want to print just a certain portion of your document or change a few printing options, you need to access the Print dialog box. To do this, open the **File** menu and select the **Print** command. From the Print dialog box, you can control the various printing options.

What to Do When You Finish with Your Document

Now I'm going to give you a few tips on what to do when you finish working with your Word files, including some things you may not know about your Word for Windows program. I'll give you some quick steps for saving your file and closing it so you can start another file.

Save a File, Save a Life

Once you create a document, you'll want to save it so you can use it again. To save a Word file, open the **File** menu and choose the **Save** command. This opens the Save As dialog box (which I showed you back in Chapter 5) where you can type a unique file name for your document. When you finish, click **OK** to save your file. For a faster save, you can also click the **Save** button on your toolbar.

Word has another save feature that you'll find very useful, called *AutoSave*. When activated, AutoSave automatically saves your work at specified intervals. Why would you want to do that? Well, what if you experienced an unexpected power outage? If you haven't saved your work, you will lose it, and you'll have to start over again. With AutoSave, you can instruct your computer to save your work and you won't have to worry about losing it. However, using the AutoSave feature does not mean you shouldn't save your document often; this is just a backup safety measure in case of a computer glitch.

To activate or change the AutoSave setting:

1. Open the **Tools** menu and select the **Options** command.

2. In the Options dialog box, click the **Save** tab to bring the save options to the front of the box.

3. Under Save Options, click the **Automatic Save Every** check box to place an **X** in it. Then designate the interval of time you want to use. For example, you can choose to automatically save your work every 5 minutes.

4. Once you've established a time, click **OK** to exit the dialog box. Word now saves your documents every few minutes.

The Options dialog box.

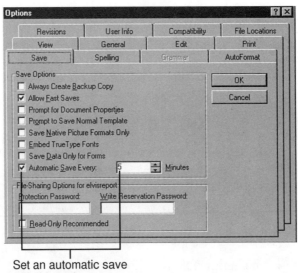

Set an automatic save with this option.

Stop the File, I Want to Get Off

When you finish working with a Word file, you'll want to close the file. There are practically a million ways to close a file, or a program for that matter. I'm not sure why Microsoft built so many ways to close into their programs; I guess it's kind of like having plenty of emergency exits in case of a fire.

Word's many exiting methods:

➤ To close a file the long way, open the **File** menu and select the **Close** command. This removes the file from your screen, but leaves the Word toolbars and such. It doesn't close the Word program, just the document you were working on.

➤ Click the second **Close** button on your screen. It appears right beneath the program Close button.

➤ Double-click the tiny **Control-menu** icon next to the menu bar (to the left of the File menu title). Don't mistake this box for Word's Control-menu icon in the upper left corner of the screen, which closes the entire Word program.

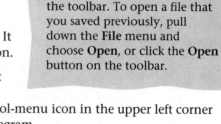

New File! To start a new file any time, open the **File** menu and choose **New**, or click the **New** button on the toolbar. To open a file that you saved previously, pull down the **File** menu and choose **Open**, or click the **Open** button on the toolbar.

If you haven't saved your file, Word will ask you to do so before closing the file.

Don't Forget, You Can Use Multiple Files

You don't have to work with just one Word file at a time; you can open up several and jump back and forth. Back in Chapter 4, I told you how to use the Window menu to move between open files. I also told you how to view several windows at the same time. Go back to Chapter 4 for tips on how to work with multiple windows.

To stop the entire Word program, open the **File** menu and choose the **Exit** command. You can also click the program's **Close** button or double-click Word's **Control-menu** icon in the upper left corner of the screen.

Outstanding in Your Fields

Fields? You may be wondering what agriculture has to do with word processing. Well, stop wondering. A *field* in Word is a special code that retrieves information from another location and displays it in your document. Fields can be used to insert the current date into your text, number figures and tables sequentially, insert titles into the document, or automatically maintain page number references. As you can guess, fields make it unnecessary to manually update many types of information in your Word documents.

There are many types of fields available. When you choose a field and place it in your document, Word evaluates the field and prints the results in its designated place. Any time you select a field in your document, it appears with gray instead of black.

To plant a field in your document, get in your little Word tractor and plow through these steps (I was just dying to work those words in):

1. Move the insertion point to the place in your document where you want the field to appear.

2. Next, open the **Insert** menu and choose the **Field** command.

3. In the Field dialog box, choose a field type from the **Categories** list box. To find more information about what a particular field in the list does, select the field name and press the **F1** key.

4. Choose a specific field from the **Field Names** list box.

5. After you choose a field, click **OK** to exit the dialog box. The field and its results immediately appear in your text.

Now that you know what fields are, go have fun planting them in your own Word documents. You'll use fields again in Part 4 when you learn how to create a form letter.

Use the Address Book!

Fields aren't the only things you can insert into your Word documents. Word 7 now comes with an **Insert Address** command, a button on your Standard toolbar, which lets you insert online and network contact information that you've stored in an electronic Address Book. The key to using this feature is making sure you've entered information into an electronic address book, such as the Schedule+ Contact List (turn to Chapter 21 for steps on creating a Contact List). If you're hooked up to a network, you may have access to other address lists.

To insert an address from your personal address book, follow these steps:

1. Click in your Word document where you want the address inserted.

2. Click the **Insert Address** button on the toolbar.

3. Choose an address book or contact list from the **Show Name from the** box.

4. Enter a name into the **Type Name** or **Select from List** box. That's all!

Be sure to consult your manual for more information about using this feature.

The Least You Need to Know

That's enough words about Word. Hopefully, after five jam-packed chapters, you know the basics of using the program to create documents with your own unique flair and style.

➤ You can change the way your documents appear with the views available on the **View** menu.

➤ Use the spelling feature to proof your text.

➤ AutoCorrect automatically corrects commonly misspelled words. Be sure to take advantage of this incredibly helpful feature.

➤ Use fields to insert information such as dates and sequential numbers into your document.

Chapter 12

Building Spiffy Spreadsheets with Excel

In This Chapter

➤ Acclimate yourself to your Excel surroundings

➤ Discover changed or added features

➤ Learn how to zip in and out of worksheets and cells

➤ Template tips for all

A spreadsheet program can turn anyone into an instant accountant. Contrary to popular belief, you don't have to be a mathematical wizard or need an MBA from one of those big name universities in order to crunch a few numbers. All you need is a good spreadsheet program such as Excel and a little instruction, and soon you *too* will be juggling numbers into complex formulas and calculations, balancing budgets, and doing other high-profile tasks to impress your friends and co-workers.

You see, a funny thing happens to people when they see facts and figures organized in nicely aligned columns and rows with totals, subtotals, pie charts, percentages, and averages: they start taking the data *very* seriously. All of Excel's automated features will help you make that data accurate and easy to read. There's a real beauty in the presentation of data on a spreadsheet—and once you understand how Excel works, you'll truly appreciate this beauty, too.

You don't have to use Excel only for accounting purposes; you can also create databases, figure out your mortgage payments, whip up a household budget, catalog collections, track your credit card bills, and much, much more. Don't be limited in your perception of what a spreadsheet can do. The more creatively you think, the more you'll get out of your Excel program.

Why Call Them Spreadsheets?

For those of you who are true software novices, spreadsheet programs may require a bit of an explanation. The very name stems from the green paper ledgers that accountants use to keep track of information. The paper forms have tidy little rows and columns in which one can neatly record all manner of data. Basically, it's one big table or chart with data spread out all over the page, hence the name *spreadsheet*.

What's New with Excel?

I'll bet you veteran Excel users are chomping at the bit to learn about Excel's changed or added features. I've created a list of features for you to preview. If you're a new Excel user, this will give you some idea of how great your Excel program really is.

There are dozens of ways you can now chart your Excel data. You can use the Chart-Wizard, Drag-and-Plot charting, and even the new Answer Wizard. (See Chapter 15 for tips on building Excel charts.)

➤ And speaking of dragging things, the new Excel lets you drag and drop data from one worksheet to another, across workbooks, onto other applications, and even onto your Windows 95 desktop.

➤ Tired of entering repetitive data over and over again? Use Excel's AutoComplete and PickLists features to speed up the process.

➤ Try out the new AutoCorrect spell checker to automatically correct your most common spelling errors.

➤ Do you use notes in your spreadsheet cells to help you organize your data? If so, you can now use Cell Tips to help you add notes to your cells, which will then automatically appear when you pause your mouse pointer over the cell.

➤ There are more spreadsheet templates to work with, which you'll find when you select the **New** command from the **File** menu. (More about templates later in this chapter.)

➤ Turn your made-from-scratch spreadsheets into templates for more spreadsheets using the Template Wizard, and you can categorize your spreadsheet's fields in a separate database using the Data Tracking feature.

➤ Use the Data Map icon to insert geographical information into your spreadsheet data. (When you installed Office 95, you may have noticed an option to install the Data Map feature.)

➤ All of your critical spreadsheet operations, such as the recalculation of formulas, perform a lot faster than the previous version of Excel (depending on how your own computer is configured, of course).

➤ You'll find it easier to work with list items by using a filter to view top 10's; it's called AutoFilter. It lets you see the highest or lowest items in a list of Excel data. You can add a filter from the Data menu to look at the top 10 items of each list you create.

➤ Keep track of your data totals with Excel's AutoCalculate feature. Use it to quickly update the sum of a range of cells and view the sum in the status bar.

➤ Ever need to have several people add data to the same worksheet? Excel's Shared Lists let you do this.

➤ When you go to insert a row or column now, you'll see the insertion animated. When you insert a column, for example, you'll see your Excel worksheet visibly scoot the other columns over and insert the new one—it's an animated procedure. Try it and see for yourself!

What Version Are We On?
In case you're wondering, your Office 95 package comes with version 7.0 of Excel.

Those are just some of the many new features and changes you'll find in your Office 95 copy of Excel.

Let's Open This Baby and Take It for a Spin

How do you start Excel? First, you have to know where to find the Excelerator. Get it? Excel-erator! Okay, enough of that. Although I told you how to start the Office programs back in the first part of this book, I'll tell you again. To run Excel, use one of these methods:

➤ Open the **Start** menu; choose **Programs**, Microsoft **Excel**.

➤ Click the **Start a New Document** button on your Office Shortcut bar at the top of your screen (if you haven't rearranged the default icons yet). Click the **Spreadsheet Solutions** tab to bring it to the front of the New dialog box. Choose from one of the Excel spreadsheet templates (the ones with giant Xs on them), and then click **OK** to open Excel.

Other Routes to Excel

You can also launch Excel from the Windows Explorer by double-clicking the Excel executable file in the Office folder. Or open Excel from the My Computer window by opening the drive and folder containing the program, and then double-clicking the **Excel** icon.

➤ If you set up your Office Shortcut bar to show an Excel icon (see Chapter 6), you can click the **Excel** icon to open the program.

After Excel starts, you're left staring at a big, blank workbook (shown in the next figure) full of worksheet pages. The area surrounding the workbook shows you all the typical program elements you learned about previously, including toolbars, menu bars, scroll bars, and so on. (The Office Shortcut bar may or may not appear on your screen, depending on what you decided to do with it back in Chapter 6.)

Excel's main screen. Doesn't it just take your breath away?

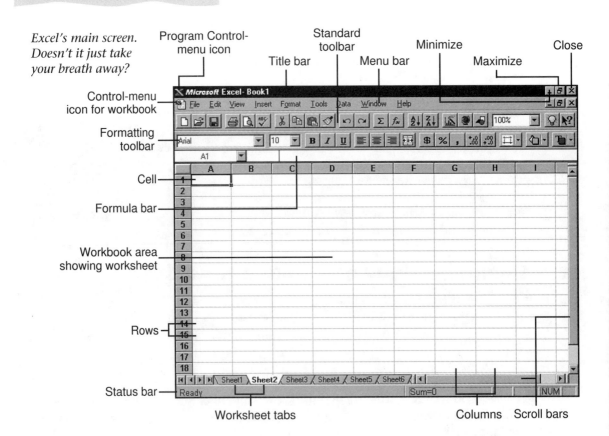

Don't Forget About TipWizard

When you learned about Word (in the previous chapters), I told you how to use the TipWizard feature to help you work with your program. There's a TipWizard in Excel, too. Click the **TipWizard** button (the one with the light bulb on it) in your Standard toolbar and a tip appears in a toolbar of its own. To turn it off, just click the TipWizard button again. The TipWizard can offer you some good advice for working with your Excel spreadsheets, so don't hesitate to use it.

What's with These Worksheets?

In Excel, each individual spreadsheet is called a *worksheet*. So just what is a worksheet then? It's a page in a workbook in which you can enter data, perform calculations, organize information, and more. Worksheets look like grids, with intersecting columns and rows that form little boxes, called *cells*.

If you worked with earlier versions of Excel, you may remember that a single worksheet appeared on your screen when you started the program. With today's latest version of Excel, you have 16 worksheets on your screen at once, all arranged into a workbook file. (You can even add more sheets if 16 isn't enough; you'll learn how later in this chapter.)

See those little tabs at the bottom of the Excel screen? Each one represents a single worksheet. If you scroll through these, you'll find there are 16 of them. And why do you have 16 worksheets in a workbook file, you may ask? That's just the default number the fine programmers at Microsoft picked out. Maybe they think you have a lot of work to do.

Here are a few pointers to help you fiddle with your worksheets:

➤ To move to a new worksheet in the workbook, just click the worksheet tab at the bottom of the worksheet area.

➤ The active worksheet's tab always appears to be on top of the tab stack.

➤ To scroll through the tabs, use the arrow buttons to the left of the horizontal scroll bar.

Use these arrow buttons to scroll through your worksheet tabs

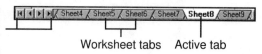

Worksheet tabs   Active tab

Use the arrow keys next to the tabs to scroll back and forth between your worksheet tabs.

153

How Many Sheets Can I Have in a Workbook?

An Excel workbook can hold as many as 256 worksheets (you'll learn how to add more sheets later in this chapter). If you're Mr./Ms. Super-Accountant, there's a possibility you might use all 256; for most of us, however, two or three at a time are quite enough. As long as I'm reeling off silly Excel trivia, a worksheet can contain as many as 256 vertical columns and 16,384 rows. Rather staggering, isn't it? The majority of these columns and rows remain blank for the vast majority of spreadsheet users.

How Do I Move Around in Here?

You can move around an Excel worksheet using the mouse or the keyboard. As you move your mouse pointer around on-screen, you'll notice it changes shape. Sometimes, it's the arrow pointer you've come to know and love, and other times, it's a strange-looking giant plus symbol. Don't be alarmed. When the mouse pointer is inside the worksheet area of your screen, it takes the shape of a plus sign, but it's still the same old mouse pointer you use to select and point at things. Anytime you move the mouse pointer outside the worksheet area, it becomes the old pointer arrow shape again.

To move from cell to cell, simply click the cell to which you want to move. The cell you click becomes highlighted, or *selected*. A dark line always surrounds a selected cell (this is called a *selector* in some areas of the country). When you select a cell, it is active and ready to accept any numbers or text you type.

Here's what a selected cell looks like.

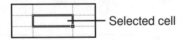 ── Selected cell

You can also use the scroll bars to move your view from place to place on your worksheets. (See Chapter 5 for more instructions on using scroll bars.)

Using the keyboard to move around is a little more complicated. Lucky for you, I've included this helpful chart of key combinations you can use to zip around your worksheets.

Moving Around the Screen with the Keyboard

Press	To Move
←	Left one cell
→	Right one cell
↑	Up one cell
↓	Down one cell
PgDn	Down one screen
PgUp	Up one screen
Ctrl+PgDn	To the next sheet
Ctrl+PgUp	To the previous sheet
Home	To the beginning of the current row
Shift+End+any arrow key	In the indicated direction, to the last cell with data
Ctrl+Home	To the first cell in the worksheet
Ctrl+End	To the last cell in the worksheet

Techno Talk

blah blah
blah bla
h bl
b

Got an Extra Toolbar?

When you first open Excel, you may see an extra toolbar, called the WorkGroup toolbar. This toolbar includes buttons that you allow to perform tasks in a networked environment, such as send and receive e-mail, write-protect your workbook, update a read-only workbook (assuming someone on the network or work group makes changes you want to save), find a file, and add a routing slip to the current workbook. To remove this toolbar, click the **View** menu; then click on **Toolbars**. In the Toolbars dialog box, click the **WorkGroup** check box to remove the check. Click **OK**, and the toolbar disappears.

Where Am I?

Sometimes, you can get lost in the vast forest of worksheet cells. Therefore, unless you've left a trail of bread crumbs on your screen, it's a good idea to learn about cell names, called *references* or *addresses*. These worksheets are laid out like grids, and each cell in the grid has a name or reference based on which row and column it's in.

Reference area or Name box
(the you-are-here marker)

*Each cell has a name
based on what
column and row
it's in.*

Column headings

This cell is in column
B, row 4, so its name
is B4.

Row headings

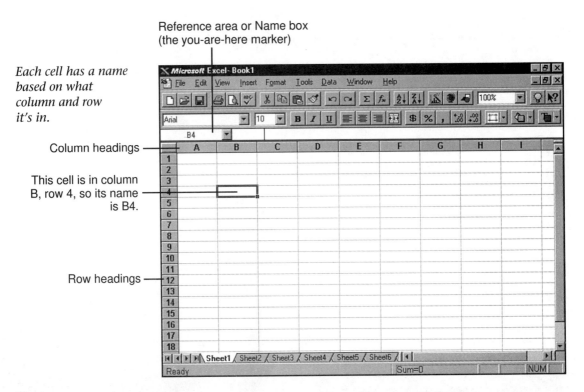

Go To You
can move to a
specific cell in
the worksheet
by selecting
the **Go To**
command from the **Edit** menu.
In the **Reference** text box, type
the name of the cell to which
you want to move, and click **OK**
or press **Enter**. If you've designed a particularly complex
work- sheet utilizing zillions of
rows and columns, you'll find
the Go To dialog box helpful in
zipping around a vast
worksheet.

Pop quiz time—guess what the top left cell's name is? If you
said A1, you're right. Excel labels columns with alphabet
letters, and rows with numbers. Cell names always reference the column letter first, and then the row number. So
the cell named A1 is the top left cell in a worksheet. If you
become confused about which cell you're in, look at the
reference area below the menu bar, called the Name or
Reference box. This is kind of like a "you-are-here" marker.

Working Out with Workbooks

Now that you're sufficiently warmed up, let's really work up
a sweat with these spreadsheets. Put down that bag of chips
and listen up. There are a few more basics you need to
know about working with workbooks (also referred to as
files and *documents*) before you start filling those cells with
important facts and figures.

You need to know how to open, close, and exit workbooks, how to display more than one workbook at a time, and how to move them around. I'll also remind you how to print, even though you learned that in Chapter 5. This part of the chapter goes over all the gory workbook details. Do a quick couple of knee-bends and we'll begin.

Workout Routine 1: Open Up

Anytime you want to open a new workbook:

➤ Open the **File** menu and choose the **New** command. This will open the New dialog box from which you can choose to start a new spreadsheet from scratch or build on a ready-made template.

➤ If the New dialog box takes too much effort for you, just click the **New Workbook** button on the toolbar. This will open the basic bare-bones template you can modify.

If you have already created and saved some workbooks, you'll want to know how to open them up again. Unless, of course, you plan on starting a spreadsheet from scratch every time you use Excel, in which case, you can skip this info.

To open existing workbook files:

➤ Pull down the **File** menu and choose the **Open** command. In the Open dialog box, select the name of the file you want to open and click **OK**. As you've probably noticed, this dialog box is pretty standard for all the Microsoft Office 95 products. (For a rundown on how to use the Open dialog box, turn back to Chapter 6.)

➤ You can also open the Open dialog box more quickly by clicking the **Open** button on the toolbar.

> **There's a New New Dialog Box**
> Seasoned Excel users will quickly notice the New dialog box. There are tabs and a preview area where you can sample the spreadsheet templates before committing to one.

➤ Excel keeps track of which files you worked on in the past and will display them at the bottom of your File menu. You can quickly open a previously worked on worksheet by selecting it from the File menu list.

What Do I Do with the Toolbars?

The icons on your Excel toolbars should look very familiar to you if you read the previous chapters. Anytime you want to know what a button does, move your mouse pointer over it, and a ToolTip name appears identifying the button (as long as you haven't turned off the ToolTip feature). If you need a refresher course on how to use the Office toolbars, go back to Chapter 5.

Workout 2: Close the Workbook

To close a workbook:

New Buttons!
Windows 95 adds Close buttons to all the dialog boxes and windows, and so your Office 95 programs use the Close buttons, too. The Control-menu icon replaces the old Windows 3.1 Control-menu box, but the function is still the same.

➤ Pull down the **File** menu and choose the **Close** command. This closes the file you were working on, but leaves Excel running. If you haven't saved the file, you'll be prompted to do so.

➤ For a faster close, click the workbook's **Close** button in the upper right corner of the workbook window area (not to be confused with the Excel program's Close button).

➤ Or double-click the workbook's **Control-menu** icon located in the upper left corner of the workbook window (don't confuse this with the program's Control-menu icon).

Workout 2 ¹/₂: Close the Whole Program

What if you want to exit the entire Excel program? Okay, then do one of these:

➤ Open the **File** menu and choose the **Exit** command. (If you haven't saved your work, a dialog box will appear asking you if you want to.)

➤ Click the **Close** button in the upper right corner of the screen, the one with an X in it.

➤ Or double-click the program's **Control-menu** icon in the upper left corner of the Excel screen.

The difference between closing and exiting is simply this: when you close a workbook, you are still in Excel and you can keep working in Excel by creating a new workbook or opening a previously saved workbook. When you exit, you leave Excel completely and end up back at your Windows 95 desktop.

Workout 3: Save It

Save workbook files in the same way you save a document in any other Office program:

➤ Open the **File** menu and choose the **Save** command. In the Save dialog box, give the file a name. (Yes, it's the same Save dialog box you use with all the other Office 95 programs, see Chapter 5 for details.) Click **OK** to exit the box.

➤ You can also click the **Save** icon on the toolbar to save your file.

➤ If you're saving a previously saved file and giving it a new file name, open the **File** menu and select **Save As**. Give the file a new name and click the **Save** button.

Workout 4: Print It

And while we're talking about things that are the same for all Microsoft Office 95 products, I might as well mention the printing process. To print a workbook:

➤ Open the **File** menu and choose **Print**.

➤ Or click the **Print** icon on the toolbar.

Two—Count 'Em Two—Open Workbooks

Sometimes, you may want to have more than one workbook open at a time. Why? You might want to flip back and forth between them, or maybe you want to copy or move text from one to the other. So let me tell you how.

You start out with one workbook open on your screen. Then open another workbook without closing the first one. When you have multiple workbooks open, only one of them is *active* (in use) at a given moment. It's one of those computer rules that you're just going to have to live with. Excel displays the active workbook on-screen, and any commands you issue affect this workbook only. You can have many workbooks open at a time (based on their size and your computer's memory), and you can switch back and forth between them at will.

> **Faster!** To quickly cycle through your open workbooks, especially if you have more than two open, press **Ctrl+F6**.

Now try switching between workbooks. I'll help you:

1. Select the **Window** menu, which lists all the open workbooks. A check mark is next to the name of the active workbook.

2. Choose the workbook name you want to make active either by clicking it with the mouse or pressing the corresponding number key that appears next to the name. The selected workbook becomes active and appears on-screen.

Viewing Two Workbooks at Once

There may come a day when you will want to have two or more open workbooks visible on-screen at the same time. That way, you can compare the information in each, or drag-and-drop data from one into the other. When that day comes, use these steps to display the workbooks:

1. Open the **Window** menu and choose the **Arrange** command. The Arrange Windows dialog box appears on-screen.

2. Select from any of the four options to display the workbooks on the same screen. The option names describe how the workbooks will appear. (Don't worry, if you pick one you don't like, you can always come back to the Arrange Windows box and change it.)

3. Click **OK** to exit the dialog box and arrange the multiple workbooks on your screen.

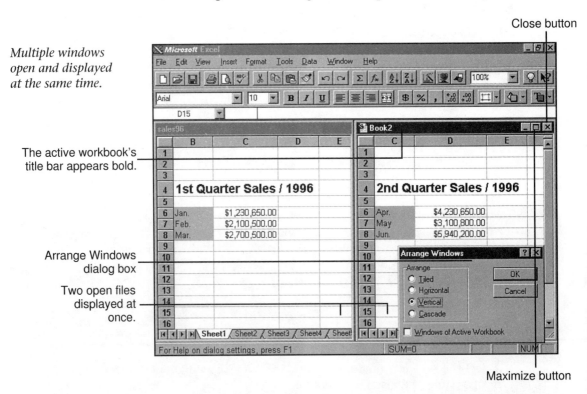

Close button

Multiple windows open and displayed at the same time.

The active workbook's title bar appears bold.

Arrange Windows dialog box

Two open files displayed at once.

Maximize button

To return to having only one workbook displayed on-screen, close the other window(s) and click that active workbook window's **Maximize** button.

Doing the Worksheet Shuffle

Let's say you've filled in as much as you want on the first worksheet on your screen. Now you're ready to work on another worksheet in the same workbook. How do you move to the next worksheet? That's easy, just click the tab of the worksheet you want to open. The selected worksheet now appears in the work area of your Excel screen.

The numbered tabs at the bottom of the workbook window represent other worksheets. Although, by default, each workbook starts out with 16 worksheets, you can easily add more worksheets to a workbook with the Insert Worksheet command. Follow these steps:

1. First, select the worksheet before which you want to add the new worksheet. (For example, if you select Sheet 6, the new worksheet will be inserted before Sheet 6.)

2. Open the **Insert** menu and select the **Worksheet** command. Excel inserts the new worksheet where you told it to. It's fast, painless, and very easy to do.

Don't Forget to Right-Click
If you click the right mouse button while your mouse pointer is on a worksheet tab, a shortcut menu appears. This menu contains commands you can use to quickly insert, delete, move, copy, and rename worksheets, or select them all.

To really confuse you, Excel gives the new worksheet you inserted the next available default name. So if your workbook has 16 worksheets and you add another, it's named Sheet 17—even though you made it appear before Sheet 6.

Deleting Worksheets

To delete worksheets you no longer need in your workbook, use the Delete Sheet command. Use these steps:

1. Start by selecting the worksheet or sheets you want to delete.

2. Then open the **Edit** menu and click **Delete Sheet**.

3. A dialog box appears, asking you to confirm the deletion. Click **OK** or press **Enter**, and it's done.

Moving Worksheets

What if you want to move a worksheet to another workbook, or copy a worksheet from one workbook to another? Here are some more steps:

1. Select the worksheet you want to move or copy.

2. Open the **Edit** menu and choose the **Move or Copy Sheet** command. The Move or Copy dialog box appears.

The Move or Copy dialog box.

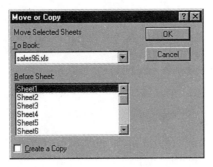

3. To move the worksheet to a different workbook, select the workbook's name from the **To Book** drop-down list.

4. In the **Before Sheet** list box, choose the worksheet before which you want the selected worksheet placed. To copy the selected worksheet instead of moving it, do the same thing, and then click the **Create a Copy** check box.

5. When you finish with the dialog box, click **OK**. You have successfully copied or moved the selected worksheet.

Rename Your Tabs By default, Excel names your worksheets Sheet1, Sheet2, and so on. You can rename your worksheet tabs at any time. To do so, select the worksheet you want to rename, open the **Format** menu, choose **Sheet** and **Rename**. (A faster way to rename is to click the right mouse button on the worksheet's tab and choose **Rename**.) When the Rename Sheet dialog box appears, type in a new name and click **OK**. You can also just double-click the tab name and type in a new name.

Copying Worksheets

What if you want to copy several of your worksheets into another file? How do you select more than one worksheet at a time? To select several neighboring worksheets, use one of these methods:

➤ Click the first tab in the group, press and hold down the **Shift** key, and click your mouse over the last worksheet's tab.

➤ To select several worksheets that are not in sequential order, click the first tab in the group, press and hold down the **Ctrl** key, and click each of the other worksheets' tabs that you want selected.

Template Time

If you need to build a spreadsheet fast and don't want to create one from scratch, use Excel's spreadsheet templates. You can also turn an existing spreadsheet into a template.

When you first open Excel, that blank spreadsheet you see is actually a simple no-frills template. You can use this model to build an elaborate spreadsheet form. However, Excel also comes with several pre-made spreadsheet templates. Depending on what installation option you chose, you may have a few templates or a lot (you can always go back to the setup program and add any you missed). You'll find the spreadsheet templates tucked away in the New dialog box.

1. Open the **File** menu and select **New**. The New dialog box appears.

Templates

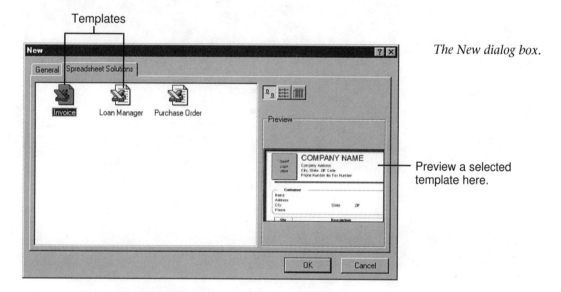

The New dialog box.

Preview a selected template here.

2. Search through the tabs to find a spreadsheet you want to use. Look in the **Spread-sheet Solutions** tab.

3. Click a spreadsheet icon, and a preview of what the spreadsheet looks like appears in the Preview area.

4. To actually select a template, double-click its name, or highlight it and click the **OK** button. The template opens onto your screen and you can begin filling it in with your own data.

You can also turn an existing spreadsheet into a template using the Template Wizard. When you do this, the new template will appear in the New dialog box under the General tab. You can then create new spreadsheets based on this template by opening the New dialog box and choosing the appropriate icon.

To use the Template Wizard, open the spreadsheet that you want to turn into a template; then pull down the **Data** menu and select **Template Wizard**. You'll then be led through

New Feature Alert! Excel 7 now uses Data Tracking with the Template Wizard to let you build databases of template fields. It's all part of the Template Wizard feature.

a series of boxes that let you link your spreadsheet data into a database and turn your spreadsheet into a template design.

You can also save any spreadsheet as a template using the Save As dialog box. Pull down the **File** menu, and select **Save As**. When the Save As dialog box appears, give the file a name, and select **Template** from the **Save as Type** drop-down box. Click **Save**, and the file is now a template.

The Least You Need to Know

You should now know your way around Excel worksheets and the various ways to manipulate them. For those of you seeking closure, let's summarize:

➤ Excel spreadsheets are worksheets collected into a workbook file.

➤ Every cell on a worksheet has a name based on its specific location.

➤ You can click any of the worksheet tabs to display a particular worksheet.

➤ You can open and view several workbooks at once.

➤ Use Excel templates to save time creating spreadsheets, or turn your own spreadsheet files into templates.

Chapter 13

Dealing with Spreadsheet Data

In This Chapter

➤ An explanation of the different types of data

➤ Find out how to enter data into your workbooks

➤ Learn your way around Excel's ranges

You got your Excel feet wet in the last chapter; now you might as well dive in. Don't be afraid; the water's fine, and there are no sharks in sight. Besides, if there were, I'd tell you about them. Keep reading this chapter and I'll help you keep your head above the murky worksheet waters. I'll even toss you a life preserver if you start to go under, okay?

What Kind of Information Do You Put in These Workbooks?

Basically, you want to put *data* into your workbooks. What constitutes data? Text, numbers, dates, times, and formulas are all forms of data. For the sake of simplicity, you can summarize data into three categories: *labels*, *values*, and *formulas*.

Excel refers to text data as a *label*; Excel cannot perform calculations on entries that are labels. For example, if you type the word **February** into a cell, you won't be able to perform a mathematical function with it—it's just a word.

Excel refers to numerical data as a *value*. Excel *can* calculate value entries. Values include numbers, dates, and times. For example, if you type the number **1024**, you can do something with that, such as multiply or add.

The third type of data is a *formula*, which is simply an entry that tells Excel to perform calculations on the values in a cell or group of cells. (You'll learn everything you need to know about entering formulas in the next chapter.) You're not limited to only using values found in cells in a formula. You can also just enter numbers or values you want to add up in a formula. For example, you can enter a formula like =24+158+12.

Excel usually knows which data category you're using and guesses what you're going to do with it. For that reason, you'll notice that Excel displays different data types in different positions in your worksheet cells. For example, plain old text always lines up to the left of the cell it's in, and numbers always line up to the right of the cell.

The cell's actual mathematical
formula appears in the formula bar.

Formula bar

*There are three
categories of data:
labels (text), values
(numbers, dates, and
times), and formulas
(calculations).*

Text data (labels)

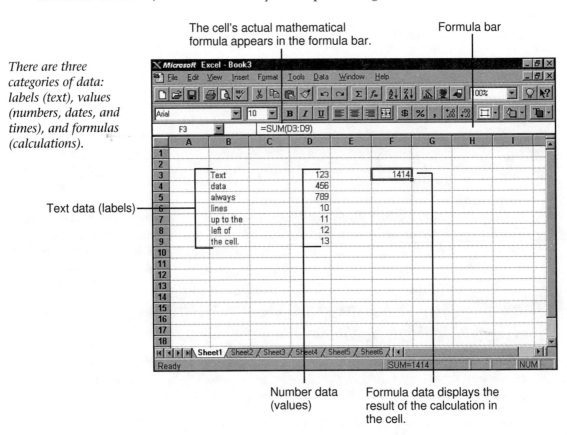

Number data
(values)

Formula data displays the
result of the calculation in
the cell.

The key to using spreadsheets is understanding the various types of data. You also need to know about the rules that apply to entering different kinds of data. If you're nice to me, I'll tell you about them.

Entering Data

To enter data, you first have to select a cell. Clicking in a cell automatically selects it (or use your keyboard arrow keys to select a cell). A bold line always surrounds the selected cell. When you start typing data into a selected cell, the data immediately appears in that cell and also in the Formula bar above the worksheet window.

My Text Corrected Itself!

Microsoft has added Word's handy AutoCorrect feature to Excel 7. It automatically corrects common misspellings immediately after you type them and press the **Spacebar** or **Enter** key. To add your own misspellings to the list, open the **Tools** menu, select **AutoCorrect**, and use the AutoCorrect dialog box to add words, turn off the feature, or control capitalization.

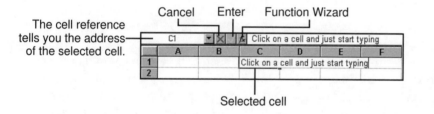

The cell reference tells you the address of the selected cell.

Cancel   Enter   Function Wizard

Selected cell

When you start entering data, the Formula bar reveals three buttons you can use.

Three new buttons appear in the Formula bar as you enter data:

➤ The left button is the **Cancel** button. It's easy to identify because it has a red X in it. Click it to cancel your entry.

➤ The middle button (with the green check mark) is the **Enter** button. Click it to confirm that you want to enter your values into the cell.

➤ The third button with the funny **fx** symbol in it is the **Function Wizard** button. I'll tell you what it does in Chapter 14.

When you finish typing in data, press **Enter** or click the **Enter** button (the button with a check mark) on the Formula bar. You can also click in the next cell in which you want to enter data. If you type in text data, it's automatically left-aligned; if you type numeric data, it's automatically right-aligned.

Part of My Data Disappeared!

Don't panic; remain calm. If your text is too lengthy to fit into the cell's column width, it might appear to be cut off. It's still there; you just can't see it. You need to widen your column—that's all. Open the **Format** menu, choose **Column**, and choose **AutoFit Selection**. This command automatically widens the column so that your text will fit. You can also move your mouse pointer between the column headings until it becomes a double-headed arrow; then double-click.

Are Your Numbers Valid?

Entering text data is pretty straightforward, but numeric data is a little more complicated. When you enter numbers as data (remember, they're called *values*), you need to know the difference between valid numbers and invalid numbers. (Here come the rules.)

Valid numbers include the numeric characters 0–9 and any of these special characters: . + – ( ) , $ %

Invalid numbers would be any other characters not mentioned as valid numbers. So the letter Z, for example, would not be considered a valid number because it's a letter.

Perhaps you're wondering why special characters, such as a percentage sign, are recognized as numeric data. It's because you use special characters to write mathematical problems, equations, formulas, and so on. When you enter numeric values, you can include commas, decimal points, dollar signs, percentage signs, and parentheses.

Although you can include punctuation when you enter numeric values, you may not want to. How come? Because you can apply formatting that adds punctuation for you. For example, rather than type a column of hundred dollar amounts including the dollar signs and decimal points, you can type numbers such as 700 and 19.99, and change the column to Currency format. Excel will change your entries to $700.00 and $19.99, adding your beloved dollar signs where needed. (You'll learn how to do this in Chapter 15.)

Numbers as Text

What if you want your numbers to be treated like text? You know, say you want to use numbers for a ZIP code instead of a value. To do this, you have to precede your entry with a single quotation mark ('), as in '90210. The single quotation mark is an alignment prefix that tells Excel to treat the following characters as text and left-align them in the cell.

Check This Out...

Something's Wrong with My Numbers!

If you enter numbers and they suddenly become number signs (######) in your cell, you haven't goofed up. The numbers are okay, they are just too wide to fit in your column. You'll have to widen your column. Open the **Format** menu, choose **Column**, and select **AutoFit Selection**. You can also move up your mouse pointer to the column headings and drag the column border with the mouse to make it wider.

Numbers as Dates and Times

What about dates and times? Dates and times are data, too, and there are a variety of ways to enter them. They're values because you can perform calculations on them (for example, you can have Excel calculate how many days until your birthday).

To use any date or time values in your spreadsheet, type them in the format you want them to appear. I made a table to help you out with this, and I cleverly labeled it *Valid Formats for Dates and Times*.

When you enter a date using one of the formats shown in the following table, Excel converts the date into a number that represents how many days it falls after January 1, 1900. (Don't ask me why. I didn't invent this stuff!) But you'll never see this mysterious number. Excel always displays a normal date on-screen. I thought you ought to know that.

Check This Out...

We're in the Army Now?
Unless you type AM or PM, Excel assumes that you are using a 24-hour military clock. Therefore, Excel interprets 8:20 as AM (not PM) unless you type 8:20 PM. Watch out, this is tricky.

Valid Formats for Dates and Times

Format	Example
MM/DD/YY	9/9/96 or 09/09/96
MMM-YY	Aug-96
DD-MMM-YY	16-Sep-96
DD-MMM	29-Mar
HH:MM	16:50
HH:MM:SS	9:22:55

continues

Valid Formats for Dates and Times   Continued

Format	Example
HH:MM AM/PM	6:45 PM
HH:MM:SS AM/PM	10:15:25 AM
MM/DD/YY HH:MM	11/24/96 12:15
HH:MM MM/DD/YY	12:15 11/24/96
Month Date, Year	February 5, 1996

You can use either dashes or slashes with your dates. It doesn't really matter, either one will suffice. You don't have to worry about capitalization either. Excel ignores it when it comes to dates.

Make a Few Changes

Need to change your data entry? No problem, you can easily perform edits in the Formula bar. Use these steps:

Yikes! I Didn't Mean to Do That! If you change your mind about the edit you made before exiting the Formula bar, click the **Cancel** button in the Formula bar to forgo the edits. (You can also press the **Esc** key on the keyboard.) If you've already made a change and pressed **Enter**, you can click the **Undo** button on the toolbar to undo your last edit.

1. Click the cell containing the data you want to change. This causes the entry to appear in the Formula bar.

2. To enter Edit mode, position the insertion point (the blinking vertical line that indicates where you enter text) in the Formula bar entry with a click of your mouse. (If you're using the keyboard, press **F2** to enter the Edit mode.)

3. Make any necessary editing changes.

4. When you finish editing the entry, press **Enter** or click the **Enter** button on the Formula bar.

Now you know what kinds of data you can put into your worksheets and how to type it all in. Believe it or not, there are a couple of other data types (called *formulas* and *functions*) to tell you about, but I'll save them for the next chapter. In the meantime, let me tell you about a few more ways you can enter data.

Secret Data Entry Techniques

Actually, there's nothing secret about these techniques at all. I wanted to make sure I had your attention. In this next section, I'm going to show you some shortcuts for entering data.

Fill 'Er Up

Let's say you want to copy existing data into several surrounding cells. Is there an easy way to do that, other than retyping? Why yes, there is. One way you can copy an existing entry into surrounding cells is by using the Fill feature. (It's even faster than the Copy and Paste commands.)

Here's what you want to do:

1. Select the cell whose contents and formatting you want to copy.

2. Next, position the mouse pointer over the cell, press the left mouse button and drag the mouse pointer over all the cells into which you want to copy the cell entry. After the cells are highlighted, release the mouse button.

3. Open the **Edit** menu and select **Fill**. The Fill submenu appears.

4. Select the direction in which you want to copy the entry. For example, if you choose **Right**, Excel inserts the entry into the selected cells to the right. Once you've selected the direction—blam, the cell data appears in the selected cells.

Can I Do This to Cells in Different Worksheets?

Yes, you can copy the contents and/or formatting of cells from one worksheet to one or more worksheets in your workbook. First, select the worksheet you want to copy from and the worksheets you want to copy to. Next, select the cells you want to copy. Open the **Edit** menu, select **Fill**, and select **Across Worksheets**. The Fill Across Worksheets dialog box appears. Select **All** (to copy the cells' contents and formatting), **Contents** or **Formats**, and then select **OK**. How about that?

A Faster Fill 'Er Up

Oh sure, the previous steps were a lot of fun and all, but there's an even easier way to use the Fill feature. Here we go again:

1. Move your mouse pointer on the lower right corner of the cell selector, or fill handle. This corner looks like a tiny square dot on the selected cell. The mouse pointer becomes a solid plus sign shape when positioned over this corner of the cell. (If you're copying a group of cells, you'll also find a fill handle when you select all of the cells.)

Look for the fill handle on any selected cell or cell group.

 —— Handle

2. Press the left mouse button and drag the mouse to highlight the cells anywhere around the selected cell (or cells) into which you want to copy the entry.

3. When you release the mouse button, the contents and formatting of the original cell (or group of cells) appear in the selected cells. What a keen technique.

Secret Cell Editing Technique Number Two: AutoFill

The amazing AutoFill—what is it, why use it? Here's why. Unlike Fill, which merely copies an entry to one or more nearby cells, AutoFill copies with logic. Say you want to enter the days of the week (Sunday through Saturday) into your worksheet. If you're using AutoFill, all you have to do is type the first entry (Sunday), and AutoFill inserts the other entries for you.

To see this in action, type the word **Monday** into a cell. Next, drag the fill handle up, down, left, or right to select six more cells. When you release the mouse button, Excel will insert the remaining days of the week, in order, into the selected cells.

How does Excel create an AutoFill? Excel has the series data stored as an AutoFill entry. Data that appears in a logical sequence, such as the days of the week, is considered *series data*. By default, Excel has the days of the week and months of the year already stored as series data. However, you can create your own list of series data to use with the AutoFill feature, which I'll show you next.

Create Your Own AutoFill Series Data

You can store your own series as AutoFill entries. Follow these steps:

1. Open the **Tools** menu and select **Options**.

2. When the Options dialog box appears, click the **Custom Lists** tab.

3. Click the **Add** button. An insertion point appears in the **List Entries** text box where you can type the entries you want to use for your AutoFill entries (for example, Item1, Item2, and so on). Press **Enter** at the end of each entry.

4. When finished, click the **OK** button.

As soon as you finish adding your own AutoFill entry, you can type any item in your series list and use the AutoFill command to insert the remaining entries.

Can I Turn Existing Text I've Already Typed into AutoFill Entries?

Sure. If you have already typed the entries you want to use for your AutoFill entries, select the text and choose **Options** from the **Tools** menu. Click the **Custom Lists** tab and select the **Import** button. Excel copies the selected entries from your worksheet and places them in the **List Entries** text box. Click **OK** and you're done!

It's New, It's Daring, It's AutoComplete

Many spreadsheet users spend a lot of time entering repetitive data, or the same labels over and over again in their columns. Excel 7 offers you a new way to speed up such entries: AutoComplete. It works like this: Excel keeps track of your column entries for each cell. Instead of retyping an entry, you can right-click the next cell and display a list of words you've already used in previous cells. You can then choose from the list, which is a lot faster than typing the word again.

Try it yourself and see how it works. Let's say you're typing in a column of labels, using the same words over and over again:

1. Type the labels in the first cells of the column.

2. When you're ready to enter a duplicate label in another cell, right-click the empty cell to open a shortcut menu.

3. Select **Pick from List**. A list of previously typed words appears beneath your cell.

4. Choose the word you want from the list and it's automatically inserted into the cell.

Note This
You may notice the AutoComplete feature kicking in while you enter text. If you repeat the first few letters of a previous entry, AutoComplete guesses that you're typing in repeat information and finishes your word for you. If it's not the correct word, however, keep typing and ignore AutoComplete.

After selecting Pick from List on the shortcut menu, a drop-down list of words appears.

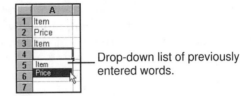

Drop-down list of previously entered words.

Throw in Some Cell Tips

For those of you who like to include notes in your spreadsheets that explain what's going on with the data, Excel has a Cell Tips feature for you (also called Cell Notes). You insert notes into any cell you like. The notes don't need to have anything to do with the data inside the cell; the note won't affect the data and they don't print out (unless you want them to). Anytime you pass your mouse pointer back over the cell, its note pops up on-screen next to the cell.

Try this yourself using these steps:

Another Improvement! Yes, the Cell Tips feature is new and improved in Excel 7. In the previous version of Excel, you had to open the Insert menu again to see your note. Now you glide your mouse pointer over the cell and it appears. When you build complex spreadsheets, this helps you organize data, post reminders to yourself, and even add comments. Think of Cell Tips as your spreadsheet footnotes.

1. Click your mouse in the cell you want to add a note to.

2. Open the **Insert** menu and choose **Note**. The Cell Note dialog box appears.

3. Type in your note text in the **Text Note** box. (You can even add a sound to the note that will play whenever you move your mouse over the cell! Check your manual for information about sounds.)

4. Click **OK** to exit the dialog box. A red dot now appears in the upper right corner of the cell with the note attached. Whenever you move your mouse over the cell, a tiny note box appears with your text.

Those are some of the other ways in which you can enter data into your worksheet cells, but that's not all you can do with your cells. You can also turn them into ranges, which is our next topic.

Roaming the Range

Well, cowpokes, now that you're working out here in Excel country entering all those data types, there are a few more basics you need to know about, such as branding your range (you know, puttin' yer own name on it). And what is a range you ask? A *range* is a rectangular group of connected cells that you can connect in a column, a row, or a combination of columns and rows. You can connect them in a number of ways, but they always have to be contiguous and they must form a rectangle. Rectangles: that's what ranges are all about. Take a look at this figure to see what I mean.

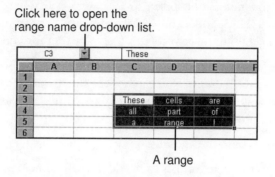

Click here to open the
range name drop-down list.

A range

A range is any combination of cells that forms a rectangle.

Why use ranges? For example, you can select a range and use it to format a group of cells with one simple step. You can use a range to print only a selected group of cells. Ranges are also handy when you use them with formulas (which I'll explain in Chapter 14).

We refer to ranges by specific anchor points: the top left corner and the lower right corner. For instance, the range shown in the preceding figure is C3:E5. (Doesn't this sort of remind you of that game Battleship? You know, A5:D10—You sunk my battleship! Remember that game?) A range with more than one cell uses a colon to separate the anchor points.

Rounding Up a Range

The first thing you need to learn about ranges is how to select them. (This is the fun part, rounding up those cells to make a rectangle.)

1. Move your mouse pointer to the upper left corner of a range you want to select.

2. Press and hold the left mouse button, and drag the mouse to the lower right corner of the cell range you are selecting.

3. Let go of the mouse button and you have selected your range.

If you want to select the same range of cells on more than one worksheet, select the worksheets (hold down the **Shift** key and click each of their tabs), and follow the same steps.

> **Check This Out...**
>
> **Another Shortcut!** You can turn an entire row or column into a range, or even the whole worksheet. You can quickly select a row or a column by clicking the row number or column letter at the edge of the worksheet. To select the entire worksheet, click the rectangle above row 1 and to the left of column A.

Brand Those Cells

Now that you've rounded up a range, you're probably wondering what to do with it, right? Brand it with a name, of course. Up to now, you've referred to cells by their cell addresses, such as B5, F12, and so on. That's fine, but there's a more convenient way to name cells that make them more recognizable and easier for you to work with.

For instance, you can name a column **JAN**, which holds data for the month of January. Whenever you refer to that data, you can use the range name instead of the name of each cell location. This makes it much easier to manage formulas. Naming ranges also makes it easier to cut, copy, and move blocks of cells.

Now, you're ready to name a cell range.

1. Select the range of cells, and click inside the cell name box, or reference area Name box (on the left side of the Formula bar).

2. Type a range name of up to 255 characters. Valid names can include letters, numbers, periods, and underlines; spaces are *not* allowed.

3. When you finish, press **Enter**.

Or you can use the **Insert** menu to name a range (but it's not nearly as much fun).

1. Select the range.

2. Open the **Insert** menu, select **Name**, and select **Define**. Excel displays the Define Name dialog box.

3. Type a name in the **Names in Workbook** text box, and click **OK** or press **Enter**. (You can also delete range names from this dialog box.)

The Least You Need to Know

Dealing with data may seem complex when you build Excel worksheets and workbooks. However, once you know what's what, it doesn't seem that bad at all.

➤ Categorize your data as labels, values, or formulas.

➤ Excel refers to text data as a *label*, numerical data as a *value* (include numbers, dates, and times), and mathematical equations as *formulas*.

➤ Try these special features: the *Fill* feature, which copies data into surrounding cells; the *AutoFill* feature, which completes entry lists of related data; the *AutoComplete* feature, which enters repeat text into your column cells; and the *Cell Tips* feature, which adds footnotes to your cells.

➤ A *range* is a rectangular group of related cells; use ranges to simplify your worksheet work.

Chapter 14

Formulas—
The Key to
Your Excel
Chemistry Set

In This Chapter

➤ Learn how to concoct formulas without the use of chemicals, test tubes, or Bunsen burners

➤ Find out about functions and how they can speed up your work

➤ Tips for finagling your own formulas

Don't get too excited or anything, but I'm about to show you the essence of your Excel spreadsheet program: *formulas*. That's right, formulas are the driving force behind your worksheets; they make all the cell entries and data come to life. Without formulas, you'd still need your calculator to get anything done.

What's a Formula, Anyway?

Before we begin concocting our formulas, make sure you have your lab coat on, get those wrap-around protective goggles securely on your face, and oh, better grab that fire extinguisher while you're at it. The formulas you will be working with can be extremely reactive and dangerous. Are you ready?

Formula Rule Number 1
Every formula must begin with an equals sign (=). It's the law.

If you've never worked with a spreadsheet program before, let me introduce you to *formulas*. Workbooks use formulas to perform calculations on the data you enter. With formulas, you can perform addition, subtraction, multiplication, and division using the values in various cells. All right, so we're not working with noxious chemicals after all.

Formulas generally consist of one or more cell addresses and/or values and a mathematical operator, such as + (addition), – (subtraction), * (multiplication), or / (division). For example, if you wanted to determine the average of the values contained in cells A4, B4, and C4, you would use the following formula:

=(A4+B4+C4)/3

Want to see how formulas work? The following figure shows the preceding formula in action.

Type a formula in the cell where you want the resulting value to appear.

E4		=(A4+B4+C4)/3 ——— Formula
	A	B	C	D	E	F
1	**Average Number of Elvis Sightings 1995**					
2						
3	Jan.	Feb.	Mar.		3 month average	
4	12	23	5		13.33333 ——— Calculated average	
5						

You can use the following mathematical operators to create formulas.

Excel's Mathematical Operators

Operator	Performs	Example	Formula Result
^	Exponentiation	=A1^3	Enters the result of raising the value in cell A1 to the third power.
+	Addition	=A1+A2	Enters the total of the values in cells A1 and A2.
–	Subtraction	=A1–A2	Subtracts the value in cell A2 from the value in cell A1.
*	Multiplication	=A2*3	Multiplies the value in cell A2 by 3.

Operator	Performs	Example	Formula Result
/	Division	=A1/50	Divides the value in cell A1 by 50.
()	Combination	=(A1+A2+A3)/3	Determines the average of the values in cells A1 through A3.

Get Your Operators in Order

You're probably dying to start entering formulas to see what happens. Well, hold on a second. There's another rule to explain. Here's formula rule number 2: *operator precedence.* Excel performs a series of operations from left to right in the following order, which gives some operators precedence over others:

1st (All operations in parentheses)

2nd Exponential equations or operations

3rd Multiplication and division

4th Addition and subtraction

Another way to remember the order of how Excel calculates formulas is to remember this jingle: *"Please Excuse My Dear Aunt Sally,"* in which P stands for parentheses, E for exponential equations, M for multiplication, D for division, A for addition, and S for subtraction. (Hey, I didn't come up with that one, my editor did.) This is important to keep in mind when you are creating equations, because the order of operations determines the result.

For example, if you want to determine the average of the values in cells A1, B1, and C1, and you enter =A1+B1+C1/3, you'll probably get the wrong answer. Excel will divide the value in C1 by 3 and add that result to A1+B1. Why? Because division takes precedence over addition according to the laws of operator precedence. So how do you finally determine the average? You have to group your values in parentheses. In our little equation, we want to total A1 through C1 first. To do this, we must enclose that group of values in parentheses: =(A1+B1+C1)/3. This way, Excel knows how to handle the formula.

Check This Out...

Formula Rule Number 2
Every formula must adhere to the order of operator precedence.

Tell Me How to Put Them In Already!

You can enter formulas in either of two ways: by *typing* the formula or by *selecting* cell references.

To type a formula, use these steps:

1. Start by selecting the cell in which you want the formula's calculation to appear.

2. First, type the equals sign (=) because it won't be a formula without an equals sign. Then type the formula. You'll notice as you type the formula into the cell, it also appears in the Formula bar.

3. When you finish, press **Enter**, and Excel calculates the result and enters it into your selected cell (assuming you have entered some values to calculate).

What's a Cell Reference?

It's the name of the cell you're working in, the name of the column and row the cell is in. To quickly find out the name of a cell, click the cell and look up in the cell reference box, called the Name box, located at the far left side of the Formula bar.

Error! If you get this message, make sure that you did not enter a formula that told Excel to do one of these things: divide by zero or a blank cell, use a value in a blank cell, delete a cell being used in a formula, or use a range name when a single cell address was expected.

To enter a formula by selecting cell references, use these steps:

1. You must first select the cell in which you want the formula's result to appear.

2. Type the equals sign (remember, the equals sign identifies the data as a formula).

3. Click the cell whose address you want to appear first in the formula, and the cell address appears in the Formula bar.

4. Type a mathematical operator after the value to indicate the next operation you want to perform, and the operator appears in the Formula bar.

5. Continue clicking cells and typing operators until you finish entering the formula.

6. When you finish, press **Enter** to accept the formula or **Esc** to cancel the operation.

Techno Talk

What If You Want to Display the Formula in the Cell?

You can view the formula by selecting the cell and looking in the Formula bar, or you can change your cell options. To change the options, open the **Tools** menu and choose **Options**. Click the **View** tab to bring it to the front of the dialog box. Click the **Formulas** check box to turn it on (an **X** appears). Click **OK** or press **Enter**.

You can also use the keyboard shortcut **Ctrl+'** (the apostrophe) to toggle between viewing formulas and values. (Use the apostrophe key near the Enter key on your keyboard.)

Well, that's the basics of formulas and how to enter them. Next, I'll show you how to edit your formulas.

Making Changes to Formulas

Don't worry, editing formulas is the same as editing any entry in Excel. Simplicity goes a long way, you know.

1. First, select the cell that contains the formula you want to edit (you probably could have figured that out on your own).

2. Position the insertion point in the Formula bar with the mouse, or press **F2** to enter Edit mode.

3. As far as editing goes, there are several things you can do. Press the left and right arrow keys to move the insertion point. Press the **Backspace** key to delete characters to the left or the **Delete** key to delete characters to the right. Type any additional characters.

Check This Out...

Fast Edit You can also double-click the cell or formula to edit its contents.

4. Click the **Enter** button on the Formula bar or press **Enter** to accept your changes.

That's all there is to editing formulas.

How Would You Like to Change the Recalculation Setting?

Excel recalculates the formulas in a worksheet every time you edit a value in a cell. However, on a large worksheet, you may not want Excel to recalculate until you have entered all your changes. So to make Excel wait, you have to tell it so with the Calculation options. To change these options, open the **Tools** menu and choose **Options**. Click the **Calculation** tab to bring its information to the front of the dialog box. Select one of the Calculation options, and then click **OK** or press **Enter**.

Need an explanation of the settings? Okay. **Automatic** is the default setting. It recalculates the entire workbook each time you edit or enter a formula. The **Automatic Except Tables** setting automatically recalculates everything except formulas in a data table. **Manual** setting tells Excel to recalculate only when you say so. To tell Excel to recalculate, you must press F9 or choose **Tools/Options/Calculation/Calc Now**. If you choose **Manual**, you can turn on the **Recalculate before Save** option.

Exploring the Exciting World of Built-In Functions

Are your eyelids getting heavy? After a while, I find working with numbers to be rather hypnotic. Perhaps this happens to you as well. Working with numbers on a computer screen makes it even worse. There you are, staring into the soft glow of your monitor, counting and calculating various values in rows and columns, row after row, column after column, rows and columns, rows and columns, rows... and... col... .

What Are Functions?

Functions are complex ready-made formulas that you can use to perform a series of operations on a specified range of values. For example, to determine the sum of a series of numbers in cells A5 through G5, you can enter the function =SUM(A5:G5) instead of entering +A5+B5+C5+ and so on. Functions can use range references such as C4:F12, range names such as EXPENSES, and numerical values such as 585.86.

The =SUM function is just one of many ready-made formulas available. You'll find more functions in the Functions Wizard dialog box; there are mathematical, database, financial, and statistical functions, to name a few categories. To see what other functions Excel has to work with, open the **Insert** menu, select **Functions**, and peer into the Functions Wizard dialog box. You'll find a list of function categories and oodles of functions to choose from. (Learn more about the Function Wizard box in the next section.)

To qualify as a true function, every function must consist of three elements. It must possess an *equals sign (=)*, a *function* name, and an *argument*. The following descriptions tell what each element does:

➤ The *equals sign (=)* indicates that what follows is a formula that uses a function.

➤ The *function name* (for example, SUM) indicates the type of operation you want Excel to perform.

➤ The *argument*, for example (A3:F11), indicates the cell addresses of the values the function will act on. The argument is often a range of cells, but it can be much more complex.

To see an exhaustive list of Excel functions, consult your online Help system. Open the **Help** menu, select the **Help Topics** command. In the Help Topics dialog box, click the **Index** tab to bring it to the front. Type in Worksheet Functions; select **Index of Functions** from the word list and click the **Display** button. This opens a help screen from which you can display function categories to see lists of functions. (You can also use Help's Answer Wizard to look them up too.)

Want to see some functions yourself? I'll show you some:

Use This Function	To Get This
ABS	A number's absolute value
GCD	A number's greatest common divisor
PRODUCT	The result of multiplying two numbers with each other
ROUND	A number rounded to a specified number of digits
PMT	An annuity's periodic payment
PPMT	An investment's payment on principal
RATE	The periodic interest rate for an annuity
COUNT	A count of all the cells in a range that contain a number
MAX	The maximum value found in a list of arguments
MIN	The smallest value found in a list of arguments

You can enter functions (once you know their names) such as other data by typing them in the cells. You can also enter them using the mystical Function Wizard, which I'll explain next.

The Mystifying Function Wizard

The *Function Wizard* feature leads you through the process of inserting a function. Although you can certainly type a function directly into a cell, you'll find the Function Wizard to be much easier to use.

To use the Function Wizard, follow these steps:

1. Select the cell in which you want to insert the function. (It doesn't matter whether you're entering the function by itself or as part of a formula.)

2. Open the **Insert** menu and choose **Function**, or better yet, click the **Function Wizard** button (the **fx** button) on the Standard toolbar or Formula bar. Magically, before your eyes, the Function Wizard-Step 1 of 2 dialog box appears.

Before you can see the Function Wizard work, figure out what function you want to use.

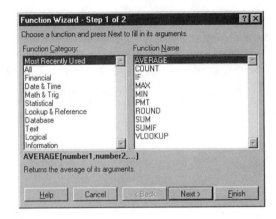

Function Rookie Tip If you're new to functions, be sure to read the function descriptions in the dialog box. Excel displays a function description whenever you highlight a function name. If you need more help, click the **Help** button or press **F1**.

3. Locate the **Function Category** list and select the type of function you want to insert. Excel displays the names of the available functions under that category in the **Function Name** list.

4. Select the function you want to insert from the **Function Name** list, and then click the **Next** button. Another dialog box, the Step 2 of 2 box, appears.

5. The second box's appearance varies depending on the function you selected. (The figure below shows the dialog box you would see if you chose the **AVERAGE** function.) Enter the values or cell ranges for the argument. You can type a value or argument, or you can drag the dialog box title bar out of the way and click the desired cells with the mouse pointer.

The second step is to enter the values and cell references that make up the argument.

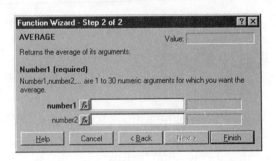

184

6. Click the **Finish** button or press **Enter**. Excel inserts the function and argument in the selected cell and displays the result.

Anytime you need to edit a function using the Function Wizard, select the cell that contains the function you want to edit. (Make sure you're not in Edit mode; that is, the insertion point should not appear in the cell.) Open the **Insert** menu and choose **Function**, or click the **Function Wizard** button. When the Editing Function 1 of 1 dialog box appears, make your edits to the function's argument. Click **Finish** or press **Enter** when you're done.

The Awesome AutoSum Tool

One of the tasks you'll perform most often is summing up values you've entered in your worksheet cells. Because summing is so popular (voted most popular function in its graduating class), Excel provides a fast way to perform this task: you simply click the **AutoSum** button on the Standard toolbar. AutoSum guesses what cells you want summed based on the currently selected cell. If AutoSum selects an incorrect range of cells, you can edit the selection.

To use this wonderful AutoSum function:

1. First select the cell in which you want to insert the sum. Try to choose a cell at the end of a row or column of data.

2. Click the **AutoSum** button. AutoSum inserts =SUM and the range of the cells to the left of or above the selected cell.

3. If you need to, you can adjust the range of cells by clicking inside the selected cell or the Formula bar and editing the range. Drag the mouse pointer over the correct range of cells, and then click the **Enter** box in the Formula bar or press **Enter**.

4. Lo and behold, Excel calculates the total for the selected range and enters it in the selected cell.

The AutoSum
function used in
the formula

The AutoSum
Button

The Function
Wizard button

*With the touch of a
button, AutoSum
inserts the SUM
function and selects
the cells to total.*

AutoSum
totaled this
row.

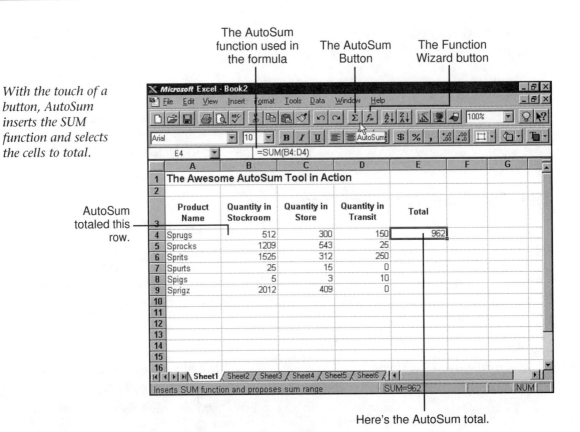

Here's the AutoSum total.

Look for the AutoCalculate Feature

Excel 7 has a new AutoCalculate feature that automatically sums up a range of cells and
displays the figure on your status bar. To see it work, just highlight a cell or range of cells
containing data you want summed up, then look down on your status bar for a running
total.

*The AutoCalculate
feature.*

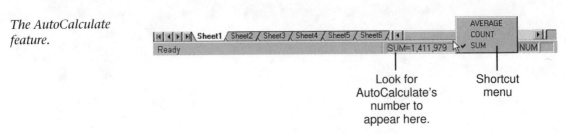

Look for
AutoCalculate's
number to
appear here.

Shortcut
menu

If you right-click the status bar, you can access a shortcut menu for viewing the average of
the selected cells, or you can get a count of the selected items.

Formula Finagling

By now, you've mastered the art of applying formulas, but don't quit reading. I'll show you how to copy formulas, work with absolute and relative formulas, and change your recalculation settings. Sound like fun? In your accountant's dreams, maybe.

What If I Want to Copy a Formula?

Copying formulas is similar to copying other data in a workbook. Use these steps:

1. First, select the cell that contains the formula you want to copy.

2. Next, pull down the **Edit** menu and select **Copy**, or click the **Copy** toolbar button.

3. Now select the cell into which you want to copy the formula. To copy the formula to another worksheet or workbook, change to it.

4. Finally, pull down the **Edit** menu again, and select **Paste**, or click the **Paste** button in the toolbar.

You can also use drag-and-drop to copy data. Simply select the cell that contains the formula you want to copy, press and hold the **Ctrl** key, and drag the cell selector border (the highlighted lines around the selected cell) where you want the formula copied. When you release the mouse button, Excel copies the formula to the new location.

It's possible you might get an error after copying a formula. Verify the cell references in the copied formula. You'll find more details about what causes this problem in a minute.

Improved Drag-and-Drop

If you're an experienced Excel user, you may be happy to know that Microsoft has improved the way in which Drag-and-Drop works in Excel 7. You can move and copy selected data across worksheets, workbooks, and even drag-and-drop the data onto your Windows 95 desktop or onto another application.

Are Your Cells Absolutely Relative and Have You Addressed Them?

Little did you know, when you copy a formula from one place in the worksheet to another, Excel adjusts the cell references in the formulas relative to their new positions in the worksheet. Let me give you an example. In the following figure, cell B9 contains the formula =B4+B5+B6+B7, which determines the total sales revenue for Fred. If you copy that formula to cell C9 (to determine the total sales revenue for Wilma), Excel automatically changes the formula to =C4+C5+C6+C7.

Excel adjusts cell references when copying formulas.

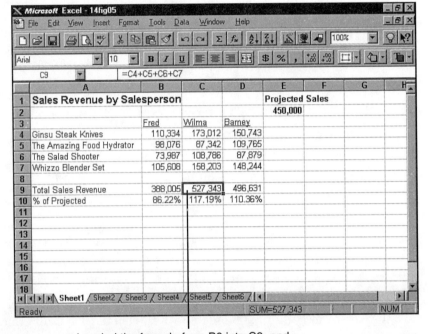

I copied the formula from B9 into C9, and
Excel adjusted it to apply to the new column.

The preceding example shows a formula in which the cell references are *relative*; they change relative to their position. However, sometimes, you may not want Excel to adjust the cell references when it copies formulas. That's when *absolute* references become important. Absolute references don't change, they always refer to the same cell.

Techno Talk

Absolute vs. Relative?

Before you get too confused, let's go over this. An *absolute reference* is a cell reference in a formula that does not change when you copy the formula to a new location. Even though the formula changed places, it still refers to the original cell specifications you typed. A *relative reference* is a cell reference in a formula that Excel adjusts when you copy the formula. The cell references change.

Let me give you an example of an absolute reference. Take a close look at the next figure.

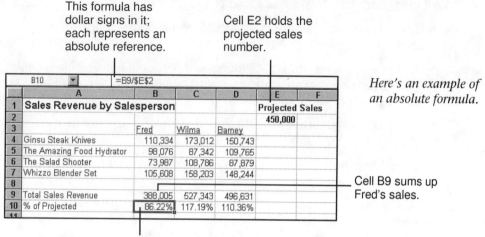

This formula has dollar signs in it; each represents an absolute reference.

Cell E2 holds the projected sales number.

Cell B9 sums up Fred's sales.

Here's an example of an absolute formula.

Cell B10 reveals how much of Fred's sales met the projected sales figure from cell E2.

The formula in cells B10, C10, and D10 (see the figure again) uses an absolute reference to cell E2, which holds the projected sales goal. (B10, C10, and D10 divide the sums from row 9 of each column by the contents of cell E2.) If you didn't use an absolute reference, when you copied the formula from B10 to C10, the cell reference would be incorrect, and you would get an error message. So, to tell Excel that the cell reference in the formula has to be absolute to cell E2, you type in a $ (dollar sign) before the letter and number that make up the cell address. For example, the formula in B10 would read as follows:

B9/$E$2

When you copy this formula into cell C9 to figure up how much of Wilma's sales meet the projected sales goal, it changes to read **C9/$E$2**. The reference to cell E2 stays fixed (it didn't change) because I told it to with the dollar sign when I first typed in the formula back in cell B10. However, the first part of the formula was not absolute, but relative, so it changed in adjustment to its new location, cell C9.

> **Check This Out...**
>
> **My References Are Mixed Up**
> A reference that is partially absolute, such as A$2 or $A2, is called a *mixed reference*. When you copy a formula with a mixed reference to another cell, only part of the cell reference adjusts—hence the "mixed" part of the name.

Of course, lots of formulas use *mixed references*. With mixed references, the column letter may be an absolute reference, and the row number may be a relative reference, as in the formula **$A2/2**. If you copied this particular formula from cell C2 to cell D10, the result would be the formula **$A10/2**. The row reference (row number) would be adjusted, but not the column reference (column letter).

The Least You Need to Know

Well now, that was a blast. In the next chapter, I'll show you how to format your data.

➤ Formulas are calculations (such as addition or subtraction) you perform on your data.

➤ Excel carries out formulas according to the rules of operator precedence, which means certain operations are performed before others. For example, Excel tackles multiplication before subtraction.

➤ You use built-in formulas, called functions, for commonly used calculations, such as averaging and summing.

➤ Depending on how you copy and place formulas, you need to code them as absolute or relative.

➤ An absolute reference is a cell reference in a formula that does not change when you copy the formula to a new location.

➤ A relative reference is a cell reference in a formula that is adjusted when you copy the formula.

Chapter 15

Formatting and Other Fun with Excel

In This Chapter

➤ Learn how to add rows and columns to your spreadsheets

➤ Make your workbook data look good with formatting

➤ Whip up a chart out of your worksheet data

➤ Build your own Excel database and generate a report from it

In the last three chapters, you learned the basics of using your Excel program and entering data and formulas into your workbooks. I realize it's going to be fairly tough to top all of that excitement, but I'll give it a shot. In this chapter, I'm going to show you how to make your data look good with formatting, charts, databases, and a few other tricks. This may seem a little mundane to you, but it's a real thrill for your spreadsheet data.

Add a Few Rows, Toss in Some Columns

When it comes to building spreadsheets and making them look good, you may run across occasions when you need to add to your worksheet structure. For example, you may need to insert more information into your workbook, right in the middle of existing data, but there's no room. Lucky for you, Excel lets you add and delete cells, rows, and columns to make room for your additions.

Make More Cells

With the commands on the **Insert** menu, you can insert one or more cells, or entire rows and columns into your spreadsheet. To insert a single cell or a group of cells into an existing workbook:

1. Select the cell or cells where you want the new cell or cells inserted. (Excel will insert the same number of cells you selected as soon as you finish with these four steps, so if you want to insert 10 cells, select 10 cells. If you only want 1, select 1.)

2. Open the **Insert** menu and choose **Cells**. The Insert dialog box appears.

The Insert dialog box.

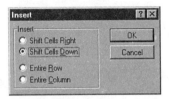

3. Select **Shift Cells Right** or **Shift Cells Down**.

4. Click **OK** or press **Enter**, and Excel inserts the cell or cells and shifts the data from the original cells in the specified direction.

Quick Insert
A quick way to insert cells is to hold down the **Shift** key and drag the fill handle (the little box in the lower right corner of the selected cell). You can drag the fill handle up, down, left, or right to set the position of the new cells.

Be careful! When you insert cells in the middle of existing data, the other cells shift over to make room, depending on what you're adding and in what direction. But be careful: if you add formulas to your worksheet that rely on the contents of the cells that you move over, it could throw off your calculations.

Inserting Rows and Columns

Not so surprisingly, inserting entire rows or columns is as easy as inserting cells. In fact, inserting cells invariably leads to inserting rows and columns. Try these steps:

1. If you want to add a row, select a cell above which you want the new row added. If you want to add a column, select a cell in the column to the left where you want the new column inserted.

2. Next, you have to select the number of rows or columns you want to insert. Open the **Insert** menu and select **Rows** or **Columns**. Excel inserts the row or column and shifts the adjacent rows down or the adjacent columns right.

Look for the Animation Effect!

Excel 7 performs a split-second animation routine anytime you insert columns or rows. The other columns and rows seemingly move over on their own accord in the extremely fast animation sequence. Look for it!

Choose the Columns command.

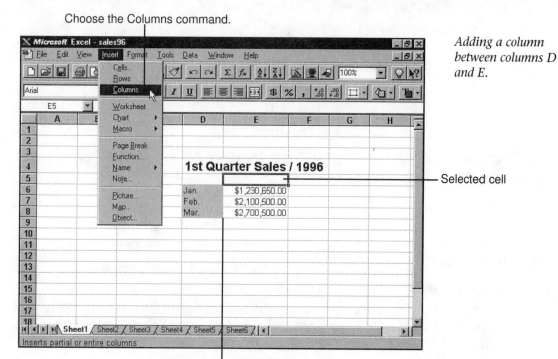

Adding a column between columns D and E.

Selected cell

I'm going to insert a new column between these columns.

Hey—There's a Shortcut Menu!

To quickly insert rows or columns, select one or more rows or columns and click one of them with the right mouse button. Choose **Insert** from the shortcut menu.

Deleting Cells: The Power to Destroy

To rid yourself of unwanted worksheet cells:

1. Select the group of cells you want to delete.

2. Open the **Edit** menu and choose **Delete**.

3. When the Delete dialog box appears, select the desired Delete option: **Shift Cells Left**, **Shift Cells Up**, **Entire Row**, or **Entire Column**.

The Delete dialog box.

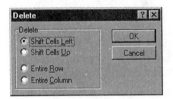

Deleting Rows and Columns: The Power to Destroy Bigger Stuff

If you think deleting cells was fun, wait until you delete a large number of columns or rows—now that's power. Deleting rows and columns is very similar to deleting cells. When you delete a row, the rows below the deleted row move up to fill the space. When you delete a column, the columns to the right shift left.

Are you ready to try it?

1. Click the row number or column letter of the row or column you want to delete. (You can select more than one row or column by dragging over the row numbers or column letters.)

2. Open the **Edit** menu and choose **Delete**. Excel deletes the row or column.

My Data Won't Fit!

Okay, you've completed a wonderful, structurally sound workbook, and suddenly you notice that your data isn't fitting into the cells. Panic sets in and your blood pressure goes up; what are you going to do? (A) Reach for an antacid tablet, (B) Slump over in your chair and stare vacuously at your monitor, or (C) Adjust your column widths and row heights. If you answered (C), you're on your way to Excel success. If you answered (A) or (B), some dietary measures may be in order. Are you getting enough vitamin C?

So, How Do I Make It All Fit?

Grab your mouse and I'll tell you. If you move the mouse pointer inside the heading for the row or column (the part where the row or column labels are) and hover it over any of the lines separating the columns or rows, it takes the shape of a double-headed arrow. When you see this shape, you're ready to drag the row or column to a new height or width. Hold down the left mouse button and drag the row or column to a new size to fit your data. Release the mouse button, and Excel adjusts the row height or column width.

Here are some more ways to readjust columns and rows:

➤ You can quickly make a column as wide as its widest entry by double-clicking the right border of the column heading.

➤ To make a row as tall as its tallest entry, double-click the bottom border of the row heading.

➤ To change more than one column or row at a time, drag over the desired row or column headings and double-click the bottommost or rightmost heading border.

➤ Let the amazing AutoFit figure out how wide your columns should be. Select the rows or columns you want to change, open the **Format** menu, choose **Column** or **Row**, and select **AutoFit Selection**. Excel makes the selected columns as wide as their widest entry or the rows as tall as their tallest entries.

➤ The Format menu offers you a variety of ways to widen columns or give your rows more height. Open the **Format** menu and choose the **Row** or **Column** option to reveal submenus with more choices for adjusting height and width. You can even choose to hide the row or column.

Okay, How Do I Make It All Look Nice?

Appearance is important. Remember what your mother said—"Dress for success." That goes for your data, too. I'll show you how to customize the appearance of numbers in your worksheet and control the alignment of data inside cells.

Use Your Formatting Toolbar!

Don't overlook a shortcut such as your Formatting toolbar. It contains buttons for changing your font type and size, selecting a number format, and aligning your text Left, Right, Center, or Center Across Columns. To do any of these things, select your cell contents and click the appropriate button, or select a button before you ever type any data.

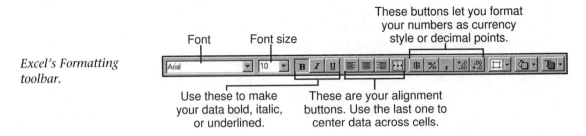

Excel's Formatting toolbar.

You can also control formatting through the Format Cells dialog box. Open the **Format** menu and select **Cells** to open the dialog box. You can easily change many of the formatting features for your data by clicking the appropriate tabs in this dialog box; the next few topics will show you how.

If you don't know how to format your spreadsheet, let Excel's AutoFormat feature give you some professional help. Select the data you want to format (or the whole worksheet); then open the **Format** menu and choose **AutoFormat**. A dialog box appears with options you can try. Look through the **Table Format** list to find a formatting style you want to use, and look at the sample to see if you like it. Click **OK** and Excel formats your data accordingly.

How to Make Your Numbers Attractive

I don't have to tell you that numeric values are usually more than just numbers. They represent dollar values, dates, percentages, and other real values. So instead of showing plain old digits on your worksheet, you can indicate what particular value they stand for. If you're working with dollars, let's see some dollar signs! If you're calculating percentages, let's see some percent signs! And how do you do this, you may ask? Well, you can use the buttons on your Formatting toolbar, or you can make additional selections in the Numbers tab of the Format Cells dialog box.

To use the Format Cells dialog box:

1. Start by selecting the cell or range that contains the values you want to format.

2. Open the **Format** menu and choose **Cells**. The Format Cells dialog box appears.

3. Click the **Number** tab to make sure it's at the front of the dialog box.

4. In the **Category** list, select the numeric format category you want to use. Excel shows you a sample of what the format looks like, and any additional Types that may be applicable to your choice. For example, if you select the **Time** category, you'll see a list of various time displays under the category of Types you can select from.

5. If you like the format, click **OK** or press **Enter**, and the format is in effect.

What You Need Is an Alignment

By default, Excel automatically aligns data, depending on what type of data it is. Text is aligned on the left, and numbers are aligned on the right. In addition, text and numbers are initially set at the bottom of the cell. But you can change all that. You can control your own alignment. Interested? I'll show you how using the Format Cells dialog box.

> **Shortcut!** You can also right-click the selected cells and choose **Format Cells** from the shortcut menu to open the dialog box for changing number formats, alignment, and such.

1. Select the cell or range you want to align. To center a title or other text over a range of cells, select the entire range of cells in which you want the text centered, including the cell that contains the text.

2. Open the **Format** menu and select **Cells**.

3. When the Format Cells dialog box appears, click the **Alignment** tab.

4. Select the alignment options you want, and click **OK** or press **Enter** to exit the box.

And speaking of options, there are plenty to choose from in the Alignment tab. Take a look at this list to help you decipher your choices:

> **Horizontal** options enable you to specify a left/right alignment in the cell(s). With the **Center across selection** option, you can center a title or other text inside a range of cells.

> **Vertical options** enable you to specify how you want the data aligned in relation to the top and bottom of the cell(s).

> **Orientation** options let you flip the text sideways or print it from top to bottom (as opposed to left to right). I'll bet you're dying to try this trick.

> **Repeat That** You can repeat an alignment format command in another cell. Use the **Repeat Alignment** command from the **Edit** menu or click the **Repeat** button in the Standard toolbar.

> **Wrap Text** check box tells Excel to wrap long lines of text within a cell. (Normally, Excel displays all text in a cell on one line.)

Text Make-Overs: Changing the Font

Does your text look drab and boring? Are you ready for a change? How about a text make-over? Use these steps to give your text a face-lift:

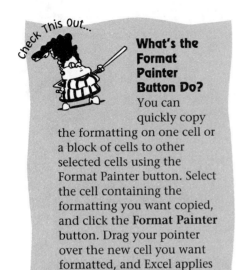

What's the Format Painter Button Do? You can quickly copy the formatting on one cell or a block of cells to other selected cells using the Format Painter button. Select the cell containing the formatting you want copied, and click the **Format Painter** button. Drag your pointer over the new cell you want formatted, and Excel applies the formatting!

1. Select the cell or range that contains the text you want to format.

2. Open the **Format** menu and choose **Cells**. (You can also right-click the selected cells and choose **Format Cells** from the shortcut menu.)

3. When the Format Cells dialog box appears, click the **Font** tab.

4. Enter your font preferences, and click **OK** or press **Enter**.

The other formatting options you see in the Format Cells dialog box allow you to change your text size and color, and even add border lines around your cells. Check out the other tabs in the Format Cells dialog box to change other aspects of how your data looks.

Excel uses a default font to style your text as you type it. To change the default font while in the Format Cells dialog box, enter your font preferences in the **Font** tab, and click the **Normal Font** option. When you click the **OK** button or press **Enter**, Excel changes the default font according to your preferences.

Fancy-Schmancy Cells

If you're looking to add special effects to your worksheet cells, then how about adding different borders or background shading to the cells? That will spruce them up for sure. You'll find all kinds of borders to try out in the **Borders** tab of the Format Cells dialog box.

If you'd like to add color or patterns to the background of your cells, look under the **Patterns** tab. Don't get too carried away with your artistic expressions. If you get too fancy with your effects, you may not be able to read the data in your cells.

Charting New Territory

The highlight of working with any type of data that involves numbers is compiling your hard work into a chart so you can show everyone else what a math wizard you are. With Excel, you can create various types of charts.

Try the Electrifying ChartWizard

You can create charts as part of a worksheet (an embedded chart) or as a separate chart worksheet. If you create an embedded chart, Excel prints it side-by-side with your worksheet data. (What a nice effect.) If you create a chart on a separate worksheet, you can print it separately. Both types of charts link to the worksheet data that they represent, so when you change the data, Excel automatically updates the graph. This is most convenient, if you ask me.

The best part of making charts is that you get to use the electrifying ChartWizard, which enables you to create a graph frame on a worksheet. To use the ChartWizard, you'll need to follow these steps:

1. Select the data you want to chart. If you typed names or other labels (for example, Qtr 1, Qtr 2, and so on) and you want them included in the chart, make sure you select them as well.

2. With the data selected, click the **ChartWizard** button on the Standard toolbar. (If you want to go the long way around, open the **Insert** menu, choose **Chart, On This Sheet**.)

3. Move the mouse pointer to where you want the upper left corner of the chart to appear in your worksheet. Hold down the mouse button and drag to define the size and dimensions of the chart. To create a perfectly square graph, hold down the **Shift** key as you drag. If you want your chart to exactly fit the borders of the cells it occupies, hold down the **Alt** key as you drag.

4. Once you set your perimeters, release the mouse button. The ChartWizard Step 1 of 5 dialog box appears, asking if the selected range is correct. If it's not, you can correct the range by typing a new range or by dragging the dialog box title bar out of the way, and dragging over the cells you want to chart. If everything's okay, click the **Next** button.

5. The ChartWizard Step 2 of 5 dialog box appears, asking you to select a chart type. Go ahead; select a chart type, and click the **Next** button.

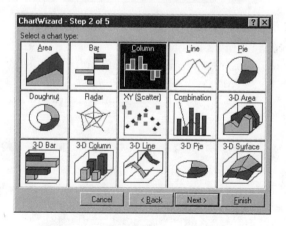

ChartWizard asks you to choose the chart type you want.

6. The ChartWizard Step 3 of 5 dialog box appears. This one asks you to select a chart format (a variation on the selected chart type). Select a format for the chosen chart type and click the **Next** button.

7. The ChartWizard Step 4 of 5 dialog box appears. Choose whether the data series is based on rows or columns, and choose the starting row and column. Click the **Next** button.

8. The ChartWizard Step 5 of 5 dialog box appears. You can add a legend, title, or axis labels, and click the **Finish** button. Your completed chart appears on the current worksheet. Whew!

A finished chart.

ChartWizard button

Floating Chart toolbar for making changes to your chart.

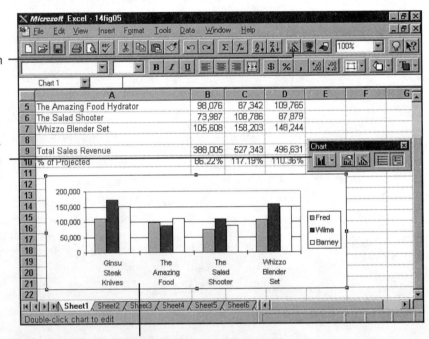

My, what a lovely chart.

A floating Chart toolbar appears on-screen with your chart. You can use it to make edits to your chart, such as changing its format. When you're completely satisfied with the chart, click the floating toolbar's **Close** button to make it disappear. If you decide to change the chart later, select it, and click the **ChartWizard** button.

I Don't Like Where My Chart Is, Can I Move It?

To move an embedded chart, click anywhere in the chart area and drag it to the new location. To change the size of a chart, select the chart, and drag one of its handles (the black squares that border the chart). Drag a corner handle to change the height and width, or drag a side handle to change only the width.

The Dirt on Spreadsheet Databases

A *database* is an organized place to put your data. Or to be more technical, a database is a tool used for storing, organizing, and retrieving information. You can use your Excel worksheets to make databases.

Let's say you want to save the names and addresses of all the people on your holiday card list; you can create a database for storing each person's first name, last name, street address, and so on. You enter each piece of information into a separate *field*. All of the fields for one person on the list make a *record*. (Hey, there are some strange parallels to baseball with this database stuff: bases, fields, records. Perhaps this has greater significance than only organizing a bunch of data?) In your wonderful Excel program, a cell is a field, and a row of field entries makes a record. Look at the next figure to see a database and its parts.

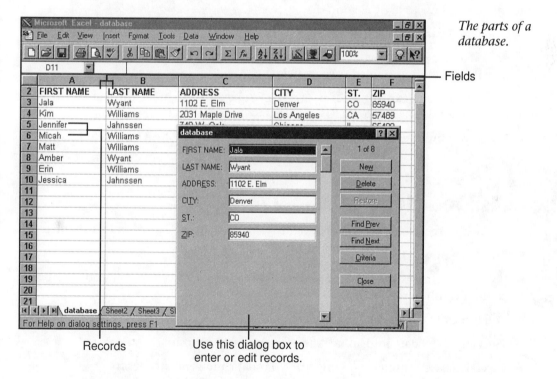

The parts of a database.

Fields

Records

Use this dialog box to enter or edit records.

Like in baseball, there are some rules to observe when entering information into your database. Peruse the following:

➤ *Field Names*   You must enter field names in the first row of the database; for example, type **FIRST NAME** for first name, **LAST NAME** for the last name. It also helps to keep your field names capitalized. Do *not* skip a row between the field names row and the first record.

➤ *Records* Each record must be in a separate row, with no empty rows between records—that's the law. The cells in a given column must contain information of the same type. For example, if you have a ZIP CODE column, all cells in that column must contain a ZIP code. (You can create a calculated field; one that uses information from another field of the same record and produces a result. But you'll have to enter a formula.)

In creating a database, you enter data into cells like you do with any other kind of worksheet.

Speedy Record Entry and Edits

To enter or edit your records more easily, be sure to use the Form dialog box. It will speed things along, especially if you're trying to edit records that are spread out across many columns. Here's how to use the Form dialog box:

1. Open the **Data** menu and select **Form**. The Form dialog box appears.

2. To add a new record to your database, click the **New** button. You can then enter new information into the displayed fields.

3. You can also edit existing records. Use the **Find** buttons to move back and forth among your database records. Use the **Delete** button to remove records.

4. When you finish editing or adding new records, click the **Close** button to exit the box.

The Least You Need to Know

Now you're an Excel expert. Feels good, right? Here's what you learned in this chapter:

➤ You can easily add cells, rows, and columns to your spreadsheets.

➤ If you're having trouble making your data fit, add to your cell space by adjusting the column width or row height.

➤ You can easily format your Excel data to look its best.

➤ Turn any Excel data into an instant chart with ChartWizard.

➤ Excel databases can help you organize your data and generate reports.

202

Chapter 16

Visualizing with PowerPoint

In This Chapter

➤ Learn your way around the PowerPoint screen

➤ Build exciting presentations using only a few short steps

➤ Apply editing techniques to make your presentations the best

It's time to introduce you to PowerPoint, the presentation graphics part of the Microsoft Office 95 programs. As you learned in the beginning of the book (unless you cheated and turned right to this chapter), presentation graphics programs help you build visuals to communicate data to others.

With PowerPoint, you can create exciting slide shows, overheads, audience handouts, and speaker notes that help convey your thoughts and ideas in a visual way. It's a pretty cool concept and surprisingly simple. In Chapters 16, 17, and 18, we'll cover all the details for creating and viewing your own presentations. With the power of PowerPoint, you should never have to give a boring old presentation speech ever again.

Techno Talk

Define Presentation Graphics Program
Coming right up.
A *presentation graphics program*, also called business presentation graphics, is a program made especially for designing visual presentations, also called *slide shows*, in a few easy steps. You supply the content, and the program helps with the design.

What's New with PowerPoint?

If you liked PowerPoint before Windows 95, you'll like it even more with version 7.0. There are several new features to tell you about, plus improvements to some old favorites.

➤ Microsoft has added an AutoClipArt feature that looks through your presentation and suggests possible clip art graphics you might include (see Chapter 17).

➤ If you're taking your PowerPoint presentation with you out of the office or across the globe, there's a new Pack and Go Wizard to help you put your presentation on disk (see Chapter 18).

➤ Microsoft improved the AutoContent Wizard, a feature for helping you decide what your presentation will say. Improvements include taking audience size and type into account, plus presentation length concerns. (More about AutoContent Wizard later in this chapter.)

➤ In case your presentation stirs up many comments from your audience, there's a Meeting Minder feature that lets you take notes during the presentation and save them with the presentation file (see Chapter 18).

➤ If you and your co-workers are networked, you'll find PowerPoint's new Conferencing features useful. Presentation Conferencing lets you and your team review the presentation at the same time through your network connection. The Presentation Conferencing toolbar lets you keep organized while giving the presentation (see Chapter 18).

Those are some of the many improvements and innovations you'll find in the new version of PowerPoint.

Acclimate Yourself

Are you ready to start the program? You gotta open it first. I told you how to do this in the first part of the book, but in case you have an attention-deficit disorder, I'll explain it again. You can use any of the following methods:

➤ Open on the **Start** menu, and choose **Programs** and **Microsoft PowerPoint**.

➤ Click the **Start a New Document** button on your Office Shortcut bar at the top of your screen (if you haven't rearranged the default icons yet). Select a PowerPoint presentation template by looking in the **Presentation Designs** or **Presentations** tabs; click **OK** to open PowerPoint. (Learn more about PowerPoint templates later.)

➤ If you set up your Office Shortcut bar to show a PowerPoint icon (see Chapter 6), you can simply click the **PowerPoint** icon.

The first time you use PowerPoint, a What's New dialog box shows up on your screen. You can use this box to learn more about PowerPoint's new features and capabilities. Simply click a topic and another box will appear where you can point and click features you want to know more about. To make the What's New dialog box go away, click the **Close** button.

Psst, Here's a Tip for You

When the PowerPoint screen opens, a Tip of the Day dialog box appears on your screen. This box contains notes for helping you get more out of your PowerPoint program. Read the box if you want, and then click **OK** to make the box go away.

> **Check This Out...**
>
> **Other Routes to PowerPoint**
> You can also launch PowerPoint from the Windows Explorer by double-clicking the PowerPoint executable file in the Office folder. Or open PowerPoint from the My Computer window by opening the drive and folder containing the program and then double-clicking the **PowerPoint** icon.

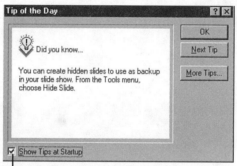

The Tip of the Day greets you every time you open PowerPoint.

Click here to stop the tip box from appearing every time you start PowerPoint.

I used to think this tip of the day concept was a really nice thing. But after a while, I found the Tip of the Day boxes to be rather annoying because they pop up *every* time you start PowerPoint. So, here's how to turn them off: click the little check box in the bottom left corner of the Tip of the Day dialog box. When there is no X in the check box, the Tip box won't be back to bother you anymore.

> **Check This Out...**
>
> **I Want It Back**
> If you disable your Tip of the Day box, and then later decide you want it back again, just click the **Help** menu and choose **Tip of the Day**. Then when the dialog box appears, make sure the check box in the bottom left corner has an X in it before exiting the box.

Start Your Presentation

Once you have the Tip box out of the way, the PowerPoint dialog box appears and awaits your instructions for creating a presentation.

The PowerPoint screen awaits your next instruction.

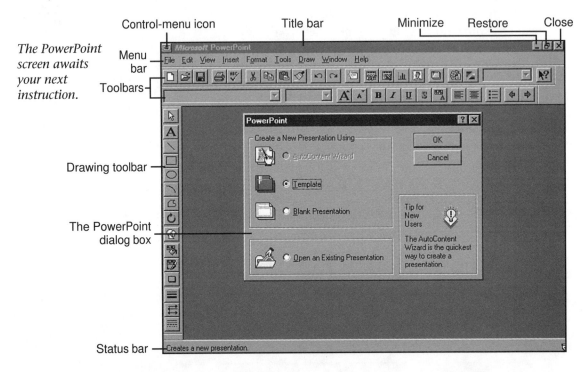

A quick glance around the screen reveals most of the program elements that you were introduced to in the first part of this book. There's a menu bar and toolbars and a new element—a drawing toolbar that appears vertically on the left side of your screen. Notice there aren't any scroll bars to use. Weird huh? (Don't worry, they'll show up when you need them.) The Office Shortcut bar may or may not appear on your PowerPoint screen, depending on what you elected to do with it back in Chapter 6.

In a Jam?
Don't forget about the Office 95 online Help system. Anytime you need assistance with a task, or want to find more information about a feature, use the Help menu to summon online help. (Turn back to Chapter 5 for tips about using Help.)

Come Up with a Plan

Before you jump in and choose a presentation, the first thing you need to do is to prepare your presentation—plan it out. You may be thinking, "What am I supposed to do with a presentation graphics program anyway?" Well, the idea here is to communicate your thoughts to some other people in a more formal, yet visual manner. What do you want to present and who do you want to present it to? Do you want to present a sales plan? An advertising campaign? A class discussion on 15th century philosophers? Your invention for an automatic toothpaste tube roller? It doesn't really matter what the content is, it's what you do with it. With PowerPoint, you can organize your contents into a really impressive visual slide show.

> **Techno Talk**
>
> **PowerPoint Also Calls These Slide Shows**
> Why? Probably because as you progress from one "page" in your presentation to the next, it sort of looks like a slide show (without the boring vacation pictures of Aunt Helga and Uncle Louie). You can even add special effects to your show to animate the slides or dazzle the audience with transitions from one topic to another.

Let's be more specific. If you're putting together an extremely important presentation for all the VIPs in your company, you'll probably want to rehearse it several times to make sure it's right. You can view it all in outline form to make sure you've covered everything. You can print out some notes to use during your actual presentation that show you what each slide is and what text goes with it. You can even print handouts for your VIPs so they have something tangible to remember your presentation by. Are you beginning to see the power in PowerPoint? Good, but you have to have some ideas about what you want to do with your presentation, so stop and plan it out first.

So, How Does It Work?

Look at that PowerPoint opening dialog box again (see the preceding figure). There are four options from which to choose. The option that you choose will effect the course of your presentation, as well as what changes you can make to it later. The top three options in the dialog box are paths for creating presentations. You select the fourth option if you've already made and saved a presentation and want to open it again.

Here's a brief description of the three presentation options:

> **AutoContent Wizard** leads you through the process of building a presentation by asking you pertinent questions about how you're going to use the presentation. Once it's asked all the important questions, it formats your responses, turning them into a slide program outline in which you enter the specific text you want to present. If you want PowerPoint to do most of the work, this option is for you.

What Are All These Wizards Doing in My Office 95 Programs?

I have no idea why Microsoft has named these various features *wizards*. I guess they want us to think this computer stuff is all magic. But we know it's not magic—it's sophisticated programming. Microsoft's wizards are dialog boxes that let you input details pertaining to the task you're trying to perform. They basically do all of the hard work for you—you just plug in the pertinent details.

A wizard can help you work a lot faster and smarter. For example, in Excel, you use the ChartWizard to make charts. Now you're using AutoContent Wizard to make presentations. But don't think you've seen the last of these wizards. They're in every Office 95 program. Remember, wizards are your friends; they speed up your work.

Template gives you a model slide on which to build a presentation. You enter the content, and PowerPoint plugs it into a predesigned format.

Blank Presentation enables you to create a presentation from scratch, designing and filling in your own information. This option is for those of you who boldly go where no presentation-planner has gone before, or for those of you who like to do things your own way.

Depending on which option you choose, PowerPoint will lead you through a variety of dialog boxes to create the presentation. Let's go over these in detail.

No More Pick a Look

In the previous version of PowerPoint, you had the choice of building your presentation using the Pick a Look Wizard, which focused on professional design and how your presentation looked instead of what it said. Pick a Look is gone now. It really didn't make much sense to use a separate design wizard when you have access to all the PowerPoint designs anyway. No great loss.

Option Number One: The AutoContent Wizard

With AutoContent Wizard, PowerPoint makes you tell it what your presentation topic is and what kind of presentation you want. It creates an outline of the presentation for you to fill in. What you type into the outline becomes your slide show. How things look isn't really a priority with this Wizard—Microsoft designed it to help you organize your content. Go ahead and select this option from the dialog box, and I'll walk you through it.

1. Click the **AutoContent Wizard** option button in the PowerPoint dialog box and click **OK**. You can also double-click the **AutoContent** name or icon—which is faster.

2. The first Wizard dialog box appears on your screen, the introduction to Auto-Content Wizard. Click the **Next** button or press **Enter** to continue.

3. The second Wizard dialog box instructs you to fill in some information. PowerPoint asks you what you're going to talk about and what kind of information you're going to display. If you're not too sure at this moment, stop and sort out what exactly it is that you're presenting. You see, PowerPoint can only help you with the visuals; you'll have to come up with the actual content. Type your name in the first text box (it may already appear there). If you know what your presentation topic is, type it in the middle text box. If you have any additional information you want to include, type it into the last text box. (To fill in the boxes, click the mouse pointer in each text box and type in your text.) Click the **Next** button or press **Enter** to move on.

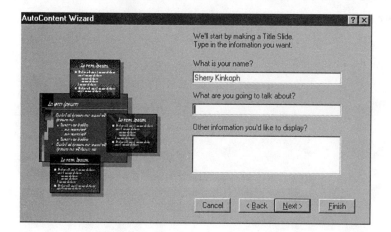

The second Auto-Content Wizard dialog box.

4. In the third Wizard box, you need to choose what kind of presentation you want to create. You can select a strategy, sales, training, reporting, bad news, or general style presentation. (If that's not enough types for you, then click the **Other** button and choose from the PowerPoint templates.) AutoContent can handle any of these styles; you just have to pick one. Click the option of your choice to select it (a bullet appears in the option button). Click the **Next** button or press **Enter** to continue.

The third Auto-Content Wizard dialog box.

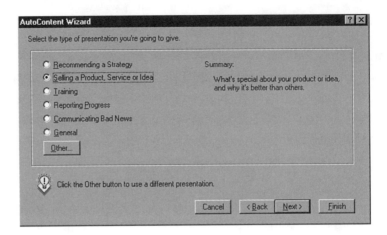

Go Back If you change your mind about any of the selections you've made so far, you can click the **Back** button to move back to the previous dialog boxes and make any changes.

5. The next Wizard dialog box lets you choose a visual style and length for your presentation. Choose from the options, and click **Next** to continue.

6. Next, choose what type of presentation output you're creating, whether it's a presentation on your computer, overheads, or actual slides and if you're using audience handouts. Click **Next** when you're ready to move on.

You can even tell PowerPoint how long you want your presentation to be.

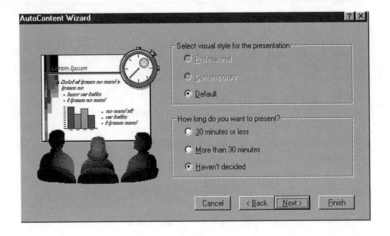

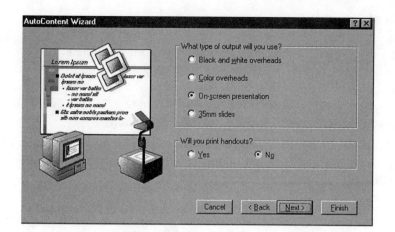

Choose what kind of output your presentation is using.

7. The final Wizard box gives you some directions to follow to finish your presentation. Click the **Finish** button to exit.

When you're done jumping through wizard dialog box hoops, your presentation appears on-screen in Slide view. By now, you're probably wondering what to do next. To add your own text, click the text you want to replace and type in some new text.

You may notice your PowerPoint view doesn't fill up the entire work area. You can easily improve this by clicking the **Maximize** button on your PowerPoint work screen (not the Maximize button in the upper right corner of the whole screen).

When you're through filling in your presentation text, you can save your slides by clicking the **Save** icon in the toolbar.

Outline View? Slide View? What's with All the Views?

It turns out that PowerPoint can display your presentation in four view modes: Outline, Slide, Notes Pages, and Slide Sorter. There are View buttons down at the bottom of your screen to the left of your horizontal scroll bar. You'll learn more about these viewing modes in the pages to come. (There's a fifth view, too, but it's for running your slide show.)

Option Number Two: The Template

There's no wizardry involved with creating a presentation from a template. The Template option let's you pick a premade design and creates the first slide for you. It leaves the content and the rest of your presentation up to you. You need to plan out your presentation before choosing this option so that you know where you're going after creating the first slide. I'll walk you through this technique, too, so keep reading.

1. First, select the **Template** option from the PowerPoint dialog box. Click the option button and click **OK**, or double-click the option name or icon. This opens the New Presentation dialog box.

The New Presentation dialog box.

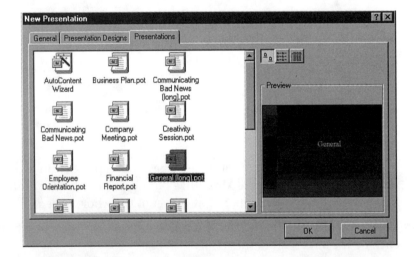

2. You'll find several different tabs to choose from, and many different templates to try. Click a tab name to bring it to the front of the box. Click a template icon to sample what it looks like in the Preview area.

Where Do I Find the Best Designs?

The Presentations tab offers you specific kinds of slide shows based on a topic or type of information; the Presentation Designs tab lists tons of specific background designs. I strongly suggest you sample each one to see what kind of background designs you have available. The General tab has a blank presentation you can use.

3. Once you've found a template you want to use, double-click its icon, or highlight it and click **OK**. The slide appears on your screen, ready for you to fill in.

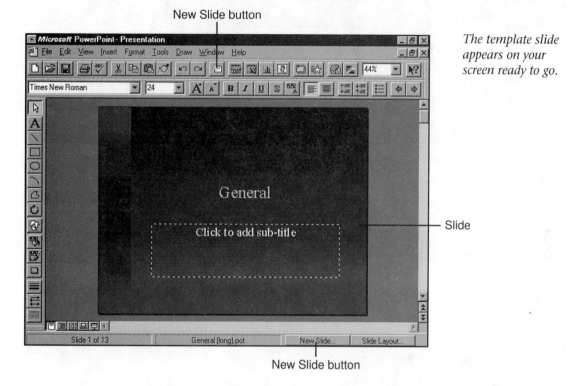

New Slide button

The template slide appears on your screen ready to go.

Slide

New Slide button

Once you complete filling in the first slide, click the **New Slide** button on the toolbar or on the status bar to add another slide based on the same template.

Option Number Three: The Blank Presentation

The last presentation option to try is the Blank Presentation. This option enables you to build your own presentations from scratch, without any help from wizards or templates. You're on your own with this option, so make sure you know what you're doing. You artistic types will love the creative freedom.

1. Start by clicking the **Blank Presentation** option button and clicking **OK**. Or double-click the option name or icon. This opens the New Slide dialog box.

2. Click a layout you want and click the **OK** button, or double-click the layout to open the presentation right away.

The New Slide dialog box.

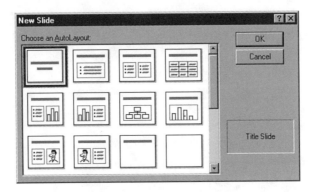

Once you open a presentation, you can fill it in with text or pictures, format it, and more. When you're ready for another slide, click the **New Slide** button on the toolbar or on the status bar. This opens the New Slide dialog box again, where you choose what kind of slide to add from the AutoLayout samples.

All right. We've covered all the options for creating new presentations. Now it's time to show you how to zip around your PowerPoint screen.

So, How Do I Move Around in Here?

As you learned, there are several different ways to get your new presentation on the PowerPoint screen. Once you get it there, you need to know how to work with it. Take a look at the PowerPoint screen again.

In the center of your screen is the presentation window, or work area. That's where your slide appears (if you're in Slide view). Around the presentation window are the typical toolbars, scroll bars, and status bar. At the left of the bottom scroll bar are some View buttons for changing your PowerPoint view. They represent Slide view, Outline view, Slide Sorter view, Notes Pages view, and Slide Show view. Click any of them to change your view. (More on these coming up.)

As in the other Microsoft Office 95 programs, you can use the mouse to move around the screen and select items, or you can use the keyboard shortcut keys and selection keys. Many of the on-screen items you work with have shortcut menus for accessing commands quickly. (You can right-click an item to display a shortcut menu, when applicable.) The toolbars you learned about in the last two Office 95 programs (Word and Excel), are very similar to those in PowerPoint. Sure, there are some new buttons on the toolbars, but you can always find out what they do by moving your mouse over the icon and reading the ToolTip name.

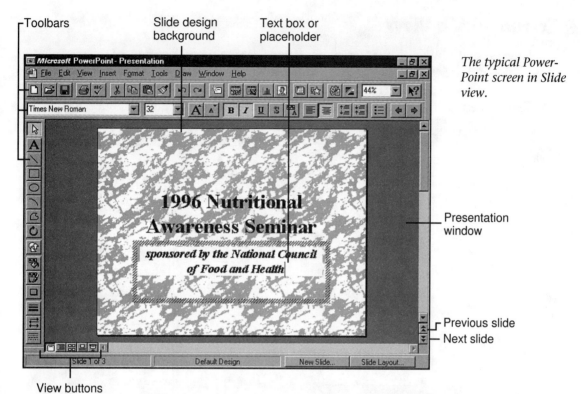

The typical Power-Point screen in Slide view.

Toolbars

Slide design background

Text box or placeholder

Presentation window

Previous slide

Next slide

View buttons

About These Vertical Toolbars on Your PowerPoint Screen...

Two toolbars share this area. When you're in Outline view, the vertical toolbar shows outline tools you can select and use. Naturally, this particular toolbar is the *Outline toolbar*. When you're in Slide view, the displayed toolbar is the *Drawing toolbar*. It has numerous tools for drawing on your slides. You can turn the display of any toolbars on or off with the **Toolbars** command on the **View** menu (you can also right-click the toolbar to view a list of other toolbars to use). Refer to Chapter 5 for a rundown on toolbars and how they work.

PowerPoint has made it easy for you to build presentations; most of the designs have instructions on them that tell you how to fill them in. You'll see many "Click here" instructions to enter text. All you have to do is click there and start typing. You can easily format and edit anything you type. In addition, you can add pictures and other cool visual materials to help you communicate to your fullest; that's what PowerPoint is all about—communicating.

A Screen with a View

Before you start filling in your own presentations, let me show you some of the screen views you can use. Take a look at the next figure to compare them (look back at the preceding figure to see what Slide view looks like). I've opened three PowerPoint presentations and they each illustrate a different way to view the presentation on your screen.

Three of the four basic views of PowerPoint presentations.

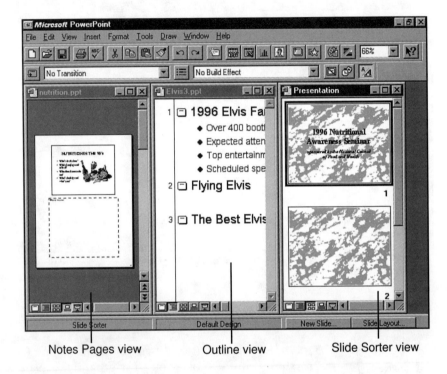

Notes Pages view   Outline view   Slide Sorter view

With each of these views you can simply perform certain tasks with PowerPoint. For example, Outline view lets you see the overall organizational structure of your presentation, and Slide Sorter view lets you see all your slides at once. You can change your view at any time by clicking the View buttons at the bottom of the screen. (There's a fifth view, called Slide Show view, but it's for running your slide show. Learn more about it in Chapter 18.)

Sliding from Slide to Slide

If you have more than one slide in your presentation, you'll want to know how to move from one to another. That depends on which view you're using.

➤ In Outline view, you can use the scroll bar to see your outline subjects. To select any of the subjects to see the slide, click the slide icon next to the subject name.

➤ If you're in Slide view or Notes Pages view, you need to click the **Previous Slide** or **Next Slide** buttons below your vertical scroll bar (the scroll bar on the right side of your screen). You can also drag the scroll bar box until the slide you want appears.

➤ In Slide Sorter view, click the desired slide to select it. When you select a slide, a dark line appears around the slide's shape.

How Do I Edit My Presentation?

The easiest way to edit your text, regardless of which option you chose to create it, is to switch over to Outline view. To edit in Outline view, select the text you want to change or position your cursor where you want to type, and make your changes.

➤ To rearrange presentation text, drag the slide icons in front of the subjects to the new location where you want them to appear.

➤ To add a new slide to the group, move your pointer and click it at the end of the last line before the place where you want the new slide inserted. Click the **New Slide** button in the toolbar, or click the **New Slide** button on the status bar at the bottom of your screen.

➤ To delete a slide, click the slide icon and press the **Del** key.

➤ The Outline toolbar, displayed vertically on the left side of your screen, has a lot of icon buttons that help you edit your work. Be sure to check them out.

The only drawback about Outline view is that you can't see what your slides look like. You have to switch to Slide view to get the big picture.

You can edit in the other views, too. Most people like to edit in Slide view because you can see what everything looks like and you know right away what will fit and what won't. When in Slide view, you can select the various objects (including graphic objects and text objects), move them around, and modify them. You can also change your slide's color and background (right-click the slide to see a shortcut menu for altering the slide's color and background).

Learn more about changing your presentation's formatting in the next chapter.

You can perform simple edits using Slide Sorter view. For example, you can rearrange the order of your slides by selecting and dragging them to new locations.

> **Check This Out...**
>
> **Don't Forget About Your Cut, Copy, and Paste Commands** You can use them to move and copy elements in your slides. You'll find the usual Cut, Copy, and Paste buttons located on your toolbar, or you can access these commands through the Edit menu.

Let's See How It Looks

To see how your entire presentation looks, switch to Slide Show view. Click the **Slide Show** icon at the bottom of your screen. To advance through your presentation, click your pointer on-screen. To stop the show, press the **Esc** key. To move back a slide, press the up arrow key, the left arrow key, or the **PgUp** key on the keyboard.

The Least You Need to Know

You now know the steps for building your own presentations. To summarize:

➤ PowerPoint offers four different options for building presentations.

➤ The AutoContent Wizard leads you step by step through the process of creating a presentation.

➤ Use the Template option to choose a predesigned presentation to use.

➤ Use the Blank Presentation option to build your own presentation from scratch.

➤ Use the Open an Existing Presentation option to open a slide show you've previously worked on and saved.

➤ Use the view icons to change how you view your presentation (whether you see all the slides or only the outline, for example).

➤ PowerPoint makes it incredibly easy to edit and add to your presentations. Many of the screens even give you instructions on what to do.

Chapter 17

Punching Up PowerPoint: Making Your Presentations Impressive

In This Chapter

➤ Format your presentation text

➤ Learn to add artwork to your slides

➤ Try a zillion editing and clip art tricks

In the previous chapter, you learned how to create a presentation. In this chapter, I'll show you all the procedures for making your presentation look good, including how to format text, add clip art, and other visual goodies. All of these options are guaranteed to punch up your presentation.

Why would you need to punch up your presentation? Let me tell you a story. A friend of mine had to give a boring sales presentation to a group of management-types. He put it together using PowerPoint, but he didn't really do much to make it very exciting or visually appealing. He just slapped the information together. Needless to say, the presentation didn't go over very well, and much of the audience dozed off, his boss included. He was asked to give the presentation to another group of management-types, but before he did, he went back into PowerPoint and jazzed everything up. He paid close attention to details, working with fonts and point sizes, adding graphics, and more. He gave the presentation again, this time receiving a round of applause. His boss was so impressed, he even gave my friend a raise. Isn't that a great story?

All right, you caught me. I made it up, but it could happen to you. Paying attention to details is what will make your own presentations stand out.

Sometimes Looks Are Everything

When you're dealing with a presentation graphics program, looks are important. Your presentation's appearance plays a big role in how your audience (whether it's a large group, small group, a collection of goofy executive-types, or just one person) responds to your message. You want your audience to respond favorably; therefore, you want your presentation to look its best.

Using Formatting Commands, Whether You Like Them or Not

Let's talk about some ways to improve your presentation's appearance. You can control fonts, sizes, and other formatting aspects of the text you type into your presentations by using the toolbar icons. These controls work like the formatting controls you used in Word and Excel. For example, if you want to make the text in one of your slides bold, select the text and click the **Bold** button. (You can also open the **Format** menu and choose the **Font** command to change formatting.) If you want to change the point size of the text, click the **Increase Font Size** button or the **Font Size** drop-down list on the toolbars.

Formatting controls are the key to making text look good in your slides. You want your text to be readable, distinct, and situated in a way that best conveys your message. With the tools on the Formatting toolbar, you have at your fingertips the ability to quickly change fonts, sizes, and positioning of text. To use any of these tools, simply click the appropriate button. You can select formatting before you type in text, or you can apply formatting to text that you've already typed in.

Here's a handy chart of formatting buttons on your Formatting toolbar. Enjoy:

Icon	Name	Description
Times New Roman	Font Face	Displays fonts
32	Font Size	Displays font sizes
A	Increase Font Size	Increases size with one click
A	Decrease Font Size	Decreases size with one click

Icon	Name	Description
B	Bold	Bolds text or numbers
I	Italics	Italicizes selected text
	Underline	Underlines text
S	Text Shadow	Creates a shadow effect
A	Text Color	Changes color of text
≣	Left-alignment	Aligns data to the left
≣	Center Alignment	Centers data
≣	Increase Paragraph Spacing	Increases the amount of space between lines and paragraphs
≣	Decrease Paragraph Spacing	Decreases the amount of space between lines and paragraphs
≔	Bullet On/Off	Turns bullet list on or off
⬅	Promote (Indent less)	Indents
➡	Demote (Indent more)	Indents

You'll also find these same formatting controls on the Format menu.

I Need a New Layout

Another thing to worry about when it comes to looks is each slide's individual layout: the placement of various elements, such as text and art, on the slide. You certainly don't want a jumbled mess of text and art, all crowded together and hard to read. You need to aim for an organized, pleasing-to-the-eye kind of layout. So, the question is, if you don't like the looks of your slide's layout, can you change it? The answer is yes. Use these steps to change a slide's layout:

1. Open the **Format** menu and choose **Slide Layout**. This will open the Slide Layout dialog box. (You can also click the **Slide Layout** button on your status bar.)

221

The Slide Layout box (looking suspiciously like the New Slide box).

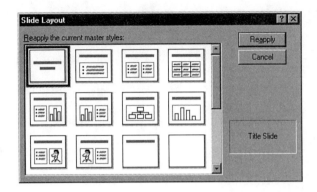

2. The Slide Layout box shows a variety of layouts you can choose from. Some layouts use a title and some text; others have columns, bulleted lists, and graphics. Select a layout from among the examples.

3. Click **OK** to exit the box. (If you're applying the new layout to an existing layout, you can click the **Reapply** button to exit the box.)

If you change a slide's layout, the existing text you've entered will attempt to fit into the new layout's elements.

Messing with Slide Designs

Aside from formatting, you can also control how your overall design looks—and by design, I mean the slide's background and color. (Remember, layout is how you position your slide elements, and design is the background and color schemes that give your slides a distinct look and feel.) PowerPoint has tons of templates, each with its own color scheme, Slide Master design (more on that coming up), and font styles. The nice thing about a presentation design is that it gives your slide show a consistent appearance.

The easiest way to assign a design is to choose from PowerPoint's many Design Templates. *Templates* are premade presentation models that you can apply to your own presentations. PowerPoint templates include designs for several different slide layouts. For example, a Design Template will include a design for a title slide, as well as a bulleted text slide. All of the slides in a template set share the same look.

To see a list of templates, open the **Format** menu and choose **Apply Design Template**. (For a faster route, click the **Apply Design Template** button on the top toolbar.) This opens a dialog box where you see a list of the various PowerPoint Design Templates, and you can preview how they look before choosing one.

This folder holds all the exciting Design Templates.

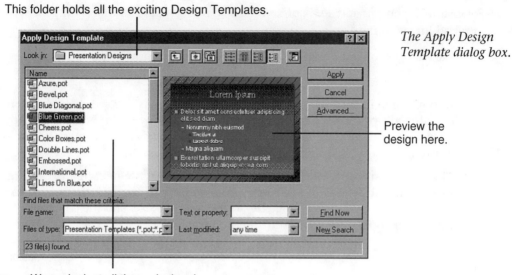

The Apply Design Template dialog box.

Preview the design here.

Wow—look at all these designs!

If the plentiful PowerPoint templates aren't enough for you to choose from, you can make your own template.

Zen and the Lost Art of the Slide Masters

For each component of your presentation (whether it's a slide, an outline, speaker's notes, or audience handouts), there's a master (original design) containing the format for an individual slide. The master includes such items as slide page numbers, title, and text placeholders. If you make a change, such as switching fonts or increasing a font size, to the Slide Master, that modification will be reflected in all the other slides in your presentation that use that master. For example, if you make a change to the slide containing a layout with a title and text, all the other slides using this layout will change, too.

So, if you're interested in changing the look of the text throughout your entire presentation and not only the slide you're currently working on, you need to fiddle with the Slide Master controls. This also holds true if you've added graphic elements to your slide show. For instance, you might have a presentation that uses your company's logo in the corner of each slide. If you make a change to the logo in one slide, you'll want to change it in all. So when you change the logo, be sure you change it in the Slide Master to keep things consistent throughout your show.

When you modify the Slide Master, you're modifying the slide's architecture; in other words, you can click the various slide elements (boxed areas) of the slide and change them. You can also add new boxed elements, called *placeholders*, to add additional text.

223

For example, you can add a box of text for placing slide page numbers on your slide page or for adding your department's name.

To make changes to your presentation's Slide Masters, follow these steps:

1. Open the **View** menu and select **Master**.

2. In the submenu that appears, choose **Slide Master**. (As you see in the submenu, you can also edit your presentation's title slides with Title Master, notes pages' appearance with Notes Master, and your audience handouts' appearance with Handouts Master.)

3. The Slide Master appears on your screen, as shown in the next figure. Click the items in the **Slide Master** and use the toolbar buttons to make changes. If you click the master text, you can change the font, the point size, and the color with the formatting toolbar buttons or the menu commands.

Here's an example of what you'll see when you switch over to view your presentation's Slide Master.

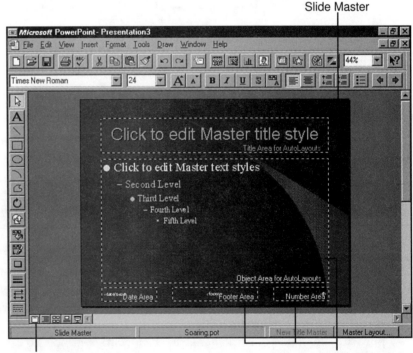

Click here to exit the Slide Master.

Slide Master Elements

Right-click for a Shortcut Menu

For faster changes to your Slide Master, use the right-click menus. For example, move your pointer over an area of the slide that doesn't include text, and right-click the mouse to open a shortcut menu. From the shortcut menu, you can choose to change the master slide's background or color.

4. To exit the Slide Master, click the **Slide View** button at the bottom of your screen, or any of the other View buttons.

But I Don't Want to Change My Whole Presentation's Design

If you'd rather change the background and fonts for one slide and not your whole presentation, by all means do it. (Make sure you're not viewing the Slide Master when you do this, or you'll change your entire presentation.) To change a single slide's design, use the formatting buttons on the toolbar to modify your text. To modify your layout and background, you can use the individual commands for layout and background, which you'll find in the **Format** menu.

Open the **Format** menu and choose the area you want to change.

➤ If you choose **Slide Layout**, the Layout dialog box appears, in which you can pick a new layout pattern for your text. (The same layout box you've seen before.)

➤ If you select **Slide Color Scheme**, a dialog box will appear for adjusting the various color schemes for your slide.

➤ Select **Custom Background** to change your slide's background, such as pattern or texture.

I have a lot of fun with these three options. My favorite is the Custom Background option for selecting some really cool, artsy background textures and patterns. Let me show you how to change your own slide's background. Follow these steps:

1. Open the **Format** menu and choose **Custom Background**. (You can also right-click and choose this command from the shortcut menu.)

2. In the Custom Background dialog box, click the drop-down box to see a list of options. Five of the options open additional dialog boxes for selecting specific patterns, textures, and other background choices.

*The Custom Back-
ground dialog box.*

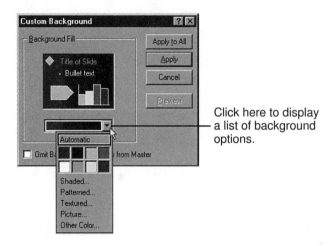

Click here to display
a list of background
options.

3. Click the **Textured** option to open the Textured Fill box. Select a texture, and click
   the **Preview** button to see how it looks. If you like it, click **OK**.

4. Click the **Apply** button to apply the background to your slide. Click the **Apply All**
   button to apply it to all of your presentation slides.

Use these same steps to change color shading, patterns, and other cool background stuff.
Use the **Slide Color Scheme** command to change your slide's color schemes. Let your
creativity soar!

*The Textured Fill
box—look at those
lovely textures!*

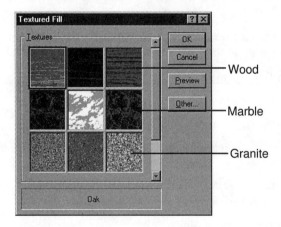

Wood

Marble

Granite

Thrill-a-Minute Editing Techniques

There's more to formatting your PowerPoint presentations than toolbar buttons and slide designs. You can also add more text blocks and even special-effects WordArt objects.

I Want to Add Some More Text

If you ever want to add text to your slide besides the text blocks predetermined in the chosen layout, you can do so by creating a text box. A *text box* is a special holding area for text that you commonly use for labels, notes, and other extraneous text.

First, switch over to Slide view. To put a text box in your slide, click the **Text** tool on your drawing toolbar (the vertical bar on the left side of your screen). Move the mouse pointer onto your slide to the upper left corner of where you want the text inserted. Hold down the mouse button and drag downward and to the right until your text box is the desired size. Let go of the mouse button, and you have an instant text box ready for your words.

Look, You Can Spell Check in Here! That's right, you can run the Microsoft Office spell check program to proof all of the text in your presentation. Click the **Spellcheck** button on the toolbar, and the spell check immediately commences.

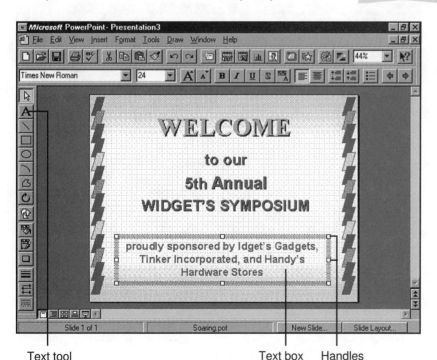

I inserted a text box in my slide (Slide view).

Text tool   Text box   Handles

Click inside your new text box and start typing. If you click your text box border, it becomes selected (handles appear around all the sides and corners of the box). You can resize it by clicking any of the handles (little black squares) and dragging the mouse, or you can move it around by dragging on the border. You can also delete it by pressing the **Del** key when it's selected.

What About Cutting and Copying?

Don't forget the handy Cut, Copy, and Paste commands. You can use them to move data, delete data, and copy text, graphics, and text boxes. Turn back to Chapter 7 to learn the basic steps for using these commands.

Put In Some WordArt Objects

With PowerPoint, you can create graphical text effects that allow you to rotate text, add shadows and borders to characters, and change the shape of the text. Want to see how?

You can create all kinds of text effects for your slides.

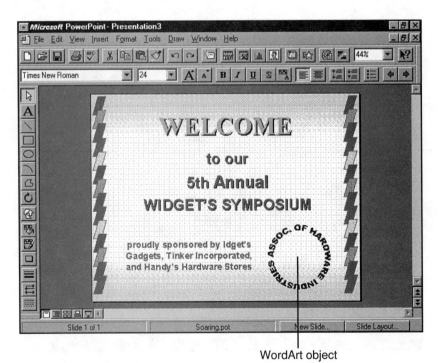

WordArt object

228

Alert!

Unless you chose the Custom installation option, you may not have installed the WordArt feature. You can go back and install it with the setup program. Check your manual for details.

1. Start by opening the **Insert** menu and selecting **Object**. This opens the Insert Object dialog box.

2. In the **Object Type** list box, click **Microsoft WordArt 2.0** and click **OK**. PowerPoint changes to display the WordArt toolbar, and an Enter Your Text Here dialog box pops up.

3. Type the text you want to create in the dialog box, and click the **Update Display** button. From any of the toolbar options, choose a special effect for your text.

Click	Results
— Plain Text	Displays a palette of shapes to use.
Arial	Fonts
Best Fit	Font sizes
B I	Formatting
Ee	Sets upper- and lowercase letters all the same height.
◁	Turns text sideways.
↔A↔	Stretches text to fit.
≡	Centers text.
AV↔	Puts spaces between characters.

continues

229

Click	Results
↻	Rotates text.
▨	Adds shadow effect to text.
▢	Adds drop shadow effect.
≡	Adds border to text.

4. When you finish, click anywhere outside the presentation window to return to your slide.

Ta-da! The WordArt effect appears in your slide. You can select it to resize it, move it, or even delete it. If you want to edit it, double-click the WordArt object to open the WordArt toolbar again. Amazing, huh?

Keeping a Tab on Tabs and Bullets

A few short paragraphs ago, I told you how to use the Slide Layout dialog box to change your slide's layout. Some of the layouts you can choose from involve columns of text or bulleted lists. But what do you do if you want to create columns or bullets in a layout that doesn't have these elements? That's easy. You get out your ruler and set some tabs.

Click inside your text box in your layout where you want the tabs set. If you've already entered your text, select it all. Follow these steps:

1. Open the **View** menu and select **Ruler**. The ruler appears at the top of your presentation window.

2. Click the **Tab** icon to the left of the top ruler to change what kind of tab alignment you want. (We covered tabs in detail back in Chapter 9, so turn back there for more tab information.)

Check This Out...

Ever Worked with Indents Before? Select the text box with the text you want indented, or select the text itself. Open the **View** menu and choose **Ruler**. On the ruler, drag the Indent marker for the indent you want changed. If you're unfamiliar with using the ruler, go back and read the Word chapter (Chapter 9) about rulers and indents.

Tab icon   Tabs

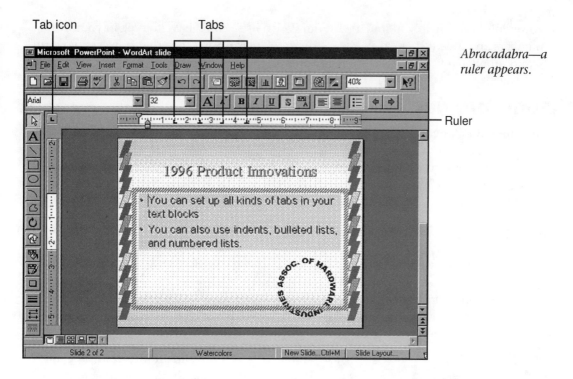

*Abracadabra—a
ruler appears.*

Ruler

3. Click your ruler in each place where you want a tab stop (or you can drag any existing tab stop to a new location on the ruler). To delete tab settings, click the tab and drag it off the ruler.

4. Turn off your ruler by opening the **View** menu again and deselecting **Ruler**.

Now you're ready to type in your tab text, if you haven't already.

What about my bulleted text? Can I change the way the bullets look? Sure you can. If you chose a slide layout with bulleted text, you don't have to settle for the default large dot bullets that PowerPoint assigns. You can change the way the bullets look. To do so:

1. Select the paragraph with the bullets.

2. Open the **Format** menu and choose **Bullet**. The Bullet dialog box opens.

3. Pull down the Bullets From list, and click the character set you want to use as a bullet.

4. Use the **Size** controls to set the new bullet's size, and choose a color from the **Special Color** drop-down list.

5. When you're all done, click **OK**.

Add Some Bullets To turn text into bulleted text, select the text and click the **Bullets** button on the Formatting toolbar.

PowerPoint can't help you much with numbered lists. You'll have to type in your own numbers and indent them as you want them to appear. Sorry, Charlie. However, you can set up numbered lists in Word and copy and paste them into PowerPoint.

Getting Graphic

Moving right along…. I showed you how to change the look of your text and even create text effects. Now let's get graphical. An important part of communicating visually is art-work. PowerPoint has many available options when it comes to adding pictures to your presentation. As you're probably expecting, I'm going to tell you about each one—that's my job.

Premade Art

PowerPoint comes with a bunch of premade art called clip art. *Clip art* is a collection of pictures that have been scanned and saved as computer data. The PowerPoint program (and many other programs) includes a clip art collection in which you'll find hundreds of clip art pictures to choose from. It's up to you to decide which one is appropriate for your slide or presentation.

Busy Art Warning
Don't get carried away with adding art to every slide. Too much art-work may distract your viewers. Use some judg-ment, and try not to pick art that conflicts with your slide design.

Other Graphics
You can also use the **Insert Object** com-mand to open other graphic libraries, or use **Insert Picture**.

Before you insert a piece of clip art into your slide, make sure you're in Slide view and display the slide to which you want to add art. When you're ready to go, use these steps to insert clip art:

1. Click the **Clip Art** button on the toolbar to open the ClipArt Gallery dialog box. (You can also select **Clip Art** from the **Insert** menu.)

2. In the dialog box, choose the particular piece of artwork you want to use. Select an art category by clicking a name in the **Categories** list box. The category you select will open available clip art pictures in the Pictures box.

3. To choose a specific picture, click it with the mouse pointer. The Description area at the bottom of the box gives you some ideas on how to use the art to convey your message.

4. To insert the art into your slide, click the Insert button. The art appears in your slide at the position of the insertion point.

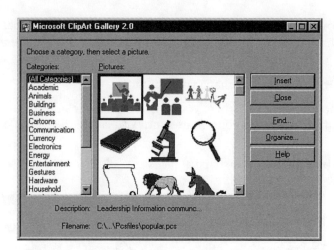

The Microsoft ClipArt Gallery dialog box.

Once the artwork appears in your slide, you can select it and do a variety of things to it. You can drag it to move it, drag its handles to resize it, or press the **Del** key to annihilate it.

In some of the slide layouts you choose, there may be a spot reserved for a clip art element. To fill this in when you come across it, double-click the clip art area on the layout to open the ClipArt Gallery dialog box and choose the clip art as you just learned.

Let AutoClipArt Decide for You

If you're not very good at deciding what clip art graphics are appropriate for your own slide shows, use PowerPoint's new AutoClipArt feature. It scans through your presentation and looks for areas that might benefit from a piece of artwork. Open the **Tools** menu and select **AutoClipArt**. PowerPoint looks for art that might be related to your presentation. You can decide if you like what it comes up with. If PowerPoint can't find any art, it offers to let you look through the clip art files. Try the AutoClipArt feature!

Draw Your Own Art

If you don't like any of the clip art that comes with your program, or if you'd like to stick with something simpler, you can draw your own art. PowerPoint has some drawing tools to help you. Maybe you'd like to design a simple logo or add a few lines or shapes to your slides. No problem, PowerPoint can do it.

233

You'll find all of PowerPoint's drawing tools located on the drawing toolbar at the left of your screen. (You have to be in Slide view or Notes Pages view to see these tools.) Let's start off by drawing a line or a shape:

1. Click the drawing tool line or shape you want to draw.

2. Move your mouse pointer to where you want the shape to appear. Hold down the left mouse button and move your mouse until you create the length or shape you want.

3. Let go of the button, and your shape appears.

It's about time I showed you how to use your drawing tools. The toolbar has all kinds of tools for drawing specific shapes.

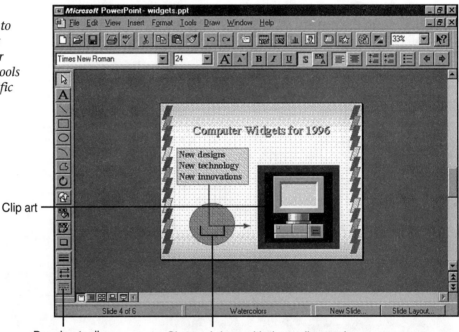

Clip art

Drawing toolbar   Shapes I drew with the toolbar tools

This is a little tricky, and it definitely takes some practice to get the hang of it.

Knowing how frustrating it can be to draw on the computer with a mouse, I'm going to reel off a bunch of tips you can use to help you.

➤ To draw a perfect shape (such as a perfect square or circle or a straight line), hold down the **Shift** key while you drag the mouse on-screen.

➤ To draw an object from the center out, press the **Ctrl** key while you drag the mouse.

➤ Double-click a tool, and you can use the mouse to create several objects of the same shape over and over without reselecting the tool each time.

234

➤ To select an object, click it.

➤ Drag the selected object's handle to resize it.

➤ Point at the selected object, hold the mouse button down, and drag it to move it anywhere on-screen.

➤ To copy a shape, click it to select it, and hold down the **Ctrl** key while moving the shape. Let go, and you have a duplicate of the original.

➤ Delete a selected shape by pressing the **Del** key.

➤ To change how your object looks, click your right mouse button and choose from the options on the shortcut menu.

You Can Undo It! Now's a good time to mention the Undo command again. On your toolbar at the top of the screen there is an Undo button. Click it to erase your line or shape, or whatever it was you drew.

Shape Up with AutoShape

The AutoShape feature enables you to add preset shapes to your slides. To use this:

1. Click the **AutoShapes** tool on your drawing toolbar (remember, you have to be in Slide view to see the drawing tools).

2. In the AutoShapes palette that appears, click the shape you want to draw.

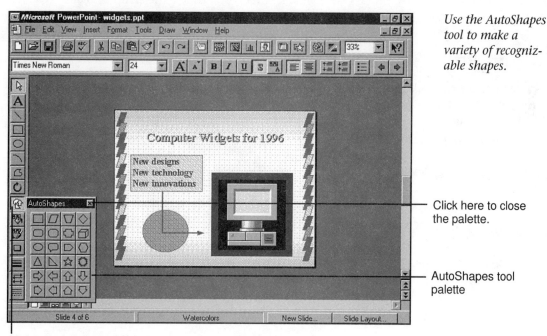

Use the AutoShapes tool to make a variety of recognizable shapes.

Click here to close the palette.

AutoShapes tool palette

Click here to open the AutoShapes tool palette.

3. Move your pointer to the slide, hold down the mouse button, and drag your mouse to create the shape.

4. Release the mouse button, and you're done.

Can I Add Pictures from Other Programs?

Yesiree, you can. You can insert graphics from other applications (even non-Microsoft applications) into your slides. Use the following steps:

1. Open the **Insert** menu and select **Picture**. The Insert Picture dialog box appears.

2. Change to the folder or drive where the picture is located. When the file list appears, scroll through the list box to find the exact picture you're looking for. Use the **Preview** button to sample the file before choosing one.

3. After you select the picture, click **Insert**, and PowerPoint inserts the picture into your slide.

You can use your mouse to reposition or resize the picture in your slide. Be sure to refer to your user's manual for specific types of graphic files you can insert into your Office 95 programs. You also need to know what graphics filters you installed. A graphics filter is what makes PowerPoint able to work with graphics from other programs. Check your manual to find out what filters are available; then you can use the setup program to install them, if needed.

Editing Your Art

If you thought there were too many ways to modify your text, you're going to be overwhelmed with the various ways you can edit art. In this section of the chapter, I'll tell you how to make your art look different with sizing, shading, coloring, and more. You can apply these editing techniques to art that you draw yourself or to clip art.

Big, Little, Distorted

If you try to resize your artwork, you may notice that some strange things happen to the way it looks. For example, if you select an object and drag it with one of the middle handles on any side, the object becomes distorted.

If you don't want a distorted object, you need to use proportional sizing. Select the object by clicking it, and drag one of the corner handles to resize the image proportionately. That means the original shape remains the same, but you enlarge or reduce it.

It's a Bountiful Crop

Cropping is another editing feature to learn about. You can trim off portions of the object off in much the same way as magazine editors trim photographs to fit.

1. To crop an object, start by selecting your image by clicking it. (You can also right-click the image to find the Crop Picture command.)

2. Open the **Tools** menu and choose the **Crop Picture** command, and your mouse pointer takes the shape of a weird-looking squarish thing.

3. Do you want to remove some of the top, bottom, or sides of the image? Decide where you want to crop your image, and move the weird pointer over one of the middle handles on your selected image.

4. Hold down the mouse button and drag the mouse until the crop lines crop the part of the artwork you want removed.

Want to remove from both the sides or the top and bottom of the image? Simply move the weird pointer over one of the corner handles on your selected image. Hold down the mouse button and drag your mouse until the crop lines crop the part you want to remove.

Do a Little Coloring

You can change the colors of your art and make it look like a completely different picture.

1. Select the image.

2. Open the **Tools** menu, and choose **Recolor**. (You can also right-click to choose the Recolor option.) The Recolor Picture dialog box opens.

3. Under the **Change** options, select **Colors** to change the image's line colors, or select **Fills** to change the colors between the lines.

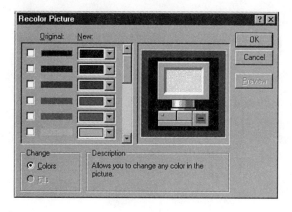

The Recolor Picture dialog box.

4. Under the **Original** list of colors options, you pick the color you want to change. Click the color's check box, and use the drop-down list under **New** to pick a new shade.

5. To see how everything looks, click the **Preview** button.

6. When the drawing meets your approval, click **OK** to exit the dialog box, and PowerPoint changes the image.

The Least You Need to Know

Formatting your text and adding art are excellent ways to polish up your presentation.

➤ PowerPoint includes numerous formatting controls that you can apply to your text one slide at a time, or to the entire presentation.

➤ You'll find plenty of clip art in PowerPoint that you can readily plug in when needed. If you prefer, you can import clip art from other applications.

➤ PowerPoint comes with a set of drawing tools with which you can create your own artwork.

Chapter 18

Put Your PowerPoint Presentation in Order

In This Chapter

➤ Learn to add graphs and charts to your slides

➤ Rearrange your slide order and polish up your presentation

➤ Apply special effects to your slide show

➤ Create speaker notes and handouts

Listen up, PowerPoint fans. This is the last chapter before I turn you loose to create your own visual presentations. I'll show you how to add graphs, charts, and a little sound to your presentation; teach you to whip up some speaker notes and handouts; and give you some tips for running through your program and putting it in order.

Adding a Graph or Chart

We covered inserting text and graphics into your slides in Chapters 16 and 17. What could possibly be left? How about graphs and charts. I'll show you how to insert graphs (also known as charts) and even create an organizational chart.

A cool feature that PowerPoint boasts about is *Microsoft Graph*. Actually, it's a small application (called an applet) that works in PowerPoint and your other Microsoft programs when called upon. Microsoft Graph takes data you enter and turns it into a great-looking graph. To use Microsoft Graph, follow these steps:

1. Display the slide to which you want to add a graph.

2. Click the **Insert Graph** button on your toolbar, or open the **Insert** menu and select **Microsoft Graph**. The Microsoft Graph window opens, displaying a Datasheet. A Datasheet is like a spreadsheet, with columns and rows intersecting to make cells. PowerPoint turns the data you type into these cells into a graph.

The Microsoft Graph window.

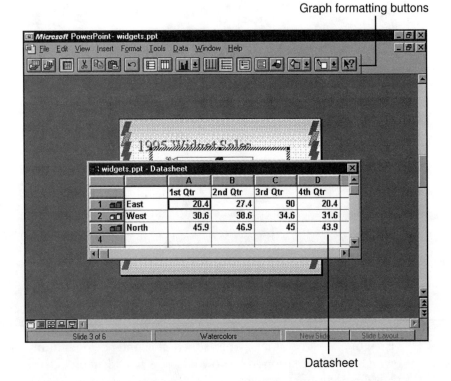

Graph formatting buttons

Datasheet

3. Fill in the Datasheet with the information you want to graph. If you need some tips on working in a spreadsheet, back up and read the chapters about Excel again.

4. Use the graph formatting buttons to apply any formatting commands to your data.

5. Once you fill in your graph data, click anywhere inside the graph window, and PowerPoint displays your new graph.

Insert Graph button

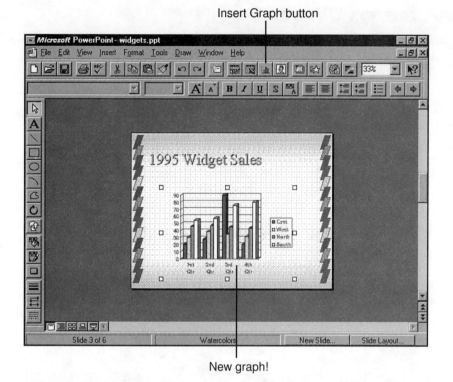

To see how your graph is going to look, click outside of the Datasheet.

New graph!

Here are a few more tips about working with graphs:

➤ To exit the graph feature, click anywhere outside the graph. When you do, PowerPoint inserts your graph into your slide.

➤ To resize the graph, select it and simply drag one of the handles until the graph reaches the desired size.

➤ To move the graph, select it, and drag the graph to a new location.

➤ To move the legend, select it, and drag it to a new location on the graph.

➤ You can easily edit your graph by double-clicking anywhere inside the graph image. This takes you to the Microsoft Graph window again, where you can make changes to your data.

➤ If the Datasheet doesn't appear in the Microsoft Graph window, you can display it by clicking the **View Datasheet** button.

I Want My Graph to Look Different!

You're not stuck with a boring old bar graph; you can select many more interesting graphs. To change your graph type:

1. Reopen the Microsoft Graph window by double-clicking your graph.

2. Open the **Format** menu and choose **Chart Type**. This opens the Chart Type dialog box, which displays a collection of graph styles from which to choose.

3. Make sure the **Entire Chart** option is selected, and click the chart type you want.

4. Click **OK** to exit the dialog box.

You can choose from 2-D and 3-D styles!

The Chart Type dialog box.

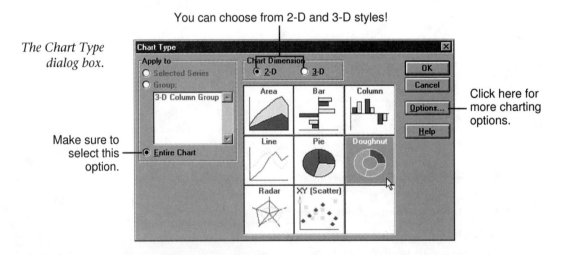

Click here for more charting options.

Make sure to select this option.

Adding an Organizational Chart

Alert! MS Organization Chart does not install during the Typical installation. If you performed a Custom installation, you may have opted to install this applet. If you did not install it, you can go back to the setup program and install it at any time. Consult your manual for details.

Another feature to know about is the Microsoft Organization Chart feature. Like Microsoft Graph, the Organization Chart is an *applet*, an application you can use in any of your Microsoft programs. It helps you create spiffy organizational charts to show a management or reporting structure. You flow-chart aficionados will love this one.

Display the slide to which you want to add an organizational chart; then follow these steps:

1. Open the **Insert** menu and select **Object**.

2. When the Insert Object dialog box appears, move your pointer over to the **Object Type** list and select **MS Organization Chart 2.0**.

3. Click **OK**.

4. In the Microsoft Organization Chart window that appears, type the names or titles of your organization (or any other information you're organizing) into the appropriate boxes. Be sure to press **Enter** after you fill each box.

5. To add more boxes to your chart, click the appropriate box style button at the top of the window.

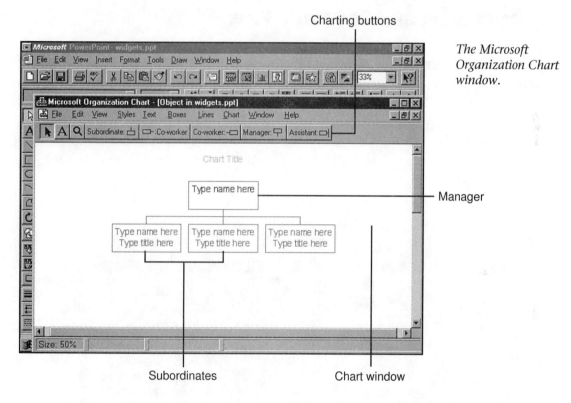

The Microsoft Organization Chart window.

6. If you don't like the family tree-like structure of the chart, you can change it. To do so, select the boxes you want to change, or select them all. Open the window's **Styles** menu and click a new style. If you don't like the way the boxes and lines look, open the **Boxes** menu and pick from those options.

7. When you finish, open the window's **File** menu and choose **Exit and Return to**. When the Exit dialog box appears, click **Yes**. Your new organizational chart appears in your slide.

You can edit your chart at any time. Double-click it to return to the Organization Chart (applet) window. Then edit the text or change the boxes' appearance as you did when you created the chart.

Rearranging Your Slides

If you've worked through the previous chapters, you should now have a presentation, complete with any necessary artwork or charts, and you're probably ready to get your presentation in order and add any additional final elements.

Rearrange Using the Slide Sorter View

The first thing you need to do is switch to Slide Sort view. In this view mode, you can see miniature versions of your slides and work with their order. Use the scroll bars, if necessary, to see them all. You can easily rearrange the slides in Slide Sorter view (and Outline view, too, as I discussed in Chapter 16).

Do you see a slide that would look better in another location? No problem. Move the mouse pointer over the slide you want to place in a new location, hold down your mouse button, and drag it to where you want it to go. When you release the button, the slide moves to the new position.

To copy a slide (instead of moving it), hold down the **Ctrl** key as you drag the slide.

Slide Sorter toolbar — When you drag a slide into a new position, an indicator line shows where you want the slide moved to.

Moving a slide in Slide Sorter view.

Rearrange Using the Outline View

Another way to rearrange slides is in Outline view. Switch to Outline view and click the slide number or the slide icon next to the subject text of the slide you want to move. This will select the entire slide's contents.

Next, move the mouse pointer over the selected slide, hold down the mouse button and drag the slide to a new location. You can use the **Move Up** or **Move Down** buttons on the Outline toolbar to help you find the right spot.

Add a Few Effects

There are a few more things to tell you about before you start viewing your slide shows. This is the fun stuff. Adding effects to your presentation can really jazz up the message, and keep your audience awake. With PowerPoint, you can decide how slides appear and disappear on-screen, how text shows up, or even how the slide sounds. Sounds? That's right, you can add sound effects, too. Slide effects are the icing on your presentation cake, so pass your plate and I'll show you how to use them.

What's on the Slide Sorter Toolbar?

First up, let's finish looking at all the details found in Slide Sorter view. Switch to Slide Sorter view by clicking the **Slide Sorter** view button at the bottom of your screen. Each slide in your presentation appears on-screen, as shown in the next figure. You also see the Slide Sorter toolbar. As you begin working with slide effects in the paragraphs to come, you'll have occasion to use the Slide Sorter toolbar to assign effects or open dialog boxes. Here's a table explaining what each toolbar button does:

Toolbar button	Name	Description
	Slide Transition	Opens the Slide Transition dialog box.
No Transition	Slide Transition Effects	Choose transition effects from this drop-down box.
Fly From Right	Text Build Effects	Use to select builds.
	Hide Slide	Use to hide slides.
	Rehearse Timings	Use to time your presentation.
	Show Formatting	Turns your presentation's formatting on or off.

I'm going to explain how to use the elements described in the table, so be patient. Keep reading this section.

I'm in a Transition Period

You can control exactly how long each slide remains on-screen and have PowerPoint automatically advance to the next slide without any prompting on your part. To automate the transition from one slide to the next, open the presentation; then follow these steps:

1. Open the **View** menu, and select **Slide Sorter**, or click the **Slide Sorter** button at the bottom of your screen.

2. To set up a controlled transition for one specific slide, select the slide. To select them all, hold down the **Shift** key and click each slide, or open the **Edit** menu and choose **Select All**.

3. Open the **Tools** menu and choose **Slide Transition**. (You can also click the **Slide Transition** button in the Slide Sorter toolbar.) The Slide Transition dialog box appears.

Transition effects are in this drop-down list.

The Slide Transition dialog box.

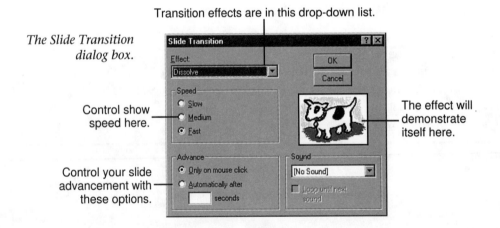

Control show speed here.

The effect will demonstrate itself here.

Control your slide advancement with these options.

4. Open the **Effect** drop-down list and pick a transition option. Look in the preview area (below the command buttons) to see a demonstration of the transition.

5. Under the Speed options, click **Slow**, **Medium**, or **Fast** to set a speed for the transition. In the Advance area, specify whether you want PowerPoint to advance the slides for you. If you do, click **Automatically After** and fill in how many seconds you want the slide to remain on-screen.

6. To add a sound to your slide, use the Sound options. Click the drop-down list to select a sound. (If you want to use a sound not found on the list, select **Other Sounds** and locate the sound file you want to use.)

7. When you finish with the dialog box, click **OK**.

Add Some Animation to Liven Things Up

PowerPoint 7.0 comes with some new animation effects you can use to liven up your slide shows. If you click the **Animation Effects** button (the one with a yellow star on it) on your Standard toolbar, you'll display the Animation Effects toolbar onto your screen. You can select from these effects to create such animations as making your slide text appear on-screen as if being typed by a typewriter, accompanied by the sound of typewriter clicking. Or how about making your slide title drop down from the top of the slide? Or maybe you'd like to add a flash of text or art? There are many possibilities, but start by looking at this table to see what kinds of choices you have.

Build It The effect of having your slide items appear at different times and in different ways on-screen is called a build. There are lots of different builds you can use with PowerPoint, such as bulleted items appearing one bullet at a time when you click the slide, or a graphic flying in from the side of the screen.

Button	Name	Description
	Animate Title	Causes the slide's title to drop down into the slide.
	Build Slide Text	Inserts slide text one sentence at a time.
	Drive-in Effect	Inserts object into slide, such as a speeding car, complete with sound effect.
	Flying Effect	Object flies into slide.
	Camera Effect	Inserts object into slide with the sound of a camera click.
	Flash Once	Flashes object onto slide and then off again.

continues

continued

Button	Name	Description
	Laser Text Effect	Writes text onto slide with a laser-like effect and sound.
	Typewriter Text Effect	Inserts slide text one character at a time, such as a typewriter, complete with typewriter sounds.
	Reverse Text Build	Builds your text block from bottom up.
	Drop-in Text Effect	Drops in each word one at a time.

I happen to think these new slide effects are the best part of PowerPoint, but I'm easily impressed with slick gimmicks. I think you're going to like playing with these effects to see how they change your presentation. The effects, after you assign them, show up when you run your slide show.

You can use the Animation Effects toolbar in Slide Sorter view or Slide view. If you're assigning effects to individual elements on your slide, you'll want to switch to Slide view and open the Animation Effects toolbar. Here's how to add effects in Slide View:

1. Click the **Animation Effects** button. This opens the Animation Effects toolbar.

2. If you want to apply an effect to a specific slide element, such as a title or art, select the item first.

3. Next, click the effect you want to assign to the element from the Animation Effects toolbar.

4. Continue selecting effects for each slide element, as needed. To close the Animation Effects toolbar, click the **Animation Effects** button again.

Check This Out...

Lookout— Shortcut!
You can also select an object on your slide (in Slide view) and right-click to view a shortcut menu; then choose **Animation Settings** from the menu.

When you're ready to run your slide show (which I'll tell you how to do shortly), the assigned slide effects will appear on your screen on command.

You can also add animation effects in Slide Sorter view, using the same Animation Effects toolbar and the Slide Sorter toolbar. You won't be able to apply effects to individual elements in the slide (use Slide view to do that), but you can apply effects to how slides appear and disappear in your presentation.

248

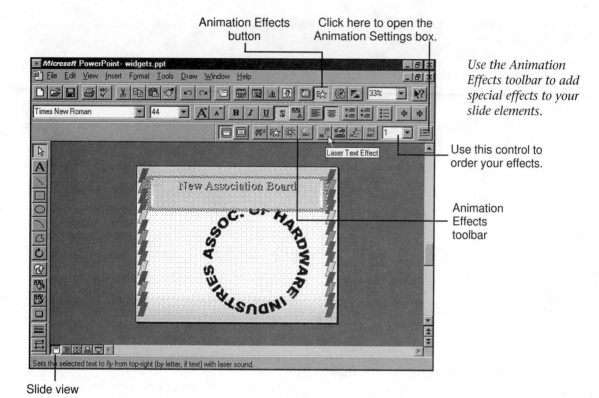

Animation Effects button

Click here to open the Animation Settings box.

Use the Animation Effects toolbar to add special effects to your slide elements.

Use this control to order your effects.

Animation Effects toolbar

Slide view

New Stuff!

The effects controls are new to PowerPoint 7. Old versions of PowerPoint let you control transitions and some builds, but Microsoft added new visual and sound effects to PowerPoint 7.0, making it even better.

Check Your Setting in the Animation Settings Box

Another way to add effects is with the Animation Settings dialog box, shown in the next figure. You'll find options for controlling how text appears (builds), as well as sound and visual effects. You can access the Animation Settings box by clicking the **Animation Settings** button on the Animation Effects toolbar, clicking the **Animation Settings** button on the Slide Sorter toolbar, or by opening the **Tools** menu and selecting **Animation Settings**.

The Animation Settings dialog box.

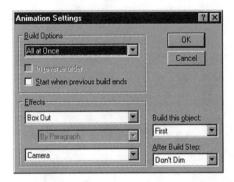

➤ Use the Build options to control how slide text appears on-screen.

➤ The Effects options (described previously) let you add visual and sound effects to the slide. Use the drop-down lists to choose from the available effects.

➤ The Build this object drop-down list can help you decide which items appear on-screen and when.

➤ The After Build Step drop-down box lets you change the color of your build text after it appears on-screen.

How About Some Sound Effects?

The new PowerPoint comes with a small collection of sound effects you can add, as I described in the preceding paragraphs. However, you may have some other sound files (WAV files) available. If you do, you can add them to your presentation, too. You can add music, prerecorded messages, sound clips, and more. Of course, your computer has to be capable of recording sounds (which it can with a sound board such as SoundBlaster Pro). If that's your scenario, I'll tell you how to perform the impressive feat of adding sound.

Display the slide to which you want to add sound, and do the following:

1. Open the **Insert** menu, and choose **Sound**.

2. In the Insert Sound dialog box, locate the folder containing the sound file you want to insert and select the file.

3. Click **OK** to insert the sound.

4. When you add a sound to a slide, a small icon appears on the slide to represent your sound. The icon may look like a speaker or another representation of the sound. You can move the icon to an inconspicuous place on your slide. When you want to play the sound, double-click the icon.

You can also use the **Insert Object** command to place sound wave files into your slides. In the Insert Object dialog box, you can select from wave sounds or other such sources.

You can even record new sounds to insert, such as someone talking, or sounds from CDs, and so on. Be sure to look through your PowerPoint manual for additional information about adding sound files to your presentation.

Sounds aren't the only dynamic effects you can add. You can also insert movie or video clips (if you're using a multimedia computer that's equipped with such things). You'll find this option also available on your Insert menu. (Consult your PowerPoint manual for more tips on using movie clips in your slides.)

It's Show Time!

This is it, the moment you finally get to see how your presentation looks and runs. I'll tell you how to electronically show your presentation, give you tips for stopping and adding notes, and even show you how to write on your slides during the presentation. Places, everyone! Cue monitor... lights, camera, action!

You're On!

When you have your show in order, take it for a spin. Starting from the first slide in the presentation, click the **Slide Show** view button on the View button bar. (You can also start the presentation by opening the **View** menu, selecting **Slide Show** and then **Show**.) Your first slide fills the screen, obscuring all the toolbars and window features, as shown in the next figure.

A slide as viewed during the course of the slide show.

Click here to view a menu of slide show controls.

251

➤ To progress to the next slide, click anywhere on the screen or press the right arrow or down arrow key on the keyboard.

➤ If you set up a specific transition time (see earlier in this chapter), it will kick in automatically.

➤ To quit the show at any time, press **Esc**.

➤ To see a menu of slide show controls, click the inconspicuous button in the lower left corner of the screen.

➤ If you selected a build effect for your slide or any slide elements, click your screen to "build" each effect.

➤ If you've inserted any sound clips, movie clips, or other special effects, you can double-click their icons to start them up during the presentation.

What's in the Slide Show Box?

You can also view specific slides in your show and how they appear with the Slide Show dialog box. To do this, pull down the **View** menu and select **Slide Show**. The Slide Show dialog box pops up on-screen. In this box, you'll find slide show options to choose from, including instructions for specifying which slides to show and how to advance from slide to slide. To start the show, click **Show**. This might come in handy when you want to practice showing a specific sequence of slides.

Slide Show Controls

Take a gander at the new PowerPoint 7 slide show controls by clicking the control button in the lower left corner of the slide screen. It opens a menu from which you can select controls for moving to the next slide, turning the arrow pointer into a pen that writes on-screen, and even ending the show.

The slide show controls menu.

Here's what each menu item controls:

Next   Takes you to the next slide or the next build effect.

Previous   Takes you back to the previous slide or build effect.

Go To   Opens a submenu for accessing the Slide Navigator box (a dialog box for specifying which slide you want to see next) or a hidden slide.

Meeting Minder   A new feature that lets you stop your slide show and compose notes, comments, and other observations made by your audience. (More about this feature coming up.)

Slide Meter   Opens a dialog box for timing your slide show.

Arrow   Lets you use the mouse pointer arrow to navigate the screen.

Pen   Turns your mouse pointer into a pen which you can then use to scribble on the slides that you show. The scribbles are not saved as part of your presentation; however, the effect is kind of like using an electronic chalkboard. (You'll learn how to do this later in the chapter.)

Pointer Options   Lets you hide the mouse pointer altogether or change your pen's color.

Screen   Opens a submenu for blacking out your current slide, pausing the show, or erasing your pen scribbles.

End Show   Puts a stop to your slide show.

> **These Are New!**
> The slide show controls are new to PowerPoint 7. I think you'll find them very useful for quickly adding to your presentation during the show, or making quick changes to the show. Be sure to familiarize yourself with these controls so your on-screen manipulations will seem fast and subtle.

Hey, I Can Write on My Screen!

Another nifty improvement to PowerPoint 7 is the ability to turn your mouse pointer into a writing pen during your show. You can use it to underline points that you make, add scribbles, notes, whatever. The potential here is to turn your slides into interactive screens where you and the audience can scribble with them like a chalkboard.

To turn your pointer into a pen during the presentation, click the slide show control button to open the menu, and select **Pen**. (If you want to change back to an arrow later, open the menu again and choose

> **Cool Pen!**   The pen feature is new to PowerPoint 7. With a little practice, this handy feature will enhance your presentation.

Arrow.) To write on the slide, move your pen (alias mouse pointer) to the place you want to "write," and hold down the left mouse button and drag. Practice this technique to get the hang of it before actually doing this during an important presentation.

You can change your pen color at any time by opening the slide show control menu again; this time select **Pointer Options**, **Pen Color**, and choose a specific color.

Quick, Get Out Your Meeting Minder

I wrote this on-screen with the pen.

The Pen feature lets you write electronically on your slides.

Turn your pointer into a pen!

Click here to display a menu of options.

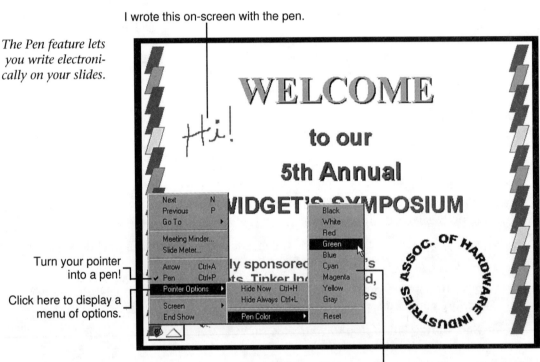

You can even change your pen color.

Microsoft has also added a feature for recording notes, meeting minutes, and action items. It's the *Meeting Minder* and you can access it anytime during your slide show. Click the slide show control button, select **Meeting Minder**, and the Meeting Minder dialog box appears.

Check out these options:

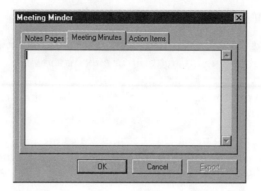

The Meeting Minder dialog box.

Notes Pages tab   Lets you view your own Notes Pages (which you'll learn how to create in the next section).

Meeting Minutes tab   Lets you type in notes to turn into meeting minutes.

Action Items tab   Lets you enter text for becoming action points after the presentation.

Choose any of the tabs, enter your information, and you can save it along with your program and export it to create meeting minutes. I found this very helpful when presenting a program that required audience feedback. By opening the Meeting Minder, I could immediately start typing in audience responses. Of course, it helps to be a fast typist and to have practiced with this feature before using it during your presentation.

To see your Meeting Minder information later, open the **Tool** menu and select **Meeting Minder**.

They've Thought of Everything!   Meeting Minder is yet another major improvement to PowerPoint 7.0, the ability to stop during your program, enter notes, and save them along with the slide show. There are plenty of uses for this feature, so be creative.

Making Notes and Handouts

In this final section of the chapter, I'll show you how to make notes for yourself and handouts for your audience members. Why would you want to do that? Because, it will make you look organized and professional and allow your audience to take the information with them to study it in detail at their leisure.

Creating Speaker Notes for Yourself

We've all witnessed presentations in which the speaker merely read the information on the slides, never elaborating on anything or making the visual meaningful. Don't let yourself fall into giving that kind of presentation. Instead, create some speaker notes to help you organize your thoughts, cover all the crucial points, and make your presentation cohesive and effective.

Notes pages consist of two parts. One part illustrates the slide, and the other part contains your notes. Since you've already put together your presentation, the only thing left is to type up the notes.

An example of a speaker's notes page.

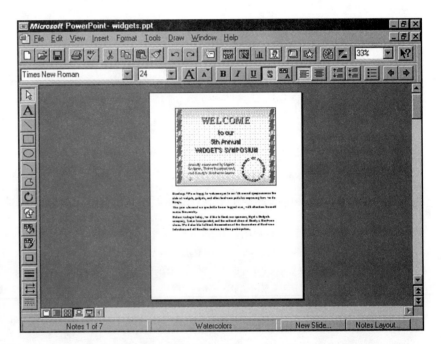

1. Open your presentation and switch to Notes Pages view.

2. On the first slide that appears, click the notes text box in the lower half of the page. This selects the notes text box so you can start typing notes. If you're having trouble seeing what you're typing, click the **Zoom** drop-down list on the toolbar to display a list of zoom percentages (if you prefer, you can use the **Zoom** command on the **View** menu). Try 100%; it's up close and personal.

3. Go ahead and type in your note text. If you're at a complete loss about what to type, consider noting supporting information, explanations and tie-ins, jokes, and so on. You can format your text any way you want it on the page.

4. When you finish with one slide, click the **Next Slide** button to move to the next one in line.

You can readjust the sizes of the slide picture or the notes text box at any time. Click either one, and a frame with handles appears around it. Drag the handles or the border to resize the frame.

To print your notes, click the **File** menu and select **Print**. In the Print dialog box, select **Notes Pages** from the Print what drop-down box at the bottom. Click **OK**, and your Notes Pages will print.

Using the Notes Master

Do you remember the Slide Master I told you about in Chapter 17? Well, there's a Notes Master, too. Essentially, it controls the architecture underlying all of your notes pages. You can design your notes pages to be uniform by summoning up the Notes Master and making all of your formatting changes.

To access Notes Master, open the **View** menu, select **Master**, and select **Notes Master**. (You can also click the **Notes Master** view button.) The screen switches to Notes Master, and you can change any of the elements on the page. To exit, click the **Notes Pages** view button.

Making Handouts for Your Audience

Slide shows go by fairly quickly, and there's rarely time for the information to sink into your audience's minds. So back up your presentation with handouts—they're easy to make.

1. Open the **File** menu and choose **Print**.

2. In the Print dialog box, pull down the **Print what** drop-down list and select the **Handouts** option you want to use.

3. When you have that squared away, click the **OK** button to print your handouts.

In Case You Want to Know... You can print out your entire presentation as an outline. In the Print dialog box, in the **Print what** drop-down list, choose **Outline View**.

Check This Out...

There's also a Handout Master you can use to make the appearance of all your handout pages uniform. Open the **View** menu, select **Master**, and select **Handout Master**. This switches your screen to Handout Master mode. Make any necessary changes to the handout page that appears. To exit, click any of the **View** buttons.

The Print dialog box.

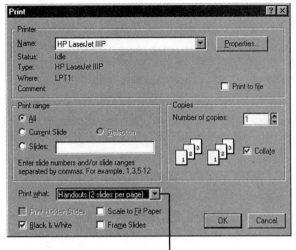

Click here to see the Print what drop-down list.

Let's Pack Up and Go

Are you ready to take your show on the road? Then you'll need PowerPoint's new Pack and Go feature. This little wizard assists you in loading your presentation onto a floppy disk, including all the relevant files that are linked to it. For example, if you're taking the presentation to an important sales meeting back at the home office in Timbuktu, you can use the Pack and Go Wizard to load the presentation files nicely onto a floppy disk to take with you. Here's how it works.

1. Open your presentation; then open the **File** menu and select **Pack and Go**. The Pack and Go Wizard box appears.

2. Click the **Next** button to proceed.

3. Choose the presentation you want to pack. By default, PowerPoint selects the current presentation that you have opened. You can choose another, however, by selecting **Other Presentations** and clicking the **Browse** command. Click **Next** to continue.

4. The next box lets you pick which drive you're packing the presentation onto. (By default, PowerPoint selects the A drive, but you can change to another.) Select a drive, and click the **Next** button.

5. The next box lets you choose to include linked files or embed TrueType fonts along with your presentation (in case the computer you're going to use to show the presentation doesn't have the same fonts you used). Make the appropriate selection; then click **Next** to continue.

258

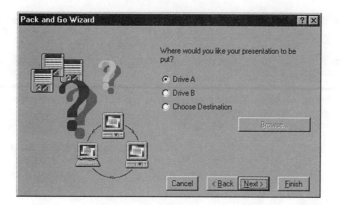

The Pack and Go Wizard.

6. If the computer you're going to use to show your presentation on doesn't have PowerPoint, the next Wizard box lets you load a PowerPoint Viewer. (The viewer will work with previous versions of Windows.) Click **Next** to continue.

7. Now click the **Finish** button in the final box, and the Wizard starts packing your data onto a floppy disk. Make sure a disk is in the appropriate drive.

Hold a Conference

PowerPoint 7.0 comes with a new Presentation Conferencing Wizard to help you manage or view presentations over a network. The participants can even add their own notes on the slides. To find this feature, open the **Tools** menu and select **Presentation Conference**. Be sure to consult your manual for more information.

The Least You Need to Know

You're a presentation pro now; get out there and visually communicate.

➤ You can easily add graphs to your slides with the Microsoft Graph feature. Selecting this feature opens up a simple datasheet for organizing graph information.

➤ Add organization charts to your presentation to help everyone see who's who and what's what.

➤ Practice running through your slide show several times, and use the Slide Sorter view to quickly move slides around.

259

➤ Experiment with the special transition and build effects and add some sound, if you like, to make your presentation more professional.

➤ Use the slide show controls during the course of your presentation to change your mouse pointer, add notes, and more.

➤ You can now write on your slides during your show with the pen feature.

➤ Keep notes about the show using the new Meeting Minder feature.

➤ Create notes pages to help you organize your material and get through your part of the presentation without fear.

➤ Print handouts of your slides that you can give to the members of your audience so they can consider your main points further.

➤ Use the Pack and Go Wizard to help you put your presentation on disk.

Chapter 19

Let Me Check My Calendar: Using Microsoft Schedule+

In This Chapter

➤ Discover what you can do with Schedule+

➤ Tips for getting around your Schedule+ screen

➤ Learn how to set up your first appointment without the help of a secretary

The last program to tell you about in your Microsoft Office 95 package is Schedule+. This helpful little program is new to the Office 95 package; it makes perfect sense to include it along with the other programs. Schedule+ is capable of acting as your own electronic secretary, keeping track of your daily schedule, appointments, and To Do lists. You can organize all your other office tasks, but don't fire your secretary yet—Schedule+ won't run the copy or fax machine or prepare your bank deposits.

What's New with Schedule+?

If you've ever worked with Schedule+ outside of Microsoft Office before, you may be curious about any improvements Microsoft made to it for Office 95. Here's a rundown of what's new:

➤ The Schedule+ new Contact Manager stores names, phone numbers, and addresses of all the people you contact the most. It's convenient, fast, and at your computer fingertips.

➤ Schedule+ is sensational if you and your co-workers are using it on a network. Use Group Scheduling to let you and your co-workers interact with Microsoft Exchange (Microsoft's e-mail software) and Microsoft Office to send memos, schedule meetings, and more.

➤ With the new Meeting Wizard, you tell the computer who needs to be at a meeting, and it takes care of the rest, including sending out reminders and solving scheduling conflicts.

➤ Use the Schedule+ information sharing technology to send out memos and attach other documents to your messages.

➤ Use the Drag and Drop technology to easily move and reposition items around on your schedule.

Those are some of the many changes and nifty features in Schedule+. Now quit wondering about them, and start organizing your own schedule.

Let's Open 'er Up

Pardon me for stating the obvious, but before you can start working with Schedule+, you first have to start the program. Back by popular demand, here are the most proven methods for opening Office 95 programs, Schedule+ in particular:

Check This Out...

Other Ways to Open Schedule+ You can also launch Schedule+ from the Windows Explorer by double-clicking the **Schedule+** executable file in the Office folder. Or open Schedule+ from the My Computer window by opening the drive and folder containing the program, and double-clicking the **Schedule+** icon.

➤ Open the **Start** menu; choose **Programs** and **Microsoft Schedule+**.

➤ If you set up your Office Shortcut bar to show a Schedule+ icon (see Chapter 6), you can click the **Schedule+** icon.

➤ If you haven't rearranged the default Office 95 Shortcut bar buttons, you can also assess Schedule+ by clicking the **Make an Appointment** button. This takes you directly to the Appointment dialog box in your Schedule+ program. (Learn more about the Appointment dialog box later in this chapter.)

➤ Click the **Add a Task** button on the Office 95 Shortcut bar, which opens the Schedule+ Task dialog box and lets you add an item to your To Do list. (Learn about the To Do list in Chapter 21.)

➤ Click the **Add a Contact** button on the Shortcut bar to open the Schedule+ Contact dialog box. You can use this to add a contact to your contact list (see Chapter 21).

What Do You Mean I Have to Logon?

The first thing you see when you start Schedule+ is a logon box. You'll see a logon box every time you open Schedule+. Depending on whether you're networked (connected to other computers) or not, your computer may show different logon boxes. If you're networked (and you share e-mail on the network with other users), you'll use a group-enabled mode box. If you're not connected to a computer network, you'll use a stand-alone mode box.

Why go to the trouble of using a logon box? Because the things you keep in your personal Schedule+ program may be personal or private, and you might not want everyone to have access to your schedule. Logons and passwords will help you keep your data safe. Logon boxes are also useful if several people are using the same computer. For example, if you're using Schedule+ at home, other members of your family can set up their own schedules and open them up through the logon box. So anyway, that's why Schedule+ uses logon boxes.

Here are instructions for handling the logon modes:

➤ In group-enabled mode, type your name in the Profile name box or select your name from the list. Type your password (if applicable), and click **OK**.

➤ In stand-alone mode, type your name, password (if applicable), and click **OK**.

The Logon box. Simple, yet effective.

How Do I Use Passwords?

Passwords are a common element with many computers and computer programs today. They help keep your data safe by only allowing certain users to log onto your files. You can set up passwords in all of your Microsoft Office 95 programs.

To create a password for your Schedule+ program, open the **Tools** menu, and select **Change Password**. In the Change Password dialog box, type in a password for yourself; confirm it by retyping it in the **Verify new password** box. Click **OK**, and Schedule+ sets your password. You'll have to use the new password to log back onto your Schedule+ program. Be sure to remember your password, or write it down and keep it somewhere safe.

Welcome to Your Schedule+ Screen

Once you've made it past the logon box, Schedule+ opens onto your screen. Schedule+ doesn't make full use of your whole monitor screen, but you can change this by clicking the **Maximize** button. Take a look at the next figure to see what Schedule+ looks like. Notice that the title bar displays your name. That's because it's your schedule. If someone else starts their own schedule on your computer, they would see their name when they logon. (Unless you logon using someone else's schedule, of course.)

As usual, you'll see the same old familiar Windows 95 elements you've been working with all along with the other Office 95 programs. Menus, toolbars, and scroll bars are scattered about, but everything looks a lot different on Schedule+. For starters, there's a big old daily schedule on the screen, accompanied by a monthly calendar and a To Do list.

Need Help?
Don't forget about the online Help system. It's always ready and waiting to help you out with any questions or tasks. Turn back to Chapter 5 for tips on using Help.

In fact, the whole Schedule+ program resembles one of those fancy personal organizer/planner books you buy at office stores, complete with tabs separating your data. However, this organizer isn't held together in an expensive leather binder, and you don't have to lug it around with you, so the chances of losing it are pretty slim. Instead, it's all electronic, simple to use, and right by your side as you sit next to your computer all day. I really think you're going to like this.

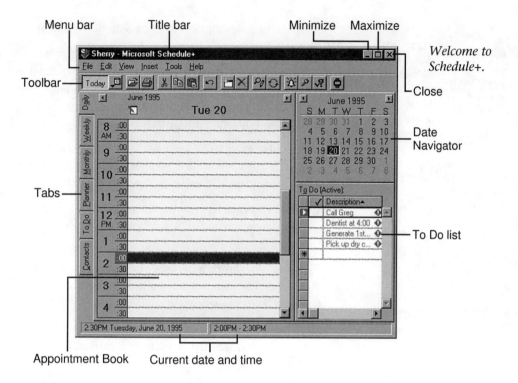

Menu bar   Title bar   Minimize   Maximize

Welcome to Schedule+.

Toolbar

Close

Date Navigator

Tabs

To Do list

Appointment Book   Current date and time

But What Am I Supposed to Do with Schedule+?

What's the matter? Haven't you ever organized yourself electronically before? It's the latest thing to do, you know. You see, your Schedule+ program is actually a Personal Information Management application, or PIM for short—at least that's what they're calling these things in nerdy social circles. PIMs are supposed to help you keep your daily life organized and free from unexpected chaos.

Schedule+ is part of the business community's newfound faith in time-management devices. Everybody who's anybody uses some kind of time-management device these days, whether it's a lug-around planner book encased in fine-grade leather engraved with the owner's name, or an electronic equivalent (which doesn't come with leather, but you can still put your name on it).

So, what's in these personal information management applications? They usually come with an appointment book, a To Do list, a place to list contacts, a planner, and an event-scheduler. As a matter of fact, those are the exact features that come with your Schedule+ program, too. How about that? Coincidence or diabolical plan—you be the judge.

Check This Out...

How Do I Start a New Schedule? Are you sharing your computer with other people, say family members? Then you'll want to know how to start new schedules for other users, right? To start a new schedule, you can type a new logon in the Logon box. This sets up a schedule for the additional user, which he can then fill to his heart's content. This information will come in handy when your entire family is sharing the program and each of them wants their own schedule.

How about a description of each Schedule+ feature? I thought you'd like that:

Appointment Book Use this feature to keep track of daily and weekly appointments, and set up reminders for yourself, too. You can even set up alarms that beep to remind you of an appointment.

To Do List Organize your daily or weekly tasks, or prioritize things you have to keep track of. (Learn more about using the To Do list in Chapter 21.)

Contacts Enter in your business contacts and keep a list of names, addresses, and phone numbers you use the most.

Planner Organize meetings and attendees with the Schedule+ Planner feature, including setting up meeting times with the Meeting Wizard.

Events Stay ahead of special occasions with the Events feature, including birthdays, anniversaries, conferences, and more.

With Schedule+ you can keep track of daily appointments, meetings, prioritize your work, and a whole lot more. Naturally, all of this organizational stuff is supposed to make your life easier—that's what the people who sell these personal organizers say.

How Do I Move Around in Here?

I'm sure this won't come as a surprise to you, but you can move around in Schedule+ using the same methods you use to move around in the other Office 95 programs. If you were expecting something different, you're out of luck.

You can use the mouse to move around the screen and select items, or you can use the keyboard shortcut keys and selection keys. Many of the on-screen items you work with have shortcut menus for accessing commands quickly. (You can right-click an item to display a shortcut menu, when applicable.)

The toolbar offers you shortcuts to common tasks, such as printing or copying. To use the toolbar tools, click the button you want to activate. There are some new buttons on the toolbar that you haven't encountered yet, but you can always find out what they do by moving your mouse over the icon and reading the ToolTip name.

To move around in your Appointment Book or any of the other features, click in the slot or select the date you want to use. There are six tabs at the left of your screen that let you open the other features. Click the tab name to open the feature. By default, Schedule+ opens to the Daily view, which opens your Appointment Book to the current date.

Setting an Appointment

Let's start out your Schedule+ adventure with a detailed look at your Appointment Book feature in the Daily view tab. After all, it's the first thing you see when you open the program (unless you used an Office Shortcut bar button to open Schedule+).

Suffering from a Concussion? In case you ever fall off your chair, hit your head, and suddenly forget what day it is, you can always look at your Schedule+ status bar for help. It always displays the current date and time.

Looking at Your Daily View Tab

There are six tabs to work with on your Schedule+ screen. By default, Schedule+ always opens to the Daily view tab where you can see your day's appointments at a glance. Take a look at the Daily view tab again in the next figure.

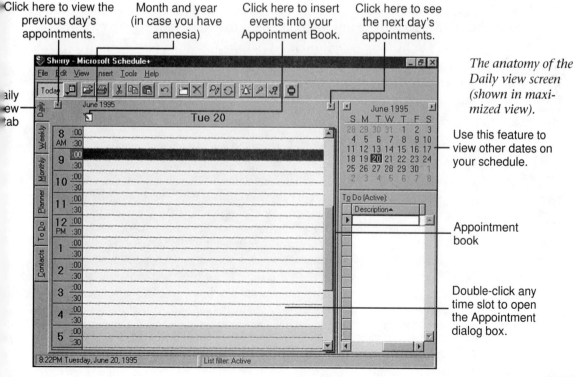

Click here to view the previous day's appointments.

Month and year (in case you have amnesia)

Click here to insert events into your Appointment Book.

Click here to see the next day's appointments.

The anatomy of the Daily view screen (shown in maximized view).

Use this feature to view other dates on your schedule.

Appointment book

Double-click any time slot to open the Appointment dialog box.

267

There are several distinct parts of your Daily tab. Three of them stand out in particular:

The **Appointment Book** (the biggest part of your screen with all the times and lines in it) shows your daily schedule.

Use the **Date Navigator** (the month displayed in the upper right corner) to change dates.

Use the **To Do list** (right underneath the Date Navigator) to display a list of what you're supposed to do on the date displayed.

Aside from these areas, you'll also note little buttons scattered about. Here's the scoop on manipulating the parts on your screen using the buttons and more:

➤ Use the two tiny buttons with arrows on them at the top of your daily schedule area to move backward and forward in your schedule.

➤ A click on the left arrow button moves your schedule back one page to the previous date.

➤ A click on the right arrow button moves your schedule forward one page to the next date.

➤ Click either arrow button and hold down your mouse button to speed through your schedule pages forward and backward.

➤ Right below the month and year at the top of your schedule section is a little white box with a pen. You can use this to insert events into your daily schedule.

➤ You can change the proportions of all three of the tab features by moving the lines that separate them. Move your mouse pointer over any line between the Appointment Book, Date Navigator, or To Do list and the pointer becomes a double-headed arrow; drag the pointer to resize the screen items.

A Word About Default Settings

All of your Office 95 programs start with default settings. These are set for typical usage, and for most of us, they work fine. However, you can always change the default settings to meet your own needs. Take for example, the Schedule+ program. Your Appointment Book typically shows an 8:00–5:00 time frame in the work window. For many folks, the week begins on a Sunday and ends on a Saturday, and the workday runs from 8:00 a.m. to 5:00 p.m. (ha—in high school, maybe). These happen to be your default settings, but you can change them to your own hours using the Options dialog box. Open the **Tools** menu, select **Options**, and zip around the four tabs to adjust settings for your schedule, screen display, and even reset your time zone. (Click **OK** to save your changes and exit the box.)

Let's Make an Appointment

Are you ready to start filling in your daily appointments? You can select any time slot in your Appointment Book to enter an appointment. Use the scroll arrows on the right side of the Appointment Book to move back and forth along your time schedule. (Yes, there are more hours than the typical 8:00–5:00; scroll up and down to find them.)

To enter an appointment, click a time slot and type in a description of the appointment. When you finish, click outside of the slot. How's that for fast? It's easier than actually writing in a paper appointment book.

In case you haven't noticed yet, the daily schedule is broken into 30-minute increments. If your appointment takes more than 30 minutes, select more than one 30-minute slot. To do this click the first slot, hold down the left mouse button, and drag to the ending time slot.

> **Check This Out...**
>
> **My Life Is Longer Than 30-Minute Increments!** If you prefer to work with increments of time other than the default 30-minute time slots, you can do so. Open your **Tools** menu, select **Options**, and click the **General** tab. In the **Appointment Book time scale** option, select a new time increment to use in your schedule. Click **OK** to exit the dialog box.

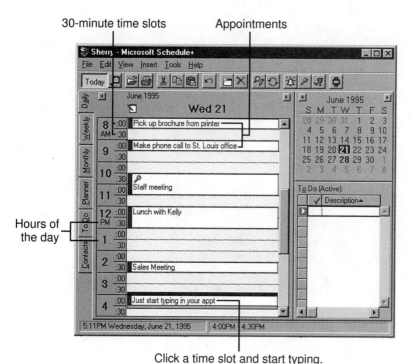

Entering appointments is easy.

Click a time slot and start typing.

Check This Out...

Toolbar Shortcut
You can return to the current date on your Appointment book by clicking the **Today** button on your toolbar.

Once you enter an appointment, you can do all sorts of things to it:

➤ You can edit it at any time.

➤ You can move it to another date or copy it.

➤ You can delete it.

➤ You can view it in weekly or monthly views.

➤ You can set it up so that it reminds you when the appointment time gets close.

I'll explain how to do each of these things in the next chapter, so hang on. In the meantime, there's another way you can enter appointments onto your schedule.

Use the Appointment Dialog Box

Another route to more detailed appointments is to open the Appointment dialog box. To do this, double-click a time slot. The Appointment dialog box will appear on your screen, as shown in the next figure.

The Appointment dialog box.

Use these buttons to change times.

Use these to change dates.

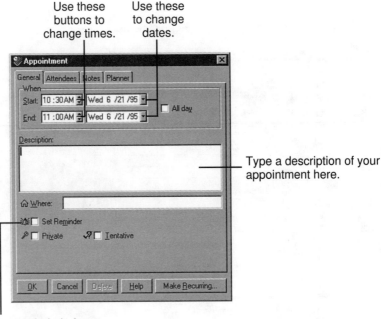

Type a description of your appointment here.

Want to be reminded of your appointment? Select this option.

270

This dialog box has four tabs for entering data. The General tab, shown in the preceding figure, has options for setting up a new appointment. Let me explain what each one of these options controls:

When   This area shows the Start and End times of your appointment. You can type in another time and date as needed. The arrow buttons next to the times let you scroll through other hours. The drop-down arrows next to the dates let you view a monthly calendar to select a new date.

Description box   This box is where you type in details about your appointment. For example, let's say you're entering your lunch date with Bob in your daily schedule. You can type **Lunch with Bob** in the description box. When you close the Appointment box, the description appears in your daily schedule.

Where   This option lets you type in the location where your appointment is taking place.

Set Reminder   If you want to be reminded of your appointment beforehand with an on-screen box and an audible beep, select the **Set Reminder** option. When selected, additional controls appear for designating when the reminder message is to appear. (The message that appears is a dialog box telling you about your appointment.) For example, you can set it up to send you a reminder message fifteen minutes before your appointment. (More about the Reminder dialog box later.) When you add a Reminder option to your appointment, a tiny bell icon appears next to the description in your schedule.

Private   To keep your appointment description away from the prying eyes of others, use the **Private** option. This options hides your appointment from other users on your computer network, but you can still see it in your schedule. When you add a Private option, a tiny key icon appears next to your appointment description.

Tentative   If your appointment is tentative, and not concrete, use the **Tentative** option. This keeps the appointment time from appearing as untouchable in your Planner, especially if you're networked and people are trying to set up meetings with you. (More about the Planner later.) When you select the Tentative option, a tiny check-question mark icon appears next to the description in your schedule.

Command buttons   The command buttons at the bottom of the dialog box are pretty standard. Use the **Delete** button to remove appointments, and the **Make Recurring** button to set up an appointment as a regular, recurring part of your schedule.

To set an appointment in the Appointment dialog box, follow these steps:

1. Set a specific time and date in the **Start** and **End** boxes. (By default, these boxes show the current date and the time you double-clicked on in your schedule.)

2. Type a description of your appointment in the **Description** box.

3. You can add any additional options, such as a reminder or a recurring appointment, by selecting those options now.

4. When you finish, click **OK** and Schedule+ sets your appointment. It will now appear on your schedule.

The Other Appointment Box Tabs

There are some other things you can do in the Appointment dialog box besides set appointments. If you're networked, the other tabs in the Appointment box can give you more information.

Use the **Attendees** tab to view a list people who are attending the appointment with you.

Use the **Notes** tab to create notes about your meeting or to type up a meeting agenda for distribution among the attendees.

Use the **Planner** tab, a miniaturized Planner feature that you'll learn about in Chapter 21, to view everyone's schedule times to help you pick a free time for all. The **Auto-Pick** button helps you locate the first free time available among the attendees.

The Least You Need to Know

Was that fun, or what? Now that you're all organized, I'll bet you're feeling free and easy, right?

➤ Schedule+ is designed especially to help you manage your time electronically.

➤ You'll logon to your schedule with a Logon box.

➤ The Daily view tab shows your schedule for the day as soon as you open the program.

➤ There are a variety of ways to set up appointments on your electronic schedule.

Chapter 20

Fiddling with Your Schedule+ Appointments

In This Chapter

➤ Tips for editing your appointments

➤ Learn how to set up recurring appointments

➤ Handle the Reminder box when it pops up on your screen

➤ View your schedule in weekly and monthly perspectives

You learned Schedule+ basics in the last chapter, but it's not enough to know how to enter appointments into a daily schedule—you have to know how to juggle the appointments, edit them, reschedule them, and much more. If you don't do all these things, you're not a good time manager, are you? Besides, you want to get your money's worth out of your Schedule+ program, don't you? That settles it; this chapter will continue your Schedule+ education.

Editing Your Appointments

You've figured out how to enter appointments into your Appointment book, right? (If not, you need to back up a chapter.) So, what if you want to change an appointment; how are you going to do that? Good question. In paper and leather organizers that you lug around, you can make changes to things you've written down by simply scribbling them out, or erasing them and scribbling them somewhere else in your schedule. In your electronic organizer, you can scribble things out too, but it works a little differently, and you won't have to worry about smudging your schedule or creating a giant ink blob on the screen.

Using the Handy Toolbar Buttons

When it comes to editing your appointments, you'll find plenty of editing options on your Schedule+ toolbar. Click the toolbar button when you want it applied. To figure out what a button does, move your mouse pointer over the button and wait. A ToolTip name appears, which should give you some idea of what the button's for.

What's Timex Doing in My Schedule+ Program?

Hey, if you're the proud owner of a Timex Data Link watch, you can use Schedule+ to download information onto your watch. What? That's right. It's a new-fangled technology that lets you export your schedule information onto your Data Link watch; that way you can take your schedule with you wherever you go. Cool, eh? It's almost like that Dick Tracy watch, but you don't talk into it. To learn more about this hip new technology, consult your Schedule+ manual or the nearest Timex Data Link watch salesman.

Getting Down to Editing

There are several different ways to edit your scheduled appointments. Take a look at the Appointment Book again, for a frame of reference.

Extra Buttons?

If you and your Schedule+ program are hooked up to a network setup, you may see two additional buttons on your Schedule+ screen: Meeting Wizard and View Mail.

As typical in computer programs such as this, there are many ways to perform a particular task. You can use toolbar buttons, menu commands, or take a more direct approach. Here's a rundown of the various editing techniques:

➤ The most direct way is to simply click the slot containing the appointment and make your changes to the text.

➤ If you want to make your edits in the Appointment dialog box, you can double-click your appointment or click the **Edit** button on the toolbar.

Use the toolbar buttons to help you edit your appointments, too.

Look at my busy schedule.

You can make edits directly into a selected appointment.

Right-click to display a shortcut menu with more editing options.

➤ To add a new appointment to your schedule with the Appointment dialog box, double-click the time slot where it's to appear, or click the **Insert New Appointment** button on the toolbar.

➤ You can increase your appointment's time length after you've already entered it into your schedule by dragging its border to a new ending time. Move your mouse pointer over the bottom border of the selected slot and the mouse pointer becomes a double-sided arrow. Hold down your left mouse button, and drag the box to a new ending time.

➤ If you want to move the appointment to another time slot, move your mouse pointer over the top border or left border and it becomes a four-sided arrow. Hold down your left mouse button and drag the appointment to a new location on your schedule.

➤ If you want to set an appointment for a future date, use the Date Navigator: the calendar in the upper right corner. Click the appropriate date on the calendar, and your Appointment book turns to the date's schedule page. The tiny arrow buttons at the top of the Date Navigator let you move back and forth between months to select other dates.

➤ You can also move appointments off of your Appointment Book daily schedule and onto another date shown in your Date Navigator calendar. Select the appointment, hold down the left mouse button, and drag the appointment over to the Date Navigator calendar to the new date. Let go of your mouse button and the appointment will now appear in the other date's daily schedule.

➤ To add a Reminder to your appointment, select the appointment on your schedule, and click the **Reminder** button on the toolbar. You can turn off a Reminder by clicking the button again.

➤ To add a Private icon to your appointment, click the **Private** button. If your appointment already shows a Private icon, you can turn it off by clicking the toolbar button.

➤ To add a Tentative icon to your appointment, click the **Tentative** button. If a Tentative icon already appears, clicking the toolbar button will turn it off.

➤ To remove an appointment from your schedule, select the appointment and click the **Delete** button on the toolbar. Or double-click the appointment's border to open the Appointment dialog box, and click the **Delete** button.

➤ You can also use your menu commands to do all of the things described in this list.

➤ Right-click anywhere on your selected appointment to open a shortcut menu for viewing editing commands.

Other Appointment Features to Know and Love

When it comes to appointments, there's plenty to do with them other than stack them into an Appointment Book. It so happens, Schedule+ has some other swell features to help you designate appointments and work with your own schedule. Here are some more scheduling tricks.

Recurring Appointments

Some of your appointments might happen every week or every day, such as a weekly staff meeting or a daily car pool. Rather than typing these appointments in over and over again, use the Recurring option. You'll find the Recurring option available all over the place. It's on your toolbar, in your Insert menu, on the shortcut menu, and even in the Appointment dialog box. I'm going to show you one way to use it.

To use the Recurring option:

1. Select the appointment on your schedule.

2. Click the **Recurring** button on your toolbar. This opens the Appointment Series dialog box.

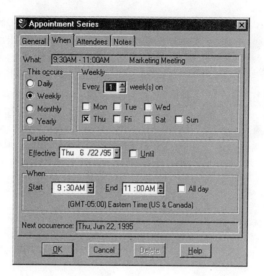

The Appointment Series dialog box. Does this look like the other Appointment dialog box to you?

3. Use the tabs to set up information about your recurring appointment. The **When** tab lets you designate when the appointment occurs (daily, weekly, monthly, or yearly) and what day it falls on. You can also set the exact time of the meeting. Make your adjustments to the settings.

4. Click **OK** to exit the box, and Schedule+ sets your recurring appointment.

A recurring appointment always appears with a circular icon symbol in your Appointment Book. If you want to set a reminder or change the appointment's description, click the **General** tab in the Appointment Series dialog box.

Dealing with the Reminder Box

Do you have any pressing appointments that you can't possibly miss? Then the Reminder feature can really help you remember them. You've already learned how to insert a Reminder icon into your appointment. But when does it get around to reminding you? It depends. What advance time did you set?

You can control when the Reminder feature reminds you when you open the Appointment dialog box. The **Set Reminder** check box, when selected, lets you control what time the Reminder feature calls your attention to the appointment. Fifteen minutes beforehand is a typical setting.

Default Reminders
Your program may be set up to remind you at a default time setting. In this case, open the **Tools** menu and select the **Options** command. In the Options dialog box, click the **Defaults** tab and deselect the **Set reminders for appointments automatically** check box to turn off the default setting.

When your appointment nears, the Reminder box will pop up on your screen (depending on when you set it to appear), as shown in the next figure. When the Reminder box appears, you'll hear an audible beep and the box suddenly interrupts what you were doing. The box itself describes your appointment and its time. The catch to using this Reminder feature, however, is you need to have your computer on, Schedule+ running (or minimized), and you need to be in the same room with your computer or you won't hear the beep or notice the Reminder box on your screen.

The Reminder box pops up on your screen to remind you about your appointment.

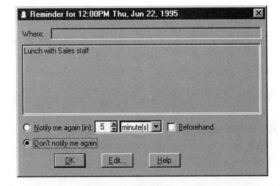

I Didn't Get a Reminder! What's Wrong?

By default, Schedule+ is set to show reminder boxes along with an audible beep. However, if you turned these settings off, you may be missing all of your reminder boxes. To check, open your **Tools** menu, select **Options**, and click the **General** tab. Make sure to select the **Set daily reminder**, **Set audible alarm**, and **Enable reminders** check boxes. Click **OK** to exit, and your reminder boxes should now work.

Your appointment will appear in the title bar of the Reminder box. Inside the box, you'll see a description of the appointment and even where your appointment is to take place (if that data was entered earlier). With the options at the bottom of the box, you can choose to remind yourself again as the appointment gets even closer. Click the **Notify me**

again option if you want another reminder before the appointment, and select a time for it. If you don't need another reminder, select the **Don't notify me again** option. When you finish with the box, click **OK** to exit.

When's the Big Event?

Need to schedule a big event or an annual event on your busy calendar? Use the Event scheduler to help you. Events show up a little differently on your schedule than appointments do. Events show up at the top of your daily schedule, right under the day and date. For example, if you set up your schedule to show your 50th wedding anniversary as an event, it will appear at the top of your schedule. (If you switch over to Weekly view, which you'll learn about later in this chapter, events appear at the top of the day of the week in which they occur.)

What constitutes a big event? I consider my vacation to be a very big event, so I'm always trying to work it into my busy schedule. Other events might include out-of-town conferences or conventions, weddings, training classes, seminars, company trips, birthdays, and more. Events can be a one-day thing, or span days and weeks. With Schedule+, you can even set recurring events so that they show up each week, month, or year.

To add an event to your own schedule, here's what you do:

1. Click the **Event** icon at the top of your schedule. (You can also open the **Insert** menu and choose **Event** or **Annual Event**.)

2. When you click this icon, a submenu appears with the option of selecting **Insert event** or **Insert annual event**. Choose the appropriate one, and an Event dialog box appears on your screen.

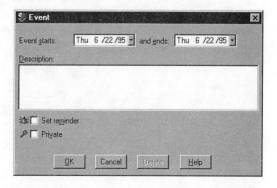

The Event box.

3. In the Event or Annual Event dialog box, choose the event start date and end dates. You can use the arrow buttons next to the dates to choose other dates, or you can type in the dates you want.

4. Click the **Description** box and type a description of the event.

5. Add any additional options, a reminder, or a private icon; click **OK** to exit the box. The event appears on your schedule as a heading at the top of the event day's column.

When you set an event into your schedule, the Event icon looks like it has writing on it. That's one way you can tell you've planned an event. You can easily edit the event by clicking the **Event** icon again; this time, your event's description appears. Select it to open the Event dialog box again and make changes.

What About the Other View Tabs?

Well, hold on. I am getting to that. For those of you who are very observant, you probably already noticed that there are two other views to see your schedule in: *Weekly* and *Monthly*. I'll cover those next.

Using the Weekly Tab

It's time to switch views. How about looking at your busy schedule in a weekly format? Okay, you'll need to click the **Weekly** tab. When you do, you'll screen will display your Appointment Book in a slightly different view.

To change to the Weekly view, click the Weekly tab.

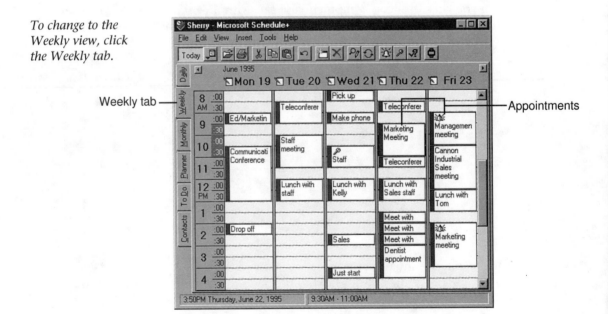

Weekly tab ⸺

Appointments ⸺

By default, Schedule+ shows you five days of the week in Weekly view. You no longer see the Date Navigator or the To Do list. Your screen looks a little crowded in Weekly view, and some of your appointments may not fit completely into your weekly columns and will look cut off. Don't forget, you can enlarge the Schedule+ screen by clicking the **Maximize** button. (If your appointment text is too long to fit in Weekly view and you still can't see the full appointment text, switch back to Daily view to read it all.)

The schedule you see in the Weekly view is the same as the schedule in Daily view; however, you see more days of the week in the Weekly view. You can perform the same functions in your Weekly view as in Daily view.

For example, at the top of the Weekly view tab are two arrow buttons, one on the left and one on the right. Like the arrow buttons in Daily view, you can use these to move your Weekly view back a week or forward a week. If you hold down your mouse button while selecting the arrow buttons, you'll move through the weeks of the month.

You can use those little boxes with pens in them next to each day of the week title to add events to your schedule (described earlier in this chapter).

Month at a Glance

Want to see your entire month of appointments? Switch over to Monthly view by clicking the **Monthly** tab. Your screen opens and you can view the entire month, as shown in the next figure.

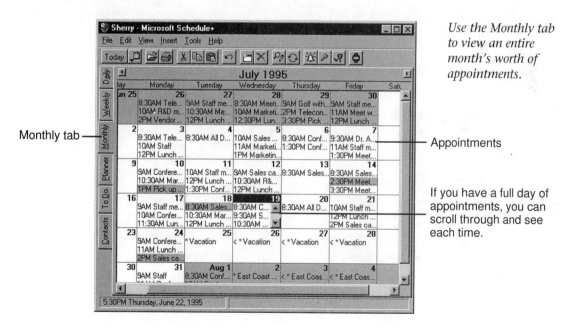

Use the Monthly tab to view an entire month's worth of appointments.

Monthly tab

Appointments

If you have a full day of appointments, you can scroll through and see each time.

Mind you, things look a little crowded when in Monthly view. At the top of the calendar, you'll see a left arrow button and a right arrow button. You can use these to view different months.

If you want to see details about any appointment listed in your schedule from Monthly view, double-click the appointment. This will open the Appointment dialog box.

The Least You Need to Know

Well, we've covered all the basics for using your Appointment Book and scheduling items. Look at all you've learned:

➤ You can set up reminders for various appointments to help you remember them.

➤ Use the Private option to keep your appointments secret.

➤ It's easy to set up regular appointment with the Recurring option.

➤ To schedule special occasions on your schedule, use the Events feature.

➤ To view your schedule in weekly or monthly form, click the **Weekly** or **Monthly** tab.

If you go to aerobics, you are going to be late for mah-jong...

SHADDUP.

Chapter 21

Using Other Schedule+ Features

In This Chapter

➤ Learn how to make a To Do list

➤ Set up group meetings with the Planner feature

➤ Compile lists of names and addresses with the Schedule+ Contacts feature

I can read your mind. I know exactly what you're thinking right now. You've finished reading two chapters about using Schedule+ to set up appointments and now you're wondering what else the program is good for. Am I right? If I am, then I'd like you to call my 1-900 psychic computer hotline; I have some more predictions to make. In the meantime, here's a chapter about other uses for your Microsoft Schedule+ program.

What to Do with the To Do List

Tired of setting up appointments? Me too. Let's check out the To Do list feature. You can use it to enter, manage, and track tasks and projects that are important to the various dates and appointments on your schedule. With the To Do list, you can assemble lists of daily things you need to do, items that you must work on to complete a project, or a grocery list of things you need to pick up on the way home. You can use the To Do list in all kinds of ways; its main purpose is to help you keep track of things you need to do.

What's a Task?

In Schedule+, a *task* is any item you list in the To Do list. A task is something you need to take care of on a particular date, or something you need to do to complete a project.

Click the **To Do** tab. This will open the screen to a To Do list format, as shown in the next figure.

The To Do tab.

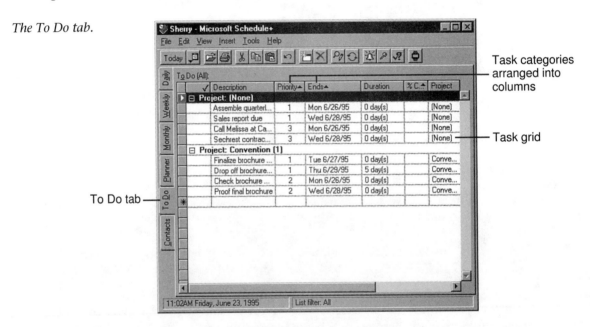

Task categories arranged into columns

Task grid

To Do tab

You've already seen the To Do list in smaller scale on the Daily view tab. (Flip back to Daily view to see the To Do list in the bottom right corner.) That particular list relates to the date on your Appointment Book schedule. It lists the tasks you need to complete that day or any held-over tasks that didn't get completed from the previous days. The To Do list shown in your To Do tab is the entire list of all the tasks you're keeping track of.

What About the Daily View To Do List?

After you enter some tasks and associate them with a particular date on your schedule, switch back to Daily view (click the **Daily** tab). The To Do list will reflect tasks that pertain to that particular date on your schedule. This can help you keep track of things you have to do each day, besides appointments to attend.

Working with Task Categories

As you can see from the preceding figure, your big To Do list appears as a grid, and the more tasks you add, the bigger your grid gets. Schedule+ organizes the tasks into columns that represent categories such as task priority, end dates, duration, and more. With these categories, and others you might assign, you can organize the tasks into groups, projects, and even filter and sort your tasks.

You can do several things to your grid columns:

➤ You can turn the gridlines on or off. Open the **Tools** menu, choose **Options**, and click the **Display** tab. Deselect the **Show gridlines** check box. The gridlines won't show up anymore.

➤ To change a column width, click its border and drag it to a new size.

➤ By default, Schedule+ shows several column categories that might relate to the tasks you want to list. However, you can change the categories at any time. Open the **View** menu, select **Columns** and **Custom**. In the Columns dialog box, you can add and remove the column categories that will appear on your grid.

Changing Grid Columns

If you don't like the column categories shown on the default grid, then change them. Follow these steps:

1. Open the **View** menu; select **Columns** and **Custom**.

2. The Columns dialog box appears, as shown in the next figure. You can change which categories appear. The Available fields list box shows remaining categories you can use. The Show these columns list box shows what categories currently appear in your grid.

3. To add a category to the Show these columns list, click the category on the left, and click the **Add** button. To remove a category from the Show these columns list, select the category and click the **Remove** button.

4. To change the order of the categories, select the category to move, and click the **Move Up** or **Move Down** buttons until the category is in the desired location.

5. To exit the dialog box and get back to your To Do list grid, click the **OK** button.

Use the Columns dialog box to change which To Do list categories appear.

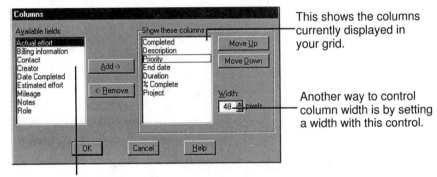

This shows the columns currently displayed in your grid.

Another way to control column width is by setting a width with this control.

Here's a list of other To Do list categories you can use.

Any changes you made in the Columns dialog box are reflected on your To Do list grid.

For a faster change of your To Do list columns, use the Columns submenu. Open the **View** menu; select **Columns**. In the submenu that appears, you have several category options to use:

➤ If want to show all the possible column categories in your grid, select **All** from the submenu that appears.

➤ To show a limited few, choose **Few** from the submenu.

➤ To go back to the original categories display, choose **Typical** from the submenu.

➤ If you don't want to see any additional categories at all, click the **Description** command from the submenu. This leaves you with just the Completed and Description columns.

Reading the To Do List Grid

Take a look at the next figure to see what kinds of things the task grid can tell you.

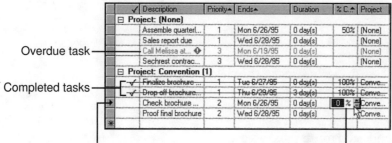

You can indicate on your task list how close your task is to completion.

Overdue task

Completed tasks

Row Selection button

Click the Completion category and enter percentages of the finished tasks.

➤ Completed tasks appear with a line through them and a check mark in the Completed column.

➤ Any tasks not completed by their specified end dates will appear with an overdue symbol, and their dates are marked in red so you can't miss them.

➤ If you're viewing the To Do list in the Daily view tab, note that uncompleted tasks from the previous day or days are held over and appear in your next day's To Do list, marked in red.

➤ If your columns are a little crowded in your To Do list, click a column border and drag the column to a new width. (You can also change which categories appear in your grid. See the previous discussion about changing grid columns.)

➤ If you sort your tasks, you'll see an arrow next to the heading indicating which direction the sorting occurred. An up arrow means it's sorted in ascending order, and a down arrow means it's sorted in a descending order.

➤ You can group your tasks under project headings. The symbols in front (plus or minus signs) of the project heading let you hide or display the tasks related to the project. The previous figure has a minus sign next to the project heading, which means all the tasks are listed.

➤ Some categories, when selected, open boxes for changing dates or percentages. These come in handy when you're editing your task's progress and status.

➤ Use the **Row Selection** button to select an entire row.

Grid Lingo

If you've already been through the chapters on Word and Excel, you know that tables and spreadsheets consist of intersecting columns and rows that form *cells*. Each row and column represents a *heading/entry* or *field/record*. In databases, which is what you're working with in the To Do list, each column is a field and each row is a record. So, if you were to see these words later in this chapter, you wouldn't be confused by anything, right? Such grid language is common among computer programs, so if you've seen one field or record, you've seen them all.

Add Your Own Tasks

Time to start adding your own tasks to the list; a task can be any item you want to accomplish or track. To add a task to your own To Do list, follow these steps:

1. Choose a row to start your task in.

2. Click the **Description** column and type in a description for your task.

3. Continue adding information in each category/column for the task row you've selected until you have filled in everything that's relevant. (You can press the **Tab** key to advance to each category in the row, or you can click the cells using your mouse.)

I Don't Like These Lines
Don't forget, you can get rid of the grid lines by opening your **Tools** menu and selecting **Options**. In the Options dialog box, select the **Display** tab. Turn off the **Show gridlines** option and the gridlines disappear.

If you want to group your tasks under a particular project name, open the **Insert** menu and select **Project**, or right-click to open the shortcut menu and select **New Project**. The Project dialog box opens. Type a name for your project, and then click **OK**. The task appears under the project heading. The project headings make it easier to organize your tasks.

When you have several projects on your To Do list, you can choose to list all the tasks under them, or hide the tasks. The tiny boxes in front of the project heading can turn your project task list on or off. A minus sign means all your tasks are listed under the project; a plus sign means the tasks are hidden in the list.

If you double-click a project heading, a Group By dialog box appears, which you can then use to list your tasks.

May I Introduce You to the Task Dialog Box?

Okay, the previous steps illustrated the simple way to add a task. Another way is to use the Task dialog box. This box lets you add more details to your task. Use these steps to add a task with the Task dialog box:

Shortcut
Another way to open the Task dialog box is to right-click the grid and select **New Task**.

1. There are two ways to open the Task dialog box; you can double-click the **Row Selection** button in front of the task (which I pointed out to you in the preceding figure), or you can click the **Insert New Task** button on your toolbar. Either method opens the Task dialog box.

Set a completion date for your task.

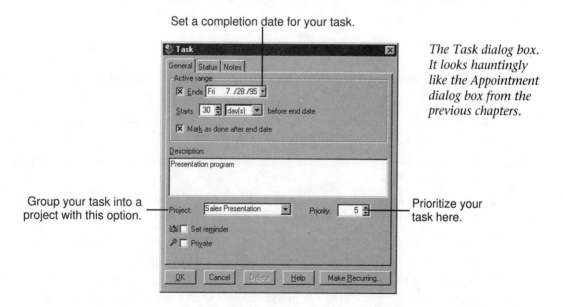

The Task dialog box. It looks hauntingly like the Appointment dialog box from the previous chapters.

Group your task into a project with this option.

Prioritize your task here.

2. In the **General** tab, enter an ending date in the Active range area associated with the task, or select a date with the drop-down arrows. You can also specify a starting date, which helps you track the duration of the task.

3. Use the **Mark as done after end date** check box to automatically mark the task when completed. By the way, this feature marks the tasks as completed after a period of time regardless of whether you yourself remember to or not.

4. Type a description of your task in the **Description** box.

5. If you want the task associated with a specific project, then type the project's name in the **Project** box.

6. If you want to prioritize the task, especially when dealing with project tasks, then mark a priority rating with the **Priority** box.

7. If you need a reminder to help you with your task, set one with the **Set Reminder** check box, and then specify when the reminder should appear.

8. If you don't want anyone else viewing your task, click the **Private** option.

9. Click **OK** to exit the dialog box and return to the To Do list; your new task appears on the grid.

You can use the **Status** tab and the **Notes** tab in the Task dialog box to add additional information about your task. You can also click the **Make Recurring** button to turn your task into a recurring item.

How Do I Change My Tasks Once They're on the Grid?

There are all kinds of ways you can make changes to your tasks. Let me run through a few for you:

➤ You can double-click the **Row Selection** button next to the task you want to edit, and make your changes in the Task dialog box.

➤ Or you can select the task fields and make your changes directly into the individual parts of your task.

➤ Depending on the column, additional controls will appear when you click a field. You can use the controls to set different percentages, dates, and so on.

➤ You can also right-click your selected task to open a shortcut menu with more commands you can apply to editing your task.

➤ If you want to rearrange your tasks on the list, such as moving them under another project heading, click the **Row Selection** button in front of the task you want to move, and then drag the task to its new location on the list. (Don't use this on grouped tasks.)

➤ To delete a task, select it and press the **Delete** key.

➤ Don't forget about those handy Cut, Copy, and Paste commands. You can select them from your toolbar or the Edit menu.

➤ To change your column headings (fields) open the **View** menu and select **Column**; then select **Custom**. This opens the Column dialog box where you can edit which columns appear in your list.

➤ To display more or less columns, open the **View** menu, select **Column**, and select the amount of columns you want displayed on your grid.

Edit the Daily To Do List, Too! You can apply the editing techniques listed here to your To Do list shown on the Daily view tab. You don't have to open the To Do tab every time to make changes.

➤ You can easily turn a task into an appointment on your schedule. Select the task, right-click to display the shortcut menu, and select **Appt. from Task**. This opens the Appointment dialog box that you can use to assign the task as an appointment.

Task Reminder Boxes

If you've added a reminder option to a task, you'll be visited by a Daily Reminder box when the time comes. Task reminders work like the reminder boxes used with your daily appointments. However, task reminders appear at the beginning of the day they're associated with. The next figure shows what one looks like.

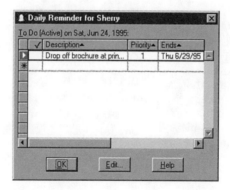

A reminder box for a task I need to complete.

Task reminders appear with an audible beep when you first start your Schedule+ program for the day. To close the box, click **OK**. You can also choose to make changes by clicking the **Edit** button.

Make Plans with the Planner

For a different perspective of your busy schedule, take a look at the Planner view. Click the **Planner** tab on the left side of your view area. This will open your schedule into Planner view, as shown in the next figure.

Planner view puts your schedule in a different perspective according to blocks of time.

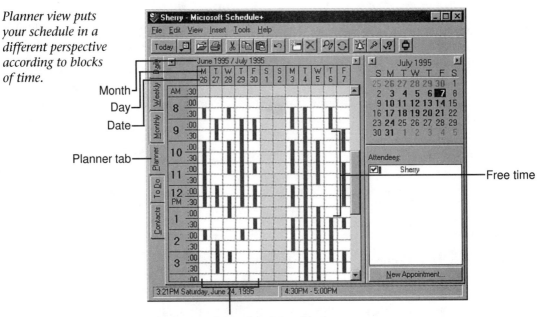

Month

Day

Date

Planner tab

Free time

A week's worth of scheduled time blocks

Hey, This Planner Looks Familiar If you've already peaked at the Planner tab in the Appointment box, then you've seen this feature already. Of course, it was a scaled-down view, but it was still the Planner.

The Planner lets you see your schedule in chunks of time, graphically displayed. The Microsoft people call this graphical depiction the *free/busy display*—what a great name for it. At least they didn't call it Date Navigator 2. Also on your screen is the old Date Navigator (number 1), which you'll recognize from the Daily view tab, and an Attendees box, which lists other networked users that you've invited to the meetings you've scheduled.

When it comes to the Planner view, I think you'll find that it's a lot easier to look at your schedule when it's spread out in blocks of time over several days. You can easily point out available time blocks. If you're networked, then you can view other users' planner views to help you organize meetings for all attendees.

I See the Planner, Now What?

What are you supposed to do with the Planner view? Check these things out:

➤ The blue lines, called bars, extending up and down on the Planner schedule represent appointments you've set. So, you can quickly see at a glance what busy times you have planned. (If you're networked, you'll see other users' planner lines displayed in other colors.)

➤ The vertical gaps between the blue bars represent open chunks of time that you haven't set aside for appointments. This lets you see when you're available.

➤ To move your daily or weekly view, click the arrow buttons at the top of the Planner screen. The left arrow takes you back and the right arrow takes you forward, date by date.

➤ To see other days in a glance, click the appropriate date on the Date Navigator calendar.

➤ To see the details concerning a particular appointment, double-click the blue bar. This reveals whose appointment it is. Click the name to reveal details about the appointment.

➤ If you're working in stand-alone mode (not connected to other computer users), your screen also shows a **New Appointment** button. You can use the New Appointment button to quickly set another appointment on your already busy schedule.

➤ If you're working in group-enabled mode (networked with other users), your screen shows a **Request Meeting** button. You can use the button to invite other networked users to your meetings.

➤ Also in group-enabled mode, you'll see little Xs appear in the Attendees box if you happen to select a time slot in which the other person is busy.

Fun with Networks

If you're using group-enabled mode, you can use the Planner view to check out the blocks of time other users have scheduled, if they've published their schedules on the network. You also have to have Read permission in order to see the schedules of other users, because, after all, they don't want any old peon knowing how busy or not-so-busy they are.

Schedule+ lets you use different levels of access permissions to view other users' schedules. The level of access permission depends upon what role is assigned to the user. Take a look at the various roles and levels available:

Role	Permissions
None	No viewing permissions.
Read	Read all appointments, contacts, tasks, events, and appointment details.
Create	Can set up appointments and add to contacts, tasks, events.
Modify	Can make changes to appointments, contacts, tasks, events.
Delegate	Can make changes to parts of schedule, except private items. Can send and receive meeting messages on your behalf.
Owner	Can make changes to the schedule, plus view and change private items, and change users' permissions to access your schedule.
Delegate Owner	Same access as Owner, plus can send and receive meeting messages for you.
Custom	You specify what permissions are allowed.

Obviously, you can control how much of your schedule others on the network have access to. All of these roles depend on your own network or office situation. For example, if you're a busy executive, your secretary might be assigned the role of Delegate Owner in order to keep your schedule organized. A secretary to another executive in another department might only be assigned the role of Read when it comes to accessing your schedule. If you work with a team of coworkers, you may all have equal or varying roles regarding each individual's schedule.

To view users' access permissions, open the **Tools** menu and select **Set Access Permissions**. To assign access permissions, open the **Users** tab and assign a user role. Select the **Global** tab to choose from options for displaying your schedule on the network. Click **OK** to exit the box when finished.

Reading a Network Planner

As I told you already, the blue bars in your Planner view indicate your schedule. However, when you're networked, you'll see other colors used as well. When you publish your schedule on the network, it shows other users a colored bar representing the times you are busy. The colored bars help differentiate between users. Depending on what access permissions you assigned, other users may or may not be able to see details about your schedule.

➤ If you see gray bars on the Planner, those are busy times of the other attendees at your meetings.

➤ The purple bars are busy times for the optional folks attending your meetings.

➤ The green bars represent busy times for resources (other people required at the meeting but not absolutely essential).

The names of attendees in the Attendees box appear with marks next to their names. A check mark appears if that person's schedule is shown in the Planner. A question mark means that person's schedule is not available. If you see an X, then the person has a prior commitment during the meeting time. Remember, you can double-click a time block to see details about an attendee's appointments.

Let's Call a Meeting

Well now, network users, what do you do when you're ready to call a meeting? You'll need to use the Meeting Request form. Mind you, everybody has to be hooked up to a mail server and the Microsoft Exchange system, but hey—if you meet those requirements, then you're ready to roll.

You can use Schedule+'s Meeting Wizard to help you call a meeting. You can also use the Request Meeting button on the Planner tab. Or... you can call a meeting through your Appointment dialog box. So many choices, so little time. But that's not all; you can turn an appointment into a meeting (by inviting others to attend), and you can reschedule meetings. It makes my head spin thinking about all the possibilities.

Probably one of the neatest tools you can use when scheduling meetings is the *AutoPick* feature. You can use it to quickly locate free blocks of time. Here's what you do:

1. Select the time slot (one or more) that you want the meeting plugged in at—try to pick the earliest date or time needed.

2. Now open the **Tools** menu and select **AutoPick**. Schedule+ goes to work and locates the earliest time available for all the attendees and highlights it on the Planner schedule.

3. If you like the time suggested, then click the **Request Meeting** button and send out your invites. If you don't like the time suggested, open the AutoPick tool and do it again.

Use the Meeting Request form to invite others to the meeting. If you follow step 3, you can send request messages to the people you want to attend the meeting. You can do the same thing using the Meeting Wizard (click the **Meeting Wizard** button on your toolbar and follow the prompts). When you set up a meeting, you must identify all the people who are invited to attend, choose a meeting time, send out request messages, and receive responses to the messages.

As each attendee responds to your meeting request, the responses show up in your Inbox (part of your network mail system). You can easily identify such responses by their Schedule+ symbols. If you happen to receive an invitation, open it up with a double-click the meeting request message; Schedule+ coordinates the request with your schedule and lets you know if you can make it or not. To automatically reply, click the Accept, Decline, or Tentatively Accept buttons. This sends your response to the originator and enters the meeting in your appointment book (if you can go).

Back on the receiving end, the originator of the meeting request can track responses to the invitations and find out who's coming to the meeting. If you're the one doing all the inviting, here's how to track the attendees' responses:

1. Double-click the meeting slot in your appointment book to open the Appointment dialog box.

2. Click the **Attendees** tab to bring it to the front.

3. As each attendee responds to the request, their names appear in the list with symbols next to them. The symbols indicate the attendees' status regarding your meeting. (I'll show you the symbols in the next table.)

4. To close the box, click **OK**.

Symbol	Indicates
✓	Accepted
✗	Declined
	Tentatively accepted
	Accepted with message response
	Declined with a message response
	Tentatively accepted with a message response
	Not responded

To learn more about using the Planner tab with networked users, and arranging meetings and schedules on a network, be sure to read your Schedule+ manual or make your network administrator give you a few lessons.

Making Contacts

Last, but not least, let's look at the *Contacts* feature of your Microsoft Schedule+ program. To take this baby out for a spin, click the **Contacts** tab. This will open your program to a screen similar to the one shown here.

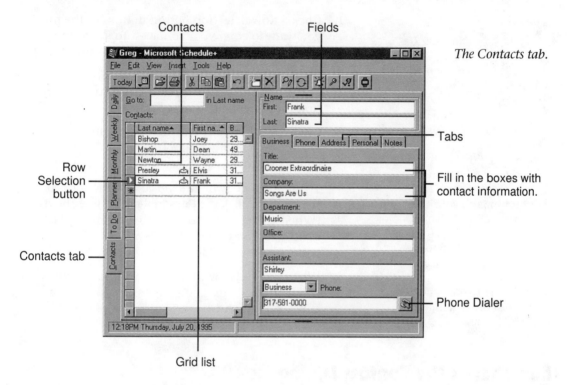

The Contacts tab.

You can use the Contacts tab to compile information about people you contact the most, such as business associates, sales leads, friends and neighbors, industrial spies, over-rated celebrities, famous computer book authors—whoever. Once you complete your Contacts list, you can keep updating it, and even use it to make appointments. You can even list each contact's birthday or other special events.

As you look around the Contacts tab, you'll see a grid listing contacts on the left and a business card format for entering data on the right. After you have started a list of contacts, you can then sort and group them. Doesn't that sound like a ton of fun?

I've Made Contact!

Quite obviously, this feature isn't going to work for you until you start compiling your own list of contacts. You can enter information about your contacts directly into the grid list, or you can use the business card tabs and fields. Let me show you one way to do it:

Check This Out...

Dial 'Em Up
Use the **Phone Dialer** button to make your computer call up your contacts via your modem. Use the little phone symbols that appear next to phone numbers you add to the contacts to dial up your contacts. Just click the **Phone Dialer** button, and your computer starts dialing for you. Cool, huh? Well, you have to have your phone hooked up to a modem to make this work for you, so it's not as easy as it sounds. Consult your Schedule+ manual for more details about using this feature.

1. Click a **Row Selection** button in front of the row you want to enter your contact into, preferably an empty row. This will display a blank business card on the right side of your screen.

2. In the business card area, start typing new information into each field as necessary.

3. Click the other business card tabs to enter more details, such as other phone numbers and the contact's address.

4. To enter birthday or anniversary information about the contact, click the **Personal** tab and set the date. (When you enter personal information about a contact, such as a birthday, a symbol will appear in your contact grid, such as a birthday cake.)

5. When you finish with the contact information, click inside the grid area and your entry appears as a contact on the list.

Then There's the Contact Dialog Box

If you don't like the direct approach to contact list building, you can use the Contact dialog box. It neatly displays the same fields from the business card side of the Contacts tab, but puts it in a dialog box. To open the Contact dialog box, follow one of these methods:

➤ Open the **Insert** menu and select **Contact**.

➤ Right-click to display the shortcut menu and select **New Contact**.

➤ Double-click an empty row's **Row Selection** button.

➤ Click the **Insert New Contact** button on your toolbar.

All of these methods open the Contact dialog box, shown in the next figure.

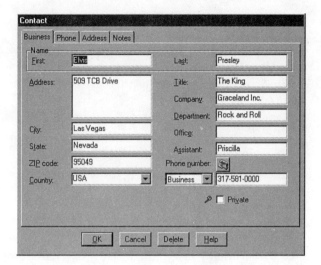

The Contact dialog box.

See, the dialog box looks like the business card format on your Contact tab, only wider and arranged differently. Proceed to fill in each field, and click **OK** when you're through.

If you want to keep certain listings in your Contact tab private (like those 900 numbers), click the Private check box in the Contact dialog box. This keeps the information safe from prying eyes.

Sort It All Out

There are several ways to sort your contacts, once you've compiled a few dozen or more. I'll give you some pointers:

➤ Open the **View** menu and select **Sort**. This opens a dialog box for determining how you want the list arranged. The Sort dialog box lets you choose three categories to sort with, and you can indicate if you want the sort in ascending or descending order.

➤ For a more direct approach, click a contact column header on the grid that you want to sort, and the list sorts in ascending order automatically. If you want to sort by descending order, hold down the **Ctrl** key while clicking the column header.

➤ Open the **View** menu and select **AutoSort**. Use this feature to sort new entries immediately after you enter them.

➤ Also on the **View** menu is a **Sort Now** command, which immediately sorts your list based on specifications set in the Sort dialog box.

Break Up into Groups

Another thing you can do with your list is to group your contacts. For instance, because some of the people on your list work for the same company, or same industry, you can group them together. The Schedule+ grouping feature lets you group items in a variety of categories and into subgroups.

Follow these steps to group items:

1. Open the **View** menu and select **Group By**. This opens the Group By dialog box.

2. Select a category to group by. The drop-down arrows display the various fields.

3. Choose ascending or descending order for each grouping you select.

4. Click **OK** to exit the box and display your groups.

The list will now display groups that you specified. The group name appears bold and above each group of contacts on the list. You can expand or collapse the list in a group by clicking the group symbol in front of the group name.

What's with the Seven Habits?

If you've been looking through your Schedule+ menus, you may have come across the Seven Habits tools or topics. Microsoft included valuable organizing information from the best-selling book *The Seven Habits of Highly Effective People*, by Dr. Stephen R. Covey. If you need some organizational help to make better use of your time and energy, then you'd better check these out. The Seven Habits Tools, found on the Tools menu, will lead you through steps for improving the way you do things. (And you don't have to buy the book to use this tool!) The Seven Habits Wizard can lead you through the process. Be sure and check these out, or read the Seven Habits Help Topics listed under the Help menu.

The Least You Need to Know

For you summary-obsessed readers, here's what you learned in this chapter:

➤ To Do lists can help you keep track of things you need to do each day. You can even add reminders to your tasks.

➤ With the Planner feature, you can view your schedule in blocks of busy/free time.

➤ Use the Planner to arrange group meetings with others on your network.

➤ The Contacts feature lets you compile lists of contacts. You can sort and group contacts to keep them organized.

Part 3
Tying Them All Together

Ever heard of OLE? The OLE I'm referring to doesn't have anything to do with bull-fighting. In this part of the book, you'll learn all about using OLE, including what exactly it stands for. Perhaps you are unaware of this, but OLE is an underlying feature that helps all of the Office 95 programs work together in an integrated way. Well, even if you're not impressed with that little nugget of knowledge, you'll still need a basic understanding of the OLE principles in order to make it through Part 4 of this book. So, put away your bullfighter's cape and start reading.

FROM THE LOOK OF THE SCREENSAVERS, MR. MURPHY COULD TELL THAT HIS POPULARITY WITH HIS EMPLOYEES HAD DIPPED JUST A BIT...

Chapter 22

All About Object Linking and Embedding

In This Chapter

➤ Connect your Office 95 programs and share data between them

➤ Finally learn the difference between linking and embedding

➤ Use the Paste Special and the Insert Object commands

An important part of using your Microsoft Office 95 programs is understanding how to link and embed objects from one program into another—the technology behind program integration. The groovy little feature that makes this possible is called *OLE*. With OLE, you can create a document in Word that incorporates a spreadsheet from Excel, or you can make a presentation in PowerPoint that uses a table you created in Word. In this chapter, we'll go over OLE and what it means to you and your Office 95 work.

What Is OLE?

The official name is *object linking and embedding*, but everybody calls it OLE for short. (Yes, you pronounce it "Oh-LAY," as if you were a bullfighter or something.) OLE is a feature that enables Windows 95 programs to share data.

Let me explain this to you with an example. Let's say you've typed up a quarterly sales report using Word. The report includes a bar chart you made in Excel that shows the results of the quarter. Are you with me so far? At the end of the next quarter, you get out your Word report again. At this point, you could insert a new Excel chart with the new sales results, but what a pain! You have to open Excel, look for the correct files, look for the right data in the files, update it, and copy and paste it into the Word document. This is truly the long and boring way to do it.

OLE to the rescue. Instead of reassembling your quarterly report the hard way, you can use OLE to automatically update your Word document with the latest data from the Excel program. Doesn't that sound a lot easier? Well, it is—I know what I'm talking about.

This Word document contains objects created in other Office programs. However, these objects aren't only copied and pasted here, they are linked and embedded.

Word document—

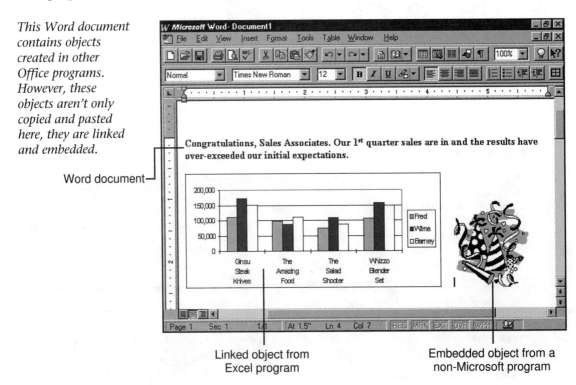

Linked object from Excel program

Embedded object from a non-Microsoft program

How Does It Work?

People sometimes confuse linking and embedding with copying and pasting. There's a big difference between the two concepts. When you share data by copying and pasting with the Windows Clipboard feature, you're just dropping in a piece of clip art or part of a text file without any information about which Microsoft Office 95 program created it.

304

When you link or embed a paragraph of text or a piece of artwork in your document, it maintains a connection to its original location (that is, the file in which you created it and the Office 95 program it's a part of). Because of this connection, you can easily trace it back and update it when needed. The catch to this is that if the programs with which you are sharing data don't support OLE as well, it's a lost cause. Luckily for you, all of the Office 95 programs support OLE.

OLE Lingo

Object linking and embedding comes with its own lingo, which you might as well learn about now. First up is the word *object*. The object is the piece of data that you link or embed in a file. An object can be a chunk of text, an entire document, a range of cells, a huge spreadsheet, a piece of artwork, or a database, among other things.

The file into which you link or embed objects is the *compound document* or the *destination document*. In our previous example, the Word document is the compound document because you have linked or embedded the Excel object into it. The Microsoft Office 95 program in which you created the compound document is the *client application*. So in our example, Word is the client program.

Are you following along? Good; there are a couple more terms you'll need to understand. The original location (the file in which you created the object) of the object you are linking or embedding is the *source document*. In our example, the source document is an Excel file. The program in which you created the linked or embedded object is the *server application*. It created the original object. In our example, Excel is the server application.

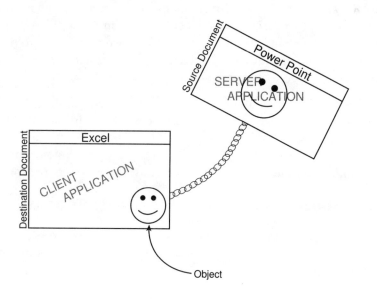

An illustration to better help you understand OLE lingo.

Let's summarize:

> ➤ An object is anything you're linking or embedding into another file.

> ➤ The file on the receiving end of the linking or embedding is the compound or destination document.

> ➤ The program in which you create the receiving file is the client application.

> ➤ The file where the linked or embedded object originates is the source document.

> ➤ The program used to create the linked or embedded object is the server application.

That's the terminology you'll encounter when we talk about OLE concepts and procedures. Flip back to this section anytime you get confused or need a refresher.

Linking and Embedding—What's the Difference?

Let's get down to the nitty-gritty. What's the difference between linking and embedding? I used to wonder the same thing. This section will explain the details of OLE.

Learning Linking

When you put a linked object in your compound or destination document, it's still linked to its original location (the source document). What this means is that any change you make to the object in its original location automatically appears in its linked location, too. Oooh, that's impressive.

Consider the quarterly report example from earlier in the chapter. The report made in Word (the compound document) contains a bar chart made in Excel (the source document). When you made the report, you linked the Excel object to your Word file. The next quarter arrives, and you get out your quarterly report document again. Somehow, the bar chart has been changed to reflect new data. How can this be?

During the course of the quarter, you or your coworkers updated the chart (the object) in its respective Office 95 program (server application). Because you linked the object back to its original source document, any changes you made to the source document appear in the compound document. Get it? The links are still there in the Word document, and the changed data from Excel automatically shows up in your Word report.

Embedding Explained

Embedding works a little differently. When you embed an object into your document, it's also connected to its original location (the source document) in that the computer knows where it came from, but it's not affected by any changes that you make there (using the server application). For example, if you embed instead of link the bar chart in our quarterly report example, someone could go into the Excel program, open the file that contains our bar chart, make changes to it, and save it, but those changes would not automatically appear in our Word document. Gee, this doesn't sound nearly as exciting as linking.

What embedding does enable you to do is to edit the object from its embedded location in the destination document. What? (You heard me right.) You don't have to open the server application (such as Excel) to change the object. Instead, you can double-click the embedded object and immediately open up its source program (Excel) without ever leaving the compound document (such as Word). This is still a big step beyond the cutting and pasting technique.

Is It Better to Link or to Embed?

Well, that depends. When you link things, you're sharing data between two or more files. When you embed things, you kind of share, but everything is put into one file. If you plan to give the destination document to someone else, and it happens to have links in it, you'll have to give him copies of the source files where the links came from, too. Not only that, but you'll also have to make sure the person has copies of the programs running on his computer.

When you hand someone a file with an embedded object, you don't have to worry about giving the person the original object file. However, the drawback to embedded files is that they tend to get rather large since the object is embedded and not linked. Why? Because you're adding items from the source file (or files) to the destination file, and the more items you embed, the larger your destination file grows. So, to determine whether it's better to link or to embed, examine how you're going to use the file.

Ye Olde Paste Special and Insert Object Commands

The secret to linking and embedding lies in the Paste Special and Insert Object commands. You can use both of these commands to link or embed objects into your files.

One Paste Special Coming Up

You are familiar, by now, with the Cut, Copy, and Paste commands? I'd like to introduce you to the Paste Special command. Both linking and embedding with the Paste Special command are very similar to using the regular Paste command. You copy the object you want to link or embed into the Clipboard. When you're ready to place it in the new location, you select the **Paste Special** command from the **Edit** menu. The Paste Special dialog box appears. (You can use the Paste Special command in other programs that support OLE functions.)

The Source area tells the name and
location of the object you want to paste.

*The Paste Special
dialog box from
Word for Windows.*

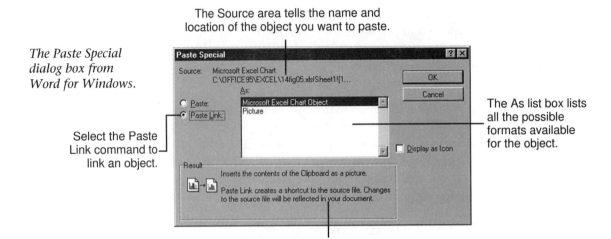

The As list box lists
all the possible
formats available
for the object.

Select the Paste
Link command to
link an object.

The Result box tells you what's going to
happen with all the options you select.

This box may look slightly different, depending on what Office 95 program you're using. However, the options are the same. Let me tell you how to read this dialog box.

In the upper left corner, the Source line tells the source of the object currently held in the Clipboard. The source includes the name and location of the object.

There are two option buttons in the dialog box. If you select the Paste option, you embed the object, but do not link it. Selecting the Paste Link option creates a link between the source document and the destination document. There's a catch to this, however. You have to save the source document in order for the Paste Link option to be available. For example, before I can paste a logo I made in PowerPoint into the Clipboard, I must save the logo as a PowerPoint file. Then the Paste Link option will be available.

Make a Note
Not all pro-
grams fully
support OLE
features. Some
may only let
you embed and not link at all.
Be sure to check other program
manuals for details about their
OLE support.

The As list box contains all of the possible formats the object can use when you paste it. These will vary, depending on the type of object you select for linking or embedding. Here's a list of formats you will come across in your own linking and embedding endeavors:

➤ **...Object** Any format that ends with the word **Object** is something you can link or embed.

➤ **Formatted Text (RTF)** This formats text in the destination document in the same manner as in the source document. This does not work with embedding.

➤ **Unformatted Text** This does not apply formatting to the object when it's linked. It also doesn't work with embedding.

➤ **Picture** This formats the object as a Windows metafile picture, a file format common in Windows (doesn't work with embedding).

➤ **Bitmap** This formats the object as a bitmap picture, like you find in the Windows Paintbrush program (doesn't work with embedding).

Under the command buttons on the right side of the box is the Display as Icon check box. (This option is only available if you select the Paste Link option button.) If you select this option, the pasted object appears in the compound document as an icon instead of as the actual object (such as a picture or chart). The icon looks like the application icon from which it's linked. This option is particularly handy for linking sounds or MediaClips. It keeps the linked data in an easy-to-find, easy-to-use format. For example, if you link a slide show to a Word document (and use the Display as Icon check box), you probably don't want to see the whole slide show on your page (it would take up too much space anyway). When you're ready to see the slide show, all you have to do is click the icon to open it up. (And who said good things didn't come in small packages?)

The Result area in the bottom left corner of the dialog box gives a description of what happens with all of the other options you've selected in the dialog box. This is kind of like a preview of what you've chosen and what it's going to do.

To exit the Paste Special dialog box and activate the options, click **OK**.

The Mysterious Insert Object Command

You can also link or embed with the Insert Object command. You use this command when you know you want to link or embed something, but you have not yet created the object in the source application. You can also use this command when you want to treat an entire document as an object.

To use this command, open the **Insert** menu and select **Object**. The Object dialog box appears. You'll notice two tabs in the Object dialog box. Use the Create New tab when you need to create an object to link or embed (and haven't done so yet). The Create from File tab reveals options for linking or embedding an entire document. Let's start by examining the Create New options. Click the **Create New** tab to see options for making an object to link or embed.

The **Object Type** list box displays a list of every OLE-supporting program on your computer by object type. If you select Microsoft Excel Worksheet, for example, Excel starts when you exit the dialog box so you can create your object.

The **Display as Icon** option makes your linked or embedded object appear as an icon in the compound file, instead of as the object in its actual form.

The **Result** area in the bottom left corner of the dialog box describes what the results will be with all of the options you choose. You'll find this bit of information helpful while learning to use the linking and embedding features. It always tells you what's going to happen based on your selections.

To finally exit the Object dialog box, click **OK**.

If you have already created the object, and you know what file it's in, click the **Create from File** tab to bring another set of options to the front of the Object dialog box.

Use the **File Name** box to type the name of the file containing the object you want to link or embed. (Remember, the object can be text, a range of cells, a graphic, and more.)

If you don't know where the file is located, use the **Browse** button to open another dialog box to help you find the correct folder and file.

The **Link to File** option will create a link between the selected object file and the document you're working in. Click the **Link to File** check box to activate this option.

The **Display as Icon** option works the same way as in the Create New tab options. It makes your linked or embedded object appear as an icon in the compound file.

The **Result** area in the bottom left corner tells you what's going to happen based on your selections. Always stop and read it to make sure your task will be carried out as planned.

To exit the Object dialog box, click **OK**.

The Least You Need to Know

In summary, you now know that linking and embedding can make you more productive with your Office programs. Your life is now complete, eh?

➤ The OLE feature enables programs to share data by linking or embedding.

➤ To link is to copy an object into a new file, yet still maintain an active connection with its original. When you modify the original object, the modification appears in the copied link object.

➤ To embed is to copy an object into a new file in such a way that the object will not reflect changes made to the original object. However, embedding does enable you to immediately access the program in which you originally created the object.

Chapter 23

Connecting with Links

In This Chapter

➤ Create your own OLE link

➤ Learn how to edit a link

➤ Find out what it takes to manage your links

Moving right along... now that you know what object linking and embedding is, you might as well put it into practice. In this chapter, I'll show you how to create a link, edit a link, break a link, and restore a link. Not only that, but we'll also explore missing links and new archeological discoveries linking us to aliens from outer space. Then, when we're through, we'll call up Art *Link*letter.

Link Up

It's time to learn how to make your own OLE link. One of the great benefits of establishing a link is that you can edit the linked object at its source (its original file and server application) and your edits will automatically appear in all of the destination documents linked to it. You don't have to do a thing to your destination document! We'll go over each step for creating a link with both the Paste Special and Insert Object commands.

Techno Talk

Can You Link with Other Programs?

Yes, you can easily link objects from other programs besides the Office applications. The only catch is all of the programs have to support OLE, or the link won't work. Use the same steps described in this chapter to link objects created in other OLE programs on your computer.

Linking with the Paste Special Command

Using the *Paste Special* command for linking is going to seem very familiar to you. No, not because you just read about it in the last chapter, but because it's so similar to the Copy and Paste routine you've used before.

The first step is to open the file that contains the object you want to link. For example, if you're planning to link an Excel chart to a Word document, start by opening Excel and opening the file that contains the chart or the information you want to link.

Open the source document and select the object you want to link. In this case, it's an Excel chart.

Open the Edit menu and choose Copy.

Selected object you want to link

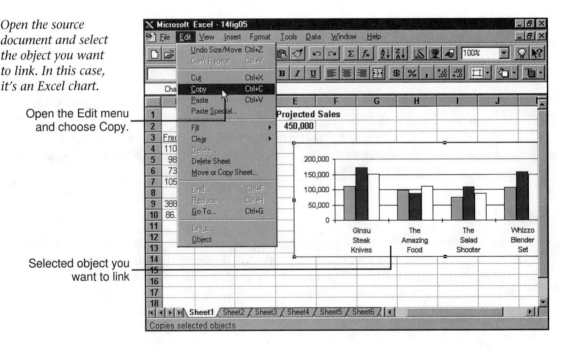

Time to link. Follow these steps:

1. Select the object you want to link. Remember, an object can be text, cells, a graphic, or database records.

2. Pull down the **Edit** menu and choose the **Copy** command. This, of course, puts a copy of the selected object into the Windows Clipboard. (Yes, you can use the **Copy** button on the toolbar if you want to.)

3. Now start the client application: open the program that you want to link the file to. (You can use your Office Shortcut bar to quickly open an Office application by clicking its appropriate icon, if you rearranged your buttons like I told you to back in Chapter 6.) If the program is already running, switch to it using the Windows 95 taskbar or by pressing **Alt+Esc**.

Wait a Minute— What Am I Linking? If you haven't created the object to be linked yet, and you're opening a new file to create the object, be sure to remember to save the file before attempting a link. You can't link from a file that hasn't been saved.

4. Make sure the destination document is open in the client application. For example, if you're linking an Excel chart into Word, make sure the Word document is open and ready.

5. Click the mouse button where you want to paste the linked object.

6. Pull down the **Edit** menu and choose **Paste Special**. This opens the Paste Special dialog box, which should look quite familiar to you since you learned about its components in the previous chapter.

Open the Edit menu and choose Paste Special.

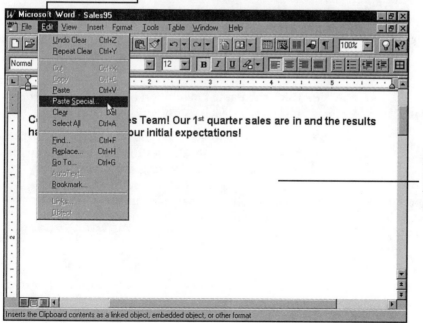

The open destination document ready for the linked object.

Make sure you clicked the mouse pointer in the place where you want the linked object inserted.

My Menu Doesn't Say Paste Special!

There's no reason to be alarmed. Some programs use different wording for the same thing. If your menu says Paste Links, choose that instead of Paste Special, okay?

7. In the As list in the dialog box, choose the data form that you want the object to appear in. (If you need any help with this, turn back to Chapter 22 to learn about object formats.)

Choose a format for the object
from the As list box.

The Paste Special dialog box.

Click here to
establish a link.

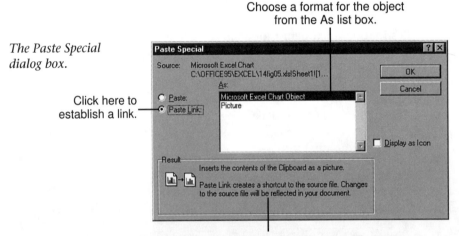

Read the description in the Result area to find out
what's going to happen with the object.

Listen Up!
You don't have to stick with linking objects from other programs. You can link from the same application, too. For example, you can link text from one Word file into another Word file. Get the picture?

8. Click the **Paste Link** option button, and read the text in the Result section of the dialog box.

9. If everything looks okay, click the **OK** button. The object appears into the destination document with an automatic link to its original location. Every time you update the object in the source document, it will automatically update in the destination document.

Linking with the Insert Object Command

Another way to create a link is with the *Insert Object* command. This is useful when you want to link an entire document. For example, whereas I previously linked an Excel chart into a Word document, this time I will link the entire Excel spreadsheet instead. The Insert Object command makes this easy to do.

You don't have to open the source document to perform this little trick. However, you do need to open the destination document in its application. So, if you're inserting an Excel spreadsheet into a Word document, open the Word document now, and use the following steps to link:

1. Pull down the **Insert** menu and choose **Object**. The Object dialog box appears. (Remember this box from the last chapter?) In it, you see a list of OLE application object types you can insert.

2. Click the **Create from File** tab to bring it to the front of the dialog box.

3. In the File Name box, type in the name of the file you want to insert and link. (If you're having trouble locating the file, be sure to click the **Browse** button to open another dialog box for locating the exact folder and file.)

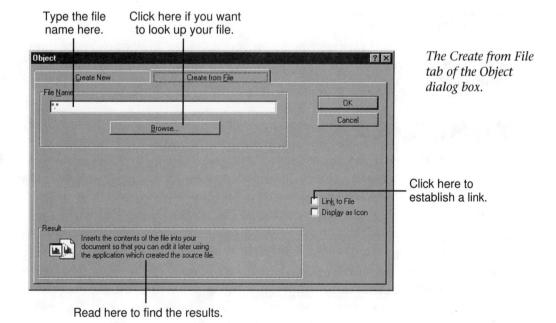

Type the file name here.

Click here if you want to look up your file.

The Create from File tab of the Object dialog box.

Click here to establish a link.

Read here to find the results.

4. Click the **Link to File** check box to establish a link between the file you selected and your current destination document.

5. Take a peek in the **Result** section for a description of what will happen.

6. Click **OK**, and the file will appear in your document. The next time you open the source document and make changes, the destination document will automatically reflect those changes.

Don't Get Confused!

Remember, the Create from File options in the Object dialog box are only good for linking entire files; you cannot use them to link individual objects. You'll have to use the Create New tab in the Object dialog box to link things like a range of cells or a block of text. To do so with the Create New tab displayed, select the object you want to link from the Object Typelist box.

Managing Your Links

Are you having fun yet? I hope so. Now that you've created a linked object, you need to know what you can do with it. You see, after you've linked something, you may want to go back and update the original object. When you do, there are several ways you can manage the link itself.

Editing the Object at the Source

You can edit a linked object in two ways: in the source document from which it came, or in the destination document that leads back to the source document. Confused? Don't be. We'll go over both ways. First, let's start with editing the object from the source document.

Open the application in which you created the object, and open the file containing the object. Make any changes to the object, and save the document. Exit the source document and open the destination document. The changes should automatically show up in the destination document as well. If the changes don't appear in the object in the destination document, your program may not be set up properly to automatically update links. I'll tell you how to fix the update settings in a few short paragraphs from now.

Editing the Object from the Destination Document

If you edit a linked object from the destination document, you don't have to remember where it came from or its original file name. The link will trace you back to the source without any stumbling around. From the destination document, double-click the object you want to edit. The server application opens and displays the source document.

Go ahead and make any necessary changes to the object. When you finish, save the file, and exit the server application with the **File Exit** command. Pow! You're back in the destination document and your changes appear in the this object as well. This is truly amazing.

Something's Wrong! If double-clicking didn't work, open the **Edit** menu and choose **Links**. In the Links dialog box, select the link you want to edit, and click the **Open Source** button. The server application should start, and you can make your changes.

Managing the Link's Update Settings

Pay attention now. I've got something new to tell you about. You can control when changes to the linked object are updated in the destination document. You can control whether the link must be updated manually or whether it updates automatically. So far, we've been talking about automatic updates. If you change that to manual update, you'll have to go through the update steps each time you change the source document containing the linked object. A manual update is convenient when you have two programs open at once, and you'd rather not see every change you make to the source document reflected in the destination document while you're working on them (besides, it slows down your computer). A manual update lets you decide when the changes take place.

To set a link to manual update:

1. Open the destination document containing the linked object.

2. Pull down the **Edit** menu and choose **Links**. The Links dialog box appears.

3. The list box lists all the linked objects in your document. Each link includes a name, the path name of the source document, and information about whether or not the link is manual or automatic. Select the link you want from the list.

4. Change the Update setting (at the bottom of the dialog box) by clicking the **Manual** option button.

317

The Manual or Automatic
information shows up here.

The Links dialog box.

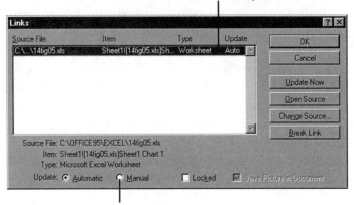

Switch to Manual by clicking here.

Lock It Up!
You can also use the Links dialog box to lock a link to prevent the object from being updated with changes made in the source document. A locked link can't be updated until it is unlocked again.

5. Click the **Update Now** button at the right of the dialog box to update the object with any changes made to the source document.

6. Click **OK** to exit the dialog box, and save the destination file to save the new link settings.

The next time you make changes to the object's source document, you'll have to open the Links dialog box and click the **Update Now** button to make those changes show up in the destination document.

Breaking the Link

There will come a time when you no longer want your linked object linked. You can leave the object in the destination document but break its link so that it is no longer associated with the source document. This turns the object into an ordinary Copy and Paste object, which has no ties to where the object came from.

To break a link:

1. Open the destination document.

2. Pull down the **Edit** menu and select **Links** (or **Link Options**). The Links dialog box appears.

3. Choose the link name for the object you want to break, and click the **Break Link** button.

4. A warning box pops up, cautioning you about your actions. Click **OK** or **Yes** to confirm your decision, and the link is broken.

Restoring the Link

Not that you want to hear this, but you can break a link without meaning to. An accidental break can occur if you move the source document to another directory, or if you change the name of the source document. If you do break a link, the next time you open the destination document, a warning dialog box tells you that the source document is missing or corrupted.

Don't worry—all is not lost. You can relink the object. One way to do this is to move the source document back to the directory where you created it or to restore the document's original name. Another way is to tell the computer the document's new location.

1. Open the destination document and deal with the warning box.

2. Open the **Edit** menu and select **Links**.

3. In the Links dialog box, select the object with the broken link from the list, and click the **Change Source** button.

4. The Change Source dialog box appears. In this dialog box, you can edit the item name or select the file name and folder to reflect the new location of the source document.

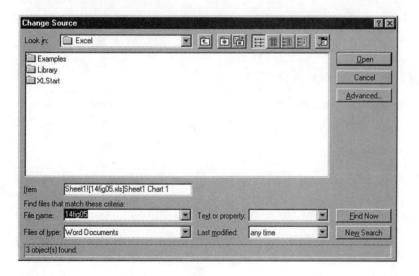

The Change Source dialog box.

5. When you finish, click **OK**, and the link is restored. Whew.

Troubleshooting Links

Up until now, object linking has seemed relatively effortless. But lest you wander off with any false hopes about how easy linking is, I'd better warn you about some problems you may encounter. Take a look at this troubleshooting section. Anytime you run into problems during your own linking efforts, flip to this section and find a solution.

Problem: In my Paste Special dialog box, the Paste Link button is dimmed, and I can't get it to work.

Solution: The source document containing the object to be linked hasn't been saved yet. You'll have to go back and save it, and then try again.

Problem: The linked object in my destination document isn't updating when I change the source document.

Solution: Your link may be set for manual update, or it might be locked. You can fix both of these problems with the options in the Links dialog box. It's also possible that you have a broken link, which you'll have to restore, or that you didn't link the object properly to begin with. To verify a link, open the **Edit** menu and choose **Links**. If the Links command is dimmed, that means you don't have a link in your document.

Problem: When I paste a linked object in Word, weird stuff appears on-screen where my object is supposed to show up.

Solution: Your **Field Codes** option is turned on in the Options dialog box. To fix this, open the **Tools** menu and choose **Options**. In the **View** options, uncheck the **Field Codes** option, and then click **OK**.

The Least You Need to Know

Linking is relatively simple and easy to manage once you know the steps.

➤ To link an object, use the Copy and Paste Special commands.

➤ To link an entire document, use the Insert Object commands.

➤ You can control when your linked object is updated with the Update settings in the Links dialog box.

➤ You can accidentally break a link by moving the source document or renaming it.

➤ You can easily restore broken links with options in the Change Source dialog box.

Chapter 24

Aiding and Embedding

In This Chapter

➤ Create your own embedded object

➤ Learn to edit an embedded object

➤ A top secret way to convert embedded objects into new file formats

You mastered the practice of linking objects in the last chapter. Feeling rather proud of yourself, you have turned to this chapter to breeze through the steps for embedding an object. Well, not so fast. This OLE business isn't just a walk in the park, you know. A lot of time-consuming thought and effort went into making it work smoothly. Just because you can waltz in here and link and embed with a few easy steps doesn't mean you're another Einstein (but it definitely proves you're not an idiot). So, you'd better just slow down and give OLE the respect it deserves. Have you got that? Good.

In this chapter, I'll show you how to embed an object using the Paste Special and Insert Object commands. I'll also tell you how to edit an embedded object, as well as convert it into another format. And I won't yell at you anymore.

Embedding with Enthusiasm

As you recall from the previous chapters, you handle linking and embedding in pretty much the same way; it's the results that really differ. Unlike a linked object, an embedded object does not reflect changes you make to its source file. However, you can easily edit embedded objects because you can pop right over to the original application without having to open one and close another.

There are two ways to embed an object. One way is with the Paste Special command; the other is with the Insert Object command. We'll go over both methods.

Embedding with the Paste Special Command

Use the *Paste Special* method to embed objects such as a range of cells, a paragraph of text, or a database record. The Paste Special method is very similar to the old Copy and Paste routine you've used before.

1. The first step is to open the program and the file that contains the object you want to embed. For example, if you're planning to embed a PowerPoint graphic into a Word document, start by opening PowerPoint and opening the file that contains the graphic.

2. Select the object that you want to embed.

3. Open the **Edit** menu and choose the **Copy** command. This copies the selected object to the Windows Clipboard.

4. Start the client application (open the program in which you want to embed the object). If the program is already running in anticipation of this big embedding endeavor, simply switch to it using the Windows 95 taskbar or by pressing **Alt+Esc**.

5. Make sure the destination document is open in the client application. For example, if you're linking a PowerPoint graphic into Word, make sure the Word document is open and ready.

6. Click the mouse button at the location in which you want to paste the embedded object.

7. Open the **Edit** menu and choose **Paste Special**. The Paste Special dialog box appears.

8. In the **As** list in the dialog box, choose the **Object** data form.

9. Click the **OK** button, and the object is embedded.

Choose the Object data
format from the As list box.

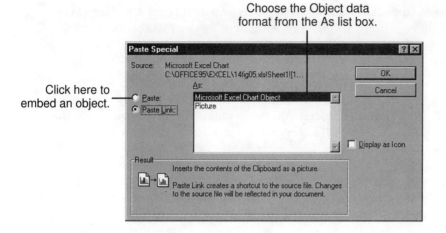

*Surprise, surprise,
surprise! The Paste
Special dialog box.*

Click here to
embed an object.

Now save the destination document. You don't have to save the source document because it's not needed to maintain the embedded object (as it is for the linked object).

You Can Use the Same Program

You don't have to stick with embedding objects from other programs into your current file. You can embed objects from the same application, too. For example, you can embed a chart from one Excel spreadsheet into another Excel spreadsheet.

Embedding with the Insert Object Command

Another way to embed an object is with the *Insert Object* command. This is handy when you want to embed an entire document. You don't have to open the source document to perform this little trick. However, you do need to open the destination document in its application.

1. In the destination document, pull down the **Insert** menu and choose **Object**. The Object dialog box appears.

2. In the Object dialog box, you see a list of OLE application object types you can embed. If you haven't created the object you want to embed, click the **Create New** tab to bring it to the front of the dialog box.

3. Choose a server application from the **Object type** list and click **OK**. The server application starts, but in a special way. Although the destination document is still on your screen, the server application appears to take over, adding its own menus and toolbars.

4. Go ahead and create the object you want to embed. When you finish, click the destination window. The server application closes, and the object you created is embedded in the destination document. (Sometimes, you may have to exit the server application to return to the destination document.) Save your destination document, and you're through.

If you already have the object you want to embed saved in another file, you can pursue a different path in the Object dialog box. Note, however, that with this method you must embed an entire file (not just an individual object).

Click the **Create from File** tab to bring it to the front. In the **File Name** list box, select the name of the file you want to embed. If you're having trouble locating the file, be sure to wind your way through the various folders to find it. Click **OK**, and the file inserts into your document.

Working with Embedded Objects

Now that you've created an embedded object, you may be wondering what you can do with it. Well, after you've embedded something, you may want to go back and make some changes to it. When you do, there are a few things you need to know.

Editing Embedded Objects

This is so easy. When you want to make some changes to an embedded object, all you have to do is double-click it in the destination document. This immediately opens the server application and takes control, adding its menus and toolbars to the screen. (If you prefer a more tedious route, you can open the **Edit** menu and select **Object**.)

Make any necessary changes to the object. When you're ready to return to the destination document, click outside of the server application window. Sometimes, you may have to close the server application by using the **File** menu and the **Exit** command.

Converting Embedded File Formats

What do you do when you have a destination document full of embedded objects, and you don't have access to the original application that created the objects? Maybe a friend gave you the destination document to work with, but you don't have the programs that created the objects loaded on your computer. Are you up a river without a paddle?

No sweat. You simply convert the embedded object into a different file format.

1. Open the destination document and select the object with which you want to work.

2. Then open the **Edit** menu and choose the **Object** command at the very bottom of the menu list (the name of this command may vary slightly, depending on what Office program you're using).

3. In the submenu that appears, select **Convert**. The Convert dialog box opens.

4. In the Object Type list, select the type of object to which you want to convert the embedded object.

5. Click the **Convert To** option button if you want to permanently change the object to the format you selected in the list box.

6. Click the **Activate As** option button if you want to temporarily change it to the selected object type.

7. Click **OK**, and the conversion is completed.

The next time you want to edit the embedded object, double-click it, and it will open in the application you selected.

Embedding Troubleshooting

This embedding business seems fairly easy, doesn't it? Well, I'd better warn you about some problems you may encounter. Take a look at this troubleshooting section. Anytime you run across a problem in your own embedding efforts, flip to this section to find a solution.

Problem: When I double-click my embedded object, it doesn't open the source application.

Solution: You may not have properly embedded the object, or you may have selected the wrong object type from the **As** list in the Paste Special dialog box. Go back and check.

Problem: When I create a new object to embed, I can't return to the destination document.

Solution: You may have to close the server application the long way. Open the **File** menu and look for a command such as **Exit and Return**, or look for a **Close Picture** box.

Problem: When I select an object type from the Insert Object dialog box, an error message appears telling me **The Server Application, Source File, or Item cannot be Found**.

Solution: The application is trying to tell you it can't find the application in which you created the object. Was the application removed from your hard drive? Check and see. You may have to change the path to the source file or convert the object to a different file type.

You're now loaded up with all the OLE information you need. In the next part of this book, you'll learn how to integrate the various Office programs, often using these OLE techniques.

The Least You Need to Know

Here's the embedding expertise you picked up in this chapter:

➤ Use the Copy and Paste Special commands to embed an individual object.

➤ Use the Insert Object command to embed an entire document.

➤ You can convert an embedded object from another program into a file format your Office programs can work with by using the options in the Convert dialog box.

Part 4
Making Office 95 Work for You

How about that—you've made it to the final section of the book. In this part, you'll learn specifics for making the Office 95 programs work together, like a happy little family (although some programs may exhibit slight dysfunctional tendencies, but you can resolve these problems with small amounts of group therapy). You'll find instructions for using Excel data in a PowerPoint slide, Schedule+ data in a Word document, PowerPoint presentations in a Word file, and much, much more. Armed with this knowledge, you can make your Office 95 package pay for itself! And isn't that what it's all about anyway?

Chapter 25

Organize Your Project Files into Binders

In This Chapter

➤ Find out how to combine your documents into electronic binders

➤ Create your own binder sections in a few easy steps

➤ Save and print your binders and share them around the office

Way back at the beginning of the book, I told you about some new Office 95 features that Microsoft added. Well, one of those features is an *electronic binder* that you can use to combine different program files into one collection—Microsoft even dubbed it "Binder." In this chapter, I'm going to tell you how to use this new feature, and you won't even have to get out a hole puncher to do it.

What Is a Binder?

The idea behind the Binder feature is that it lets you combine common files, regardless of what program they're from, and put them into an electronic version of a notebook

Definition Change Up until this point in the book, the term *document* referred to a file created in a word processing program. In computer-speak, however, a document can be anything— a Word file, a spreadsheet file, a database file, or a presentation file. So, for the remainder of this chapter, when you see the word *document*, don't think of it as only applying to word processing files. Documents in your binder can be any kind of file.

binder. The files themselves can be copies or originals. Once you combine several files into a binder, you can open them and work with them much more readily than starting and stopping Office applications. In other words, you can switch back and forth between programs without having to use the taskbar.

Most people are familiar with regular old notebook binders; you use them to hold papers and related documents. Typically, you punch holes in your papers and insert them into a metal three-ring binder device, which holds everything together. Well, the electronic version of a binder works the same way, without the holes punched in, of course. You can combine files to create reports, organizers, proposals, and whatever else you can think of that can benefit from a collection of related files. Binders will help you stay organized and keep your important files within easy reach.

Opening Your Binder Feature

Before you start using your Office 95 Binder, you have to find it. Back in Chapter 6, I recommended that you customize your Office Shortcut bar. One of the buttons you can add to the bar is the Binder button. That's what I did, so all I have to do to open the Binder is to click the Binder button on my Shortcut bar. (Turn back to Chapter 6 for steps to customize your Shortcut bar.)

Another way to open the Binder is to use the traditional route:

1. Open the **Start** button on your Windows 95 desktop.

2. Select **Programs** from the Start menu.

3. Select **Microsoft Binder**, and the Binder box appears on-screen, as shown in the next figure.

Granted, there's not much to look at the first time you open the Binder feature; it doesn't even fill up the screen. Don't be too heartbroken; you'll have to add documents of your own to create a binder. The second figure on the next page shows what happens when you start adding documents to your binder file.

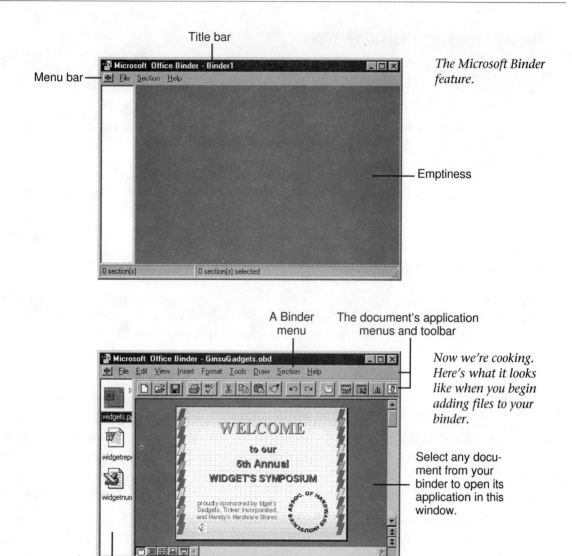

Title bar

Menu bar

Emptiness

The Microsoft Binder feature.

A Binder menu

The document's application menus and toolbar

Now we're cooking. Here's what it looks like when you begin adding files to your binder.

Select any document from your binder to open its application in this window.

The documents in your binder appear here.

The files shown in the binder in the preceding figure include a Word document, a worksheet from Excel, and a slide presentation from PowerPoint. You can even add files from other programs outside of your Office 95 package.

Navigating the Binder Box

When the Binder dialog box opens onto your screen, it's relatively small. If you don't like dealing with the small window size, you can enlarge it. Click the **Maximize** button. The menu bar at the top of the Binder box lists three menus.

The **File** menu lets you open new binders and existing binders, print binders—all the typical File menu commands.

The **Section** menu is where the binder commands hang out.

The **Help** menu holds the typical online help elements explained back in Chapter 5.

Next, I'm going to tell you how to start creating your own binders. Are you ready?

Create Your Own Binder

If you just give this binder concept some thought, I'll bet you can come up with all kinds of information you'd like to group together into your binder files. You can then pass along the entire binder to others on your network, or other Office 95 users.

Adding Sections to Your Binder

By default, a blank binder appears every time you open the Binder feature. To add files to it, use one of these methods:

➤ Drag-and-drop existing documents into the left pane of the Binder box. (Remember how to drag and drop? Click the item, hold down your left mouse button, and drag it to a new location.)

➤ Open the **Section** menu and select **Add** (use this method to start a new document).

➤ Open the **Section** menu and select **Add from File**, which lets you designate which file you want included in the binder.

New Binder, Please
Whenever you want to start a new binder, open the **File** menu and choose **New Binder**. This is different than opening a new file; it starts another binder window running.

I typically add files to a binder that I've already created with the other Office 95 programs. To do the same, follow these steps:

1. Open the Binder box. Open the **Start** menu, select **Programs** and **Microsoft Binder**.

2. Open the **Section** menu, and select **Add from File**. This opens the Add from File dialog box, which looks suspiciously like the Open dialog box you've been using all along.

3. Locate the folder and file you want to copy into a binder.

4. Click the **Add** button, and the document becomes a section in your binder dialog box.

Repeat these steps to add more files to the binder.

Remember, when you add a file to a binder, an icon appears in the left pane, and the right pane opens to reveal the document along with a menu bar and toolbar for editing the document. To view a file in the Binder box, click the file icon at the left of the Binder box. If you're having trouble seeing a file's entire name on the left side of the screen, just hover you mouse pointer over the file icon for a minute; the name appears in full.

If you prefer to create new files for the binder, use the **Add** command on the **Section** menu. When selected, it opens the Add Section dialog box, which you can then use to open any of your Office 95 programs and create new documents out of them.

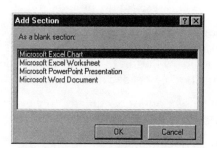

Can I Rename My Binder Sections? Like you even had to ask that... of course, you can. Select the binder document icon you want to rename and open the **Section** menu. Select the **Rename** command and type a new name for the document. This won't change the name of the original document you copied, in case you were wondering.

The Add Section dialog box.

Choose a document type from the dialog box and click **OK** to add a section to the binder and open the application in the right window pane.

Working with Binders

Okay, now that you've added some files to your binder, you probably want to know what to do with them, but first, I'll tell you a little more about using the Binder commands.

You've worked with the File menu and the Help menu before with other programs, but the *Section* menu is new. You'll use the commands on the Section menu to add documents to your binders, delete them, duplicate them, rename them, and more. When you've added a document to the binder, the menu bar changes to reflect the document's originating application. Subsequently, the File and Help menus must share commands with the application, but the Section menu stays the same. So, what I'm trying to tell you is that the three Binder menus are always available in the Binder dialog box, but the File and Help menu may reflect additional commands in them based on what application appears in the dialog box.

Once you've placed a document into a binder, its originating application opens up in the window on the right side of the dialog box. (The Microsoft people are calling the left and right side of the Binder dialog box *panes*.) The binder file appears as an icon on the left side of the box, in the left pane. They call the documents that you add to the binder *sections*. (Don't forget this; it's important.)

The application window displaying your document also includes toolbars and menu commands for making changes to the document, or in the case of new documents, adding data. (Warning: Not all of the toolbar buttons work with the program's file contents. For example, the New and Save commands will activate Binder commands, not the program's New and Save functions.) You can use these toolbar buttons and menu commands to your heart's content, but if you'd rather work on the application in its entire program window, you'll need to open the **Section** menu and select **View Outside**. This lets you see the document in its original program window, outside of the Binder box.

Here are some ways you can select documents and change your binder views:

➤ If you ever want more room to work with the document in its application window, you can close up the left pane showing the icons (alias *sections*). Just click the double-headed arrow button to the left of the File menu. To open the left pane again, click the double-headed arrow button again.

➤ You can select a section (or document) to view and work with in the binder window by clicking the document's icon in the left pane.

➤ To select several documents in a row, click the first one, and then hold down the **Shift** key and click the last document.

➤ To select noncontiguous documents, hold down the **Ctrl** key while selecting icons.

➤ To select all the documents in a binder, open the **Section** menu and choose **Select All**.

➤ To move binder documents around, drag them to their new locations, either in the current window or into another binder window. You can even move them into the Windows Explorer, My Computer, or onto the Windows 95 desktop. You can also drag files from the Windows Explorer and other places into your binder.

➤ To hide a section in the binder window, click inside the document, open the **Section** menu, and select **Hide**.

Printing and Saving Binders

After you've filled a binder with all the necessary documents, you'll want to save it. Follow these steps:

1. Open the **File** menu, select **Save Binder** or **Save Binder As**.

2. This opens the typical dialog box for saving files. Type in your binder name and designate which folder you want to save it in.

3. Click the **Save** button to save the binder and exit the dialog box.

When you save your binder, it's automatically given an OBD extension to distinguish it as a binder file. I thought you might like to know that in case there's a pop quiz later.

You can also print your binder sections. Open the **File** menu and select **Print Binder**. Make any adjustments to the Print Binder dialog box, and click **OK** to print. Under the Print What area in the dialog box, you can choose to print all of the Binder sections (all the files you've collected in the binder) or just selected sections.

Once you create a binder file, you can easily zip in and out of the files you've stored there without having to re-open applications. You can also pass along the binder file to other Office 95 users and they can access the files as well.

The Least You Need to Know

The first time I used the Binder feature, I was very impressed; it's great to be able to group related documents into one file.

➤ Use binders to combine related files into a kind of electronic three-ring notebook.

➤ The files you place into your binder become sections.

➤ You can save your binders and send them to other people on your network.

Chapter 26

Putting Word to Work

In This Chapter

➤ Insert data from Excel into Word

➤ Create an Excel worksheet without ever leaving your Word program

➤ Link an entire PowerPoint slide show into your Word document

➤ Whip up a form letter using your Schedule+ contact list

It's about time you learned how to integrate all of these Office 95 programs. In this chapter (and the chapters in the rest of Part 4), I'll go over ways in which you can make the Office 95 applications work together, combining their power and features to make computer tasks easier for you.

First up in our integration shuffle is Word for Windows. I'll show you some specific integration tasks to make Word work for you. These tasks involve some OLE, as well as some simple copy and paste techniques. Word is unique from all the Office 95 programs; it inevitably becomes the *host program* when integrating parts of the other programs

What Does Integration Mean, Anyway? *Integration* is the act of uniting different programs and program elements to make them work together.

(okay, not always, but usually). Why? Because everyone loves their word processing program; it's the easiest thing to use to build a report on your market analysis or scientific breakthroughs, to write form letters, or to create any type of textual document. You'll soon find yourself filling your own Word documents with charts from Excel, graphics from PowerPoint, lists from Schedule+, and more.

What Can I Integrate with Word?

You can integrate any of the other Office 95 programs with your Word documents. Granted, there are already a zillion things you can do with your Word documents without any help from other programs, however, when you start thinking of tapping into the features and capabilities of the other programs and combining them with Word, then the sky's the limit.

Let's talk specifics here... you can copy, paste, link, and embed data from the other Office programs into your Word documents. You've already learned about these specific commands in the previous chapters. But what about learning how to turn an Excel range into Word text, making a form letter with the help of your Schedule+ contact list, or linking an entire slide presentation to your document? Now we're talking nitty-gritty integration steps. (I'll cover these very tasks in this chapter!)

To better explain what kind of integrating tasks I'm talking about, let me give you some examples. Let's say you're creating a lovely little club newsletter using Word. In one of your newsletter articles, you want to use a chart you created in Excel as a picture in your document. You can easily copy the chart from Excel and paste it into your newsletter. If you want the chart to automatically update itself when the original changes, you can link the chart. Or, if you only want to edit the chart from its original location, you can embed it into your newsletter. There are a lot of possibilities—take a look at Exhibit A on the next page to see what I mean.

What About Integrating with Other Microsoft Programs? Good question. And the answer is: you can integrate your Office 95 programs with other Microsoft applications, such as Access (a database program), so don't hesitate to try.

As you can see, when you start branching out and using the power and capabilities of the other Office 95 programs in your Word documents, you can add to your Word program and enhance your productivity. The rest of this chapter gives you specific instructions for completing some popular integrating tasks.

The PowerPoint program showing the embedded slide

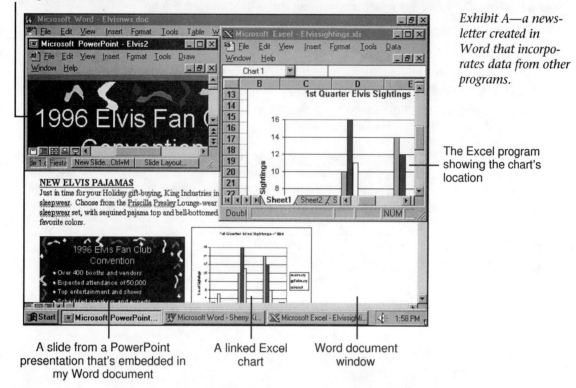

Exhibit A—a newsletter created in Word that incorporates data from other programs.

The Excel program showing the chart's location

A slide from a PowerPoint presentation that's embedded in my Word document

A linked Excel chart

Word document window

Using Excel Data in Your Word Document

There are dozens of ways to integrate Excel data. You can move, copy, link, or embed worksheet data from Excel into your Word documents. Likewise, you can insert an entire spreadsheet or only a range of cells—and that's only the tip of the iceberg. Being the considerate author that I am, I'll show you how to do all of this.

Turning an Excel Range into a Word Table

Here's something interesting for those of you who like interesting things. When you copy a range of cells from Excel and paste them into a Word document, they automatically appear as a Word table. How about that? The text retains the formatting you gave it in Excel, but you can easily edit the data at any time when it's in Word.

To copy a range of cells from Excel:

1. Open the Excel worksheet containing the cells you want to copy.

2. Select the range, and click the **Copy** button in the toolbar or open the **Edit** menu and select **Copy**.

3. Open the Word document to which you want to copy the cell data, and click in the place where you want the data to appear.

4. Finally, open the **Edit** menu and select **Paste**, or click the **Paste** button on the toolbar. The Excel range suddenly appears in your Word file as a table.

An Excel range turns into a table when you paste it into Word.

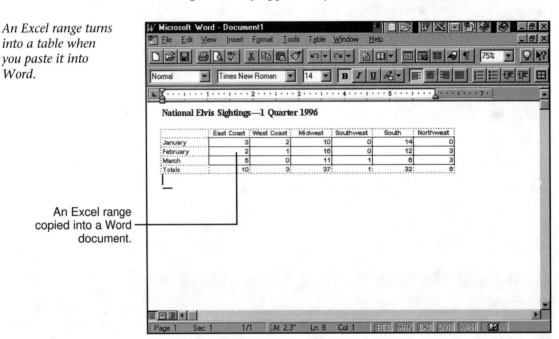

An Excel range copied into a Word document.

You can select the data for editing and use the Word calculation features to change it, but you cannot use the original Excel formulas any longer to change your data. Why? Because you used a regular copy and paste technique instead of a link.

Interested in Some Drag-and-Drop Fun?

There's another method for embedding from one program to another using the drag-and-drop technique. In order to use this, however, you have to have the two program windows open at the same time. Use the Window menu to tile the windows on your screen (see Chapter 4). For example, to drag-and-drop between Excel and Word, open both program windows on-screen at the same time. Select the Excel data you want to copy, point to the edge of the selected data, hold down the **Ctrl** key and the left mouse button, and drag the data into the Word window to where you want the data to appear. Release the mouse button and the Ctrl key, and the data is embedded. What a neat trick.

Embedding and Linking an Excel Chart into Word

When you embed a chart into Word, you can still use the Excel features to control the way it looks, and you can still use its formulas and other calculations. To embed a chart:

1. Open the Excel file containing the chart you want to embed.
2. Select the chart, and select the **Edit**, **Copy** command. (If you prefer, you can click the **Copy** button on the toolbar.)
3. Open the Word document and click in the place where you want to embed the chart.
4. Open the **Edit** menu and choose **Paste Special**. The Paste Special dialog box appears.
5. Click the **Paste** option.
6. In the **As** list box, select the **Object** type.
7. Click **OK** to exit the box and the chart appears in your Word document.

To make changes to it, simply double-click it. This opens the chart in an Excel window where you can apply all of the Excel tools.

If you link the range of cells into your Word document, you still have an active connection to the original formulas. To link the range of cells, open the Word document into which you want to paste the range, pull down the **Edit** menu, and choose **Paste Special**. The Paste Special dialog box appears. To link the range, click the **Paste Link** option button.

Inserting an Entire Worksheet into Word

You can insert an entire spreadsheet into your Word document. Use these steps to do so:

1. Open the Word document and click where you want to place the spreadsheet.

2. Open the **Insert** menu and choose **Object**.

3. In the Object dialog box, click the **Create from File** tab to bring it to the front.

4. Type in the name of the spreadsheet file you want to insert. If you're not sure of the file name, click the **Browse** button and locate the folder and file from the Browse dialog box.

5. Click **OK**; click **OK** again and the entire file appears in your Word document.

To link the entire spreadsheet to Word, click the **Link to File** check box in the Object dialog box.

Make a Worksheet Without Leaving Word

Hey, did you know you can create a spreadsheet without ever leaving your Word file? Want to know how? Use the *OfficeLinks* technology.

1. First, in your Word document, click in the location where you want to place the worksheet.

2. Click the **Insert Microsoft Excel Worksheet** button on the standard toolbar, and a drop-down diagram of columns and rows appears.

3. In the diagram, drag over the number of columns and rows you want to use, and release the mouse button. (To see even more columns and rows displayed, move your mouse pointer beyond the right or bottom diagram border.)

4. A worksheet appears in your Word document, and Excel menus and toolbars appear at the top of your window.

Add whatever data you want to the worksheet, taking advantage of Excel's tools. When you finish working on your worksheet, click anywhere outside the worksheet area to return to your Word controls.

The Insert Microsoft Excel Worksheet button

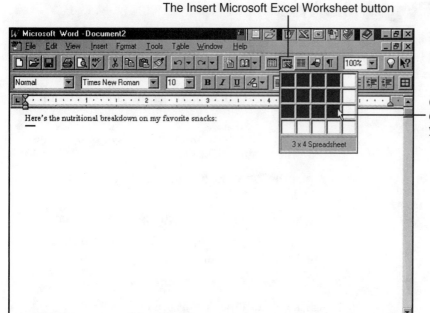

I'll bet you didn't know Word came with an automatic worksheet maker.

Choose the number of columns and rows you want to use.

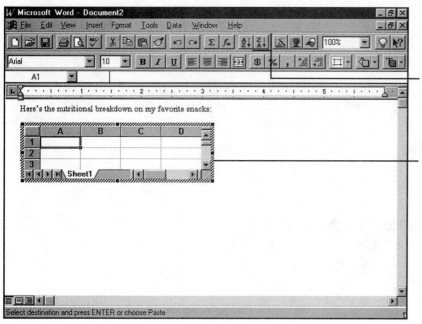

The new worksheet is empty and ready to be filled.

My Word menus and toolbars changed into Excel menus and toolbars.

The new worksheet appears as a window in my Word document.

343

Turning Excel Ranges into Text

A few paragraphs ago, you learned that any ranges you import into Word automatically become Word tables. But if you prefer, you can turn the range of cells into text instead. Follow these steps to make this scenario happen:

Oops! If you've already pasted a range of cells into Word (which turns it into a table, you can still convert it into text. Simply select the table, and open the **Table** menu. Choose the **Convert Table to Text** command.

1. Open the Excel file and select the range you want to use.

2. Click the **Copy** button on the toolbar, or open the **Edit** menu and choose **Copy**.

3. Open the Word document and click where you want the data to appear.

4. Open the **Edit** menu and choose **Paste Special**.

5. In the Paste Special dialog box that appears, choose the **Paste** option button.

6. In the **As** list box, select **Unformatted Text**.

7. Click **OK**, and the deed is done.

Treating Excel Data as a Picture in Word

Here's yet another cool trick I'm passing on to you: if you treat an Excel chart or range of cells as a picture in Word, it won't take up as much room in the file. Don't wrinkle your nose at me. If you're hard pressed for file space, a smaller file can be a blessing. However, you only want to use this technique if you don't need to edit the Excel data again.

The neat thing about making the Excel data act like a picture in Word is that you can treat it like a piece of clip art. This means you can easily crop it and resize it (flip back to Chapter 17 for tips on resizing and cropping). To insert Excel data into Word as a picture:

1. Open the Excel file and select the data.

2. Press and hold the **Shift** key, open the **Edit** menu, and select **Copy Picture**. The Copy Picture dialog box appears.

The Copy Picture dialog box.

3. Select any options you want to use and click **OK**.

4. Open your Word document and click where you want to insert the Excel data/picture.

5. Click the **Paste** button on the toolbar, or open the **Edit** menu and choose **Paste**. You can now move the data around as if it were a graphic object.

Moving PowerPoint Slides into Word

I know you won't be surprised at this, but you can easily turn your PowerPoint slides into Word data. In fact, you can even turn an entire PowerPoint slide show into a document in Word. Those good old OLE techniques will come into play again in this section.

Inserting a PowerPoint Slide into Word

Let's start with something simple, putting one of your PowerPoint slides into a Word document. Ready?

1. Open the PowerPoint presentation containing the slides you want to embed.

2. Click the **Slide Sorter** view button, and select the specific slide you want to use. To select a single slide, click it.

Check This Out...

I Want More Than One Slide

To select more than one slide to use in Word, hold down the **Ctrl** key and click each slide in Slide Sorter view.

3. Click the **Copy** button, or open the **Edit** menu and choose the **Copy** command.

4. Open the Word document and click where you want to copy the PowerPoint data.

5. Click the **Paste** button on the toolbar, or open the **Edit** menu and choose **Paste**. That's it. If you prefer to link or embed the slide instead, select the **Paste Special** command in the **Edit** menu. You can easily edit a linked or embedded slide by double-clicking it.

My Friend Doesn't Have PowerPoint

Okay, so what if you pass along your Word document with embedded PowerPoint data to someone who doesn't have PowerPoint? Don't worry, Word has a PowerPoint Viewer, a separate application for viewing PowerPoint slides while in Word. (If it wasn't installed with your Microsoft Office 95 package, use the Office Setup procedure to install it.)

If you don't want to copy a whole slide into Word, copy the text or graphic from the slide. Select the specific text or graphic you want to copy, and click the **Copy** button on the toolbar. Or open the **Edit** menu and choose the **Copy** command. Open the Word document and click where you want to insert the text or graphic. Click the **Paste** button on the toolbar, or open the **Edit** menu and choose **Paste**. You can choose to link or embed the object by using the **Paste Special** command instead.

Linking an Entire Slide Presentation

Perhaps you'd like to connect a PowerPoint slide presentation to your Word document so you can run the presentation at the click of a button while in Word. This is a handy tool, especially if you are using your Word document to instruct someone (rather like a tutorial). The student could read a few paragraphs and click a button in the text to start the show.

To set this up, follow these steps:

1. First switch over to your PowerPoint presentation.

2. In Slide Sorter view, select all the slides. (You can open the **Edit** menu and choose **Select All**, or you can click each slide while holding down the **Shift** key.)

3. Once you select your entire program, click the **Copy** button on the toolbar, or open the **Edit** menu and choose **Copy**.

4. Open the Word document and click where you want to insert the program.

5. Open the **Edit** menu and choose **Paste Special**.

6. In the Paste Special dialog box, click the **Paste Link** option button and select the **Object** type from the **As** list box.

7. Instead of inserting every slide picture into your Word document, click the **Display as Icon** check box. The presentation appears as an icon in your Word document.

8. Click **OK** to exit the dialog box.

You have now linked the presentation. To view the slide show from your Word document, double-click the icon.

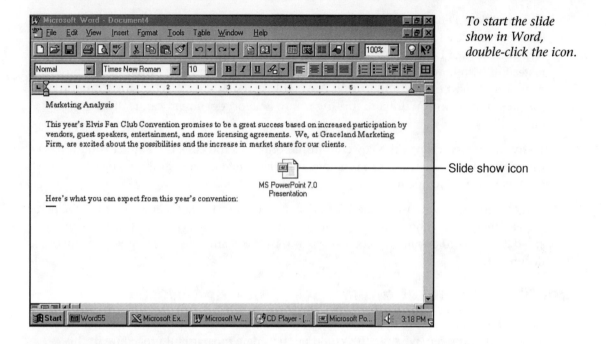

To start the slide show in Word, double-click the icon.

Slide show icon

Embedding Several Slides

You can easily insert more than one slide into a Word document using the Paste Special command. To embed several slides:

1. Open the PowerPoint presentation containing the slides and switch to Slide Sorter view.

2. Select the slides you want by holding down the **Shift** key as you click each one.

3. After you've selected your slides, click the **Copy** button, or open the **Edit** menu and choose the **Copy** command.

4. Open the Word document and click where you want to copy the PowerPoint slides.

5. Open the **Edit** menu and choose **Paste Special**.

6. In the Paste Special dialog box, click **OK**.

7. To view all of the slides you selected, open the **Edit** menu again, choose **Microsoft Office Presentation Object**, and select **Show**.

Turning a PowerPoint Presentation into a New Word Document

You can take an entire PowerPoint presentation and import it into Word in Rich Text Format to make a text-based Word document. This turns the presentation into a text format instead of individual slide boxes, and makes it look as if you created it with Word instead of with PowerPoint. Why would you want to do that? Well, what if your boss demands a report based on that swell PowerPoint presentation you designed? Importing the presentation into Word and turning it into a report document can really help you out.

To try this yourself, open the PowerPoint presentation and click the **Report It** button on the Standard toolbar. The Word program automatically launches and the PowerPoint text appears in your document.

You can now save your work as a Word document file instead of a PowerPoint file. Open the **File** menu and choose **Save As**. Name the file and save it as a Word file. Once you've saved it as a Word document, you can open it in Word and edit it as you would any other document.

Creating a Form Letter with Schedule+ and Word

Here's the part where I tell you how to make Word and Schedule+ work together to make a form letter. It's very possible this could be the single most useful procedure in this whole chapter (especially if you work for Publishers' Clearinghouse). So listen up.

Form letters (as you well know after receiving thousands of them in the mail each year) are letters in which you use the same information over and over again but change pertinent information, such as the recipient's name and address. Computers have made the art of creating form letters commonplace and practical. Okay, marketing people, pay attention.

1. Start by opening up a new Word document.

2. Select the **Tools** menu and choose **Mail Merge**. The Mail Merge Helper dialog box appears.

3. Click the **Create** button.

4. In the list box that drops down, select **Form Letters**.

5. Click the **Active Window** button in the next dialog box.

6. Back in the Mail Merge box, click the **Get Data** button. Another list box drops down.

7. Choose **Use Address Book**, and the Use Address Book dialog box appears.

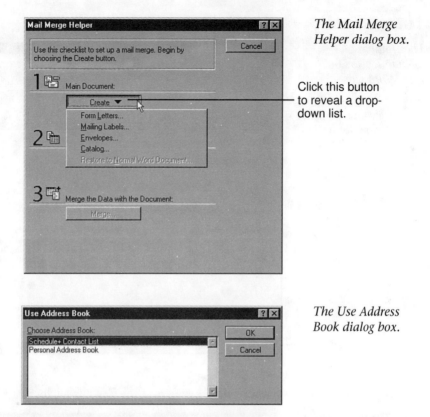

The Mail Merge Helper dialog box.

Click this button to reveal a drop-down list.

The Use Address Book dialog box.

8. From the list, select **Schedule+ Contact List** and click **OK**.

9. In the next dialog box that appears, click the **Edit Main Document** button.

10. The Database toolbar pops up on your screen. Is your head spinning yet? You're not done, so breathe deeply and keep going.

11. In your Word working area, build your form letter. Go ahead; type everything in. When you reach a place where you want to use information from your Access database, click the **Insert Merge Field** button on the Database toolbar. A list appears, showing all the fields you selected. Choose the field that contains the data you want and that will appear in your Word text with special brackets.

12. When you finish composing your letter and inserting fields from your database, click the **View Merged Data** button on the Database toolbar. You'll see how your form letter looks with real data displayed (see the following figure). Use the **Record** buttons to view different data in the fields.

349

The Database toolbar appears on your Word screen.

Click here to insert a field into your form letter.

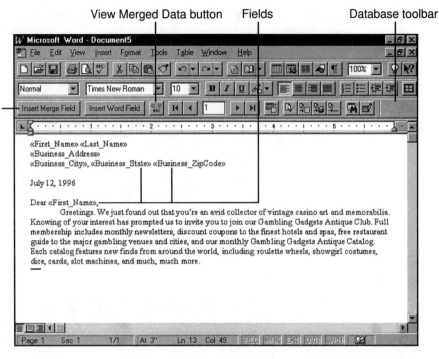

Cool! The form letter shows all the fields and even real data.

My fields are filled in with record data from Schedule+.

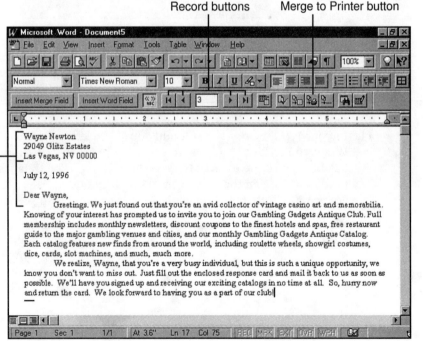

13. When you're ready to merge everything, click the **Merge to Printer** button if you want to print out every letter based on your database.

14. To save your letter, open the **File** menu and choose **Save**.

Congratulations—you're an official marketing engineer now.

Using Word as an E-Mail Editor

Hey, e-mail users—if you're using Microsoft Exchange and you chose to use the Custom installation of Office 95 and selected the option to use Word as a mail editor, then guess what? You can use Word to create e-mail messages! With WordMail, you can take advantage of all the great formatting features found in your Word program.

Here's how to install WordMail on your system (you may have to get out your Office CD-ROM or disks to do this):

1. Open the Microsoft Office setup program. You can do this from your Office Shortcut bar. Open the **Microsoft Office** menu, and select **Add/Remove Office Programs**.

2. Click **Add/Remove**, select the **Microsoft Word** check box; then click the **Change Option** button.

3. In the Options box, click the **WordMail** option.

After you install the WordMail option, you're ready to use it (as long as you have Microsoft Exchange installed). Follow these steps:

1. Open your Microsoft Exchange program. (Click the **Start** button on the taskbar, select **Programs** and **Microsoft Exchange**.)

2. Pull-down the **Compose** menu; select **WordMail Options**.

3. In the **WordMail Options** box, select the **Enable Word as Email Editor** check box.

> **Check This Out...**
>
> **Need Some Matching Envelopes?** You can also use your Word program to make mailing labels to go with your form letters. Be sure to consult your Word manual for help, or ask the Answer Wizard feature on your online Help system.

> **Techno Talk**
>
> **What's Microsoft Exchange?** It's a new program for Windows 95 that lets you organize and share all kinds of electronic mail messages. You can use it to send e-mail to other people on your network, attach files from other programs to the messages you send, and keep an Address Book of e-mail names and addresses.

The WordMail Options box.

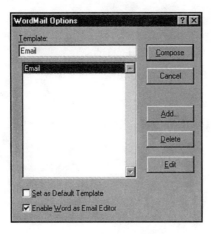

4. Choose the **Email** template, and click **Compose** to put it into effect. Now, whenever you compose an e-mail message, you can use Word's wonderful formatting controls to give your messages punch and pizzazz.

Consult your manual or network administrator for more information about sending and receiving electronic mail.

The Least You Need to Know

Integrating with Word involves a variety of commands and procedures:

➤ Word is the most commonly used host program for combining program elements.

➤ There are several ways for you to insert all or part of Excel, PowerPoint, or Schedule+ files into Word documents.

➤ You can apply Copy and Paste commands to move data from other programs into Word.

➤ You can use all of the exciting OLE features you learned about in Part 3 of this book.

Chapter 27

Excelling at Excel

In This Chapter

➤ Insert Word data into your Excel worksheets

➤ Turn a Word table into an Excel range

➤ Link a PowerPoint slide into a single cell

Integrating programs can seem a little complicated sometimes. However, I have some good news for you: you're over the worst part of the integration business. Most people do the majority of their integration work in their word-processing programs (which I covered in the last chapter). That's not to say there aren't some great integration tasks to use with the other programs, such as Excel. There are, so that's what I'll show you in this chapter.

What Can I Integrate with Excel?

You can integrate any of the other Office 95 programs with your Excel spreadsheets. Mind you, I realize there are already tons of impressive things you can do with your Excel worksheets on their own without any help from other programs. However, when you start using the amazing capabilities of the other programs with Excel, well, there's no end to what you can do.

You can perform the typical copy, paste, link, and embed functions (which you've already learned about) with data from the other Office 95 programs and place them into your Excel worksheets. But how about learning how to turn a Word table into worksheet cells, or copying PowerPoint slides into your Excel worksheet? That's real integrating, you know. I'll show you all about these very tasks in this chapter!

Take a look at the figure to see how integration can happen to your own worksheets. I've linked and embedded both data from Word and PowerPoint.

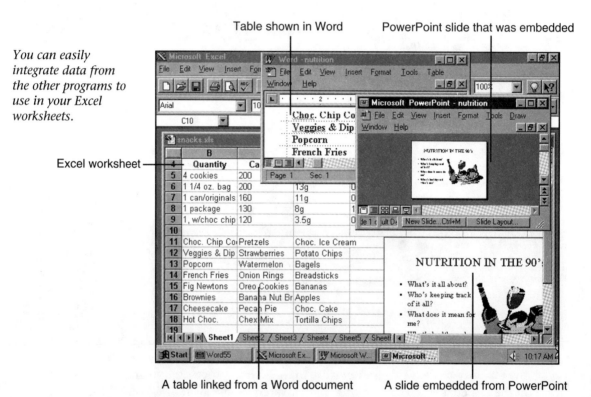

You can easily integrate data from the other programs to use in your Excel worksheets.

Don't be afraid to delve into the other programs for data to use in your Excel worksheets. You can truly increase Excel's power by tapping into the other resources. In the rest of this chapter, I'll show you some popular integrating tasks for working with Excel.

Cramming Word into Worksheets

In the last chapter, I taught you how to pull some worksheet data into Word documents. This time, we'll do the reverse: we'll move Word data into Excel. Ready?

Using Word Text in an Excel Worksheet

Naturally, you can cut, copy, and paste text from a Word document into an Excel worksheet anytime. By text, I mean a single word, a sentence, a paragraph, or an entire document. You can paste text into cells, into the formula bar, or into an Excel text box (a special box you create on your worksheet for holding text).

To copy text from Word:

1. First open the Word document and select the text you want to insert into Excel.

2. Click the **Copy** button on the toolbar, or open the **Edit** menu and choose **Copy**.

3. Then open the Excel worksheet and click where you want to insert the text.

4. Click the **Paste** button on the toolbar, or open the **Edit** menu and choose **Paste**. You can also link or embed text from Word into Excel. To do so, use the **Paste Special** command in the **Edit** menu when you're ready to paste the copied data into place.

When you link data into Excel, the cell into which you insert it contains a link formula, called an *array formula*. For more information about array formulas, check out Excel's online Help feature.

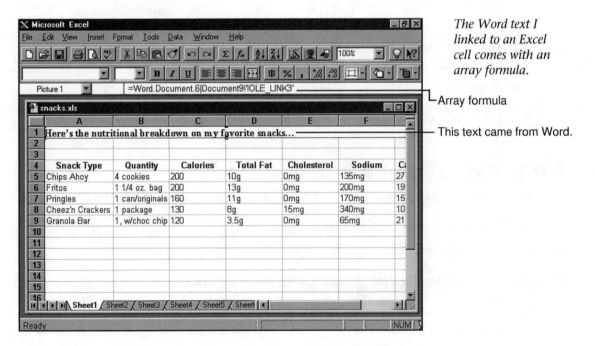

The Word text I linked to an Excel cell comes with an array formula.

Array formula

This text came from Word.

Drag-and-Drop It

Another method for embedding from one program to another is to use the drag-and-drop routine. You have to have the two program windows open at the same time to do this little trick. (Press **Alt+Esc** to view the Windows 95 taskbar; then right-click the taskbar and select one of the Tile commands to tile the windows on your screen—see Chapter 4.) For example, to drag-and-drop between Word and Excel, open both programs on-screen at the same time. Then select the Word data you want to copy, point to the edge of the selected data, press and hold the **Ctrl** key and the left mouse button, and drag the data into the Excel window to the place where you want the data to appear. Release the mouse button and the Ctrl key, and the data is embedded.

Converting a Word Table into Worksheet Cells

What if you have a table in Word that you want to use in Excel? No problem. Here are the steps:

1. Open your Word program and select the table.

2. Pull down the **Edit** menu and choose **Copy**, or click the **Copy** button on the toolbar.

3. Then open the Excel file and click where you want the upper left cell of the table to be.

4. Pull down the **Edit** menu and choose **Paste** (or choose **Paste Special** if you plan to link or embed the table instead). You can also click the **Paste** button in the toolbar. Each cell of your Word table appears in a corresponding cell in the worksheet.

Using PowerPoint Information in Excel

Word's not the only program whose data you can integrate into Excel worksheets. You can do the same with PowerPoint data. You can select specific elements from a PowerPoint presentation and copy them into a workbook at any time. You can also link an entire presentation to your Excel spreadsheet and play it when you want.

Placing a PowerPoint Slide in a Worksheet

By now, you've learned how incredibly easy it is to copy and paste bits and pieces of data from one program into another using the Windows Clipboard. You can apply the same techniques to copy text, graphics, or entire slides from PowerPoint into Excel. This time, let me show you how to embed a slide into an Excel worksheet.

1. Open the PowerPoint presentation containing the slide you want to copy.

2. Switch to Slide Sorter view and select the slide you want to use.

3. Click the **Copy** button on the toolbar, or open the **Edit** menu and choose **Copy**.

4. Then open your Excel worksheet and click in the cell where you want the slide to appear.

5. Pull down the **Edit** menu and choose **Paste Special**.

6. Select the Object type from the **As** list box, and click **OK**. The slide embeds in your worksheet. To edit the slide at any time, double-click it.

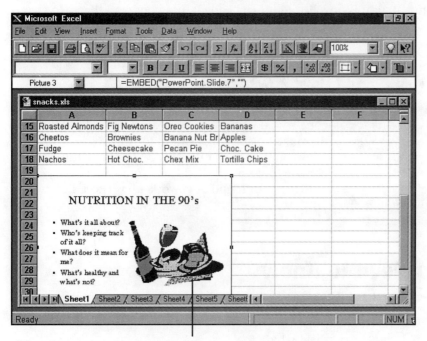

An embedded PowerPoint slide in a worksheet cell.

A slide in my Excel worksheet

Inserting an Entire Slide Show into Excel

You can link an entire PowerPoint presentation into your Excel file; you can make it appear as an icon in a cell. Then, to see the show, you just double-click the icon. Are you intrigued by this task? Good, because I've written down the instructions to tell you how to do it. You don't even have to leave your Excel program.

1. Click the cell where you want the presentation icon to appear.

2. Open the **Insert** menu and choose **Object**.

3. In the Object dialog box, click the **Create from File** tab to bring it to the front.

4. Locate the folder containing the PowerPoint presentation you want to use, and select the file name. (If you're not sure of the file name, click the **Browse** button and look for it in the Browse dialog box.)

5. Click the **Link to File** check box to link the presentation to your Excel file (if you don't select this text box, the presentation is embedded instead).

6. Click the **Display as Icon** check box.

7. Click **OK** to exit the dialog box and return to your worksheet.

The PowerPoint presentation is now linked (or embedded) into your worksheet. To view the slide show, double-click the icon.

Techno Talk

blah blah
blah bla
h bl
b

My Friend Doesn't Have PowerPoint!

Let's say you want to pass along your Excel worksheet with embedded PowerPoint data to someone who doesn't have PowerPoint. Don't worry, Excel has a PowerPoint Viewer, a separate application for viewing PowerPoint slides while in Excel. (If it wasn't installed with your Office 95 package, use the Office Setup procedure to install it. Check out your Office 95 manual for details.) Therefore, as long as your friend or coworker has Excel, he or she can still view the slide show. Isn't that nice?

The Least You Need to Know

Integrating with Excel is a breeze. You can pull a number of different types of data into your worksheets.

➤ Word tables make great worksheet tables, too.

➤ You can use the OLE power to link an entire slide show into a single cell and play it back at any time.

Chapter 28

Making PowerPoint Jump Through Hoops

In This Chapter

➤ Turn your Word text into a PowerPoint presentation

➤ The lowdown on making tables into slides

➤ Make a presentation out of Excel data

Being the dynamic presentation program that it is, PowerPoint only gets better when you start linking and embedding data from Word or Excel. In the end, your slide show is a beacon of light in the dim world of graphic presentations and boring speeches.

What Can I Integrate with PowerPoint?

That's an easy question to answer. You can integrate any of the other Office 95 programs with any presentation elements you create in PowerPoint. (You can even integrate non-Microsoft programs.) Yes, PowerPoint is a pretty impressive program all by itself, but it gets even better when you start adding components from the other Microsoft Office 95 applications. If you thought you already knew how to put together a dynamite presentation back in Chapters 16, 17, and 18, you're really going to knock 'em out by integrating features from the rest of your Office 95 software package.

Of course, you can copy, paste, link, and embed data into your slides, just like you can with Word documents and Excel spreadsheets (you learned all about using these commands in earlier chapters). But why not try turning an outline created in Word into a slide show, or making an Excel chart act like a graphic? These are the down-to-business integration steps we'll go over in this chapter.

To give you an illustration of what kind of integrating tasks I'm alluding to, take a look at the figure for some examples. It shows several forms of data used in a slide, and the programs from which the data came. See how nicely it all ties together?

When you integrate data from other programs, your slide shows know no bounds.

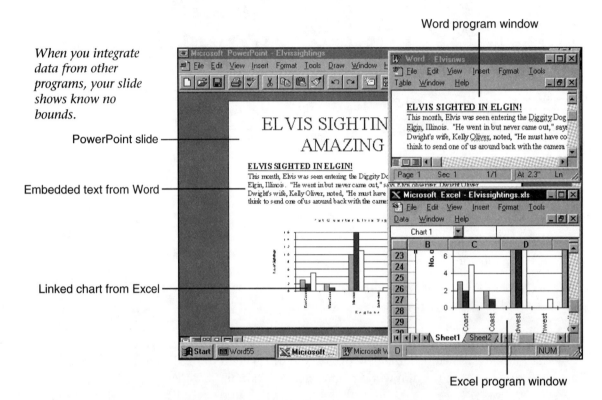

Word program window

PowerPoint slide

Embedded text from Word

Linked chart from Excel

Excel program window

You'll find many occasions to use data from Word and Excel in your PowerPoint materials, whether it's slides or handouts. The ability to link the data will keep your presentations current, and the visual potential is there to create a slide out of just about anything. The rest of this chapter goes over some popular integrating tasks you'll use with any or all of your PowerPoint presentations.

Wrestling Word into PowerPoint

Okay, don't just sit there; start integrating. Word and PowerPoint make very nice companions, and you'll probably be surprised at the various tasks they can share. The following information details those tasks. Just follow the instructions closely and the two programs will be sharing data in no time at all.

Linking Word Text in PowerPoint

As usual, we'll start out with the easy stuff. You can copy and paste Word text in its many forms into your presentation slides. Use the Copy and Paste commands for that. You can also link and embed Word text into PowerPoint. Let me show you how.

1. Open the Word document containing the text you want to copy.
2. Select the text (or graphic or whatever you're copying) and click the **Copy** button in the toolbar. You can also pull down the **Edit** menu and choose **Copy**.
3. Open your PowerPoint presentation to the slide to which you want to copy the text.
4. Pull down the **Edit** menu, and select **Paste Special**.
5. In the Paste Special dialog box, click the **Paste Link** option button.
6. Click **OK**, and your Word text links into your PowerPoint slide. Note that you may have to move the object to where you want it in the slide.

Embedding Word Tables

For your next trick, you'll embed a Word table into a PowerPoint slide without ever leaving the PowerPoint screen. Roll up your sleeves—no need to hide a table there. Follow along, you budding magicians... .

You may not have noticed this, but in your PowerPoint Slide Layout dialog box, there's a Table layout.

1. Open your PowerPoint file to the slide into which you want to insert a table.
2. Click the **Layout** button in the bottom right corner of your status bar, and the Slide Layout dialog box opens.

Table layout

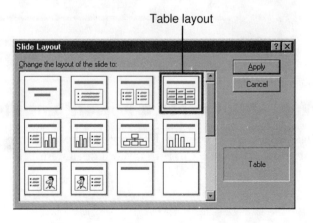

The Slide Layout dialog box.

3. Click the Table layout image (the last one in the first row of the layouts) and click the **Apply** button.

4. Back on your slide screen, double-click the Table icon, and the Insert Word Table dialog box pops up.

5. Indicate the number of columns and rows you want in your table and click **OK**.

6. Suddenly, a blank Word table appears in your slide, and your PowerPoint menus and toolbars change into Word menus and toolbars. Go ahead and enter your table information.

7. When you finish, click outside of the table window, and you return to the PowerPoint screen and menus.

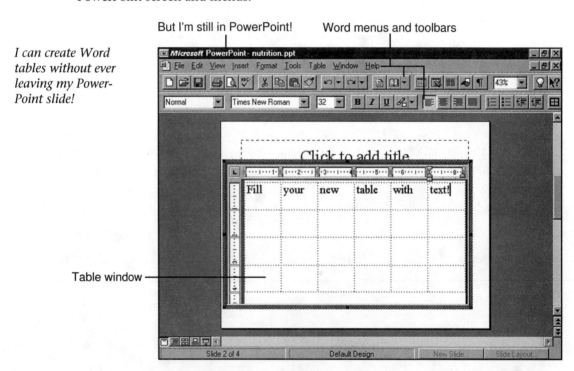

But I'm still in PowerPoint!   Word menus and toolbars

I can create Word tables without ever leaving my Power-Point slide!

Table window

Turning Your Word Outline into a PowerPoint Presentation

As you learned back in Part 2, you can build PowerPoint presentations based on outlines. What you may not know is that you can turn a Word document into a PowerPoint outline with only a few simple commands.

362

1. First, open your Word document containing the text you want to use in the outline.

2. Switch over to Outline view by pulling down the **View** menu and choosing **Outline**.

3. Fix your document as you want it to appear in the presentation and save it (make sure you close your Word document before moving on).

4. Then open your PowerPoint program.

5. In PowerPoint, pull down the **File** menu and select **Open**.

6. In the Open dialog box, locate the Word folder and the file you just saved. Under Files of type, choose **Word**. Click **Open** and your document becomes a presentation.

Psst! Over Here! Want to know another way to embed a Word table? Click the **Insert Microsoft Word Table** button on your PowerPoint toolbar. Define your table size in the drop-down diagram, and voilá—a table is born!

Excel Data Meets PowerPoint Slides

I'm getting dizzy from all this integration excitement. It's a good thing I'm sitting down in front of a computer, or I could seriously hurt myself. In the next round, Excel meets PowerPoint—this is an exciting match.

Inserting a Range into PowerPoint

I must remind you that all the copying and pasting commands enable you to insert Excel data into PowerPoint just as you would insert data from any other program. So if you feel like copying the data from an Excel cell into a PowerPoint slide, just do it. You know how. The same linking and embedding technology applies, too. However, to keep you sharp, I'll show you specific steps for linking a range of cells into a slide.

1. Open your Excel spreadsheet and access the worksheet containing the data you want to copy.

2. Select the range of cells.

3. Pull down the **Edit** menu and choose **Copy**. Or you can click the **Copy** button on the toolbar.

4. Switch over to your PowerPoint presentation and go to the slide where you want to insert the data.

5. Click where you want the data to appear.

6. Pull down the **Edit** menu and choose **Paste Special**.

7. In the Paste Special dialog box, click the **Paste Link** option button.

8. Select **Microsoft Excel Worksheet Object** from the As list box, and click **OK**. The data is inserted.

Inserting an Entire Spreadsheet into PowerPoint

Maybe copying bits and pieces of your Excel worksheet isn't enough for you. Maybe you want more; maybe you want to turn the entire spreadsheet into a slide. Okay, here's how to embed a worksheet into PowerPoint.

1. Start from the PowerPoint slide into which you want to embed the Excel worksheet.

2. Open the **Insert** menu and select **Object**.

3. In the Insert Object dialog box, click the **Create from File** option button.

4. If you know the name of the file you're inserting, type it in the **File** text box. (If you don't know the file's name, click the **Browse** button to open a dialog box from which you can select the Excel folder and file you want to use. This option is particularly handy for those of you with short-term memories.)

5. Click **OK** to exit the dialog box (if you opened the Browse dialog box, you'll have to click **OK** again).

The worksheet embeds into your PowerPoint slide.

The Least You Need to Know

Had enough integration yet? Come on now, you have to admit it has made your life easier somehow. This is what you were supposed to have learned in this chapter:

➤ You can turn your Word text and tables into powerful presentation images.

➤ You can select a Word table layout from your Slide Layout dialog box.

➤ Use object linking and embedding commands to link Excel ranges into your PowerPoint slides.

Speak Like a Geek: The Complete Archive

cell   The intersection of a column and a row in an Excel worksheet. Cells can contain data and formulas for calculations.

client   A program that receives copied, linked, or embedded data from other programs.

clip art   A collection of images that your computer stores as graphic files.

Clipboard   A temporary storage area in Windows that saves data that you copy or move until you are ready to place it in a new location. The Clipboard only holds the last item that you copy or move.

command   An instruction that tells the computer what to do.

cursor   A vertical line that appears to the right of the text characters that you type.

data   Information a computer works with and stores.

database   A computer program used for storing, organizing, and retrieving information.

desktop   The area on your Windows 95 computer screen from which you can open programs, remove files with the Recycle Bin, view other drives, and more.

destination document   The file receiving data that has been copied, linked, or embedded from another file or program.

dialog box   A smaller window/box that displays more options from which to choose. Dialog boxes usually appear when the program needs more information from you in order to carry out the task.

document (or file)   A page, or pages, created in a word-processing program.

e-mail   Stands for electronic mail. E-mail is any message sent to another network user.

embedding   An OLE feature that enables you to copy data from one program into another program, but still retain a viewing or editing connection to the original program.

Excel   A spreadsheet program made by Microsoft. You can use Excel to organize numbers and other data, perform complex mathematical operations, and much more.

field   A category of information used to build a database. A field can be a name, a number, or any type of category imaginable.

file   Anytime you save your work, such as a document or a spreadsheet, your computer stores all of the data as a file. Each file has a unique name, and you can save your files on your computer's hard disk or on a floppy disk.

filter   A technique for looking up data that involves specifying criteria and results in a temporary datasheet of records. Your computer uses filters to convert graphics files from one format to another so different programs can use them.

font   A set of characters sharing the same design.

formatting   Changing the appearance of your text characters.

formulas   Calculations that your computer performs on spreadsheet values.

graphical user interface (GUI, pronounced "GOO-ey")   A program interface that uses graphical elements such as icons, dialog boxes, and pull-down menus. Macintosh computers and the Windows program are examples of GUIs.

graphics   Electronic art and pictures. A graphic can be a drawing created on the computer, an image scanned in for digital manipulation (clip art), or various shapes, lines, and boxes created with the computer.

icon   A graphic image that represents a command, a program, or a feature.

integration   In computerese, the process of uniting different programs and program elements and making them work together.

labels   Worksheet data that is treated as text and cannot be calculated.

linking   An OLE feature that allows you to copy data from one program into another, yet still maintain an active link to the source data. Anytime you change or update the source data, you also update the linked data.

maximize   To enlarge your window to fill the entire screen.

memory   The computer's electronic storage area measured in bits and bytes of data. The computer can only hold a certain amount of bits and bytes, so you can also refer to memory as the amount of room available for use on a hard drive or a floppy disk.

menu   A list of commands. Menus appear as drop-down or pull-down lists. You can select an item on the menu list by highlighting it and pressing **Enter** or by clicking it with the mouse.

minimize   To reduce your window to a button on the taskbar.

network   Connecting several computers together for the purpose of sharing information.

OLE   Short for object linking and embedding, OLE is a technology for sharing data from different programs.

online   To be connected to another computer or network of computers.

PowerPoint   A presentation graphics program made by Microsoft. Use PowerPoint to create visual presentations on your computer.

presentation graphics program   Also called business presentation graphics, a program made especially for designing visual presentations in a few easy steps. You supply the content, and the program helps with the design.

program   A special set of instructions written for the computer, telling it how to do something. You'll hear the words *program*, *software*, and *application* used interchangeably; they all mean the same thing.

record   A collection of fields making one complete entry in a database.

Schedule+   A personal information manager program from Microsoft designed to help you manage your schedule, coordinate meetings, and keep track of to do lists and contacts.

selection letters   Specially marked letters in the menu names and menu commands that you can press in conjunction with the Alt key to activate menus or tasks. Most Windows-based programs show selection letters as underlined letters.

server   A program that acts as the source or lending program when copying, linking, or embedding data.

shortcut keys   Keypress combinations designed to circumvent a menu or command selection.

source document   The originating program or file from which you can copy, link, or embed data.

spreadsheet A program made to imitate a ledger's rows and columns, which you use to organize and display data. You can use spreadsheets to perform complex mathematical functions upon the values entered.

style A collection of specifications for formatting text.

subset A group of records created from data specified in a filter.

taskbar The bar at the bottom of your Windows 95 desktop that lets you switch back and forth between programs or launch new programs with the Start button.

template A pattern for a document page that predetermines fonts, sizes, and other formatting specifications.

text file A type of file that contains no special formatting, just plain text.

values Worksheet data that is numerical in nature and can be calculated.

virus detection A virus is a computer program written for the express purpose of vandalizing your system or harming your data files. A virus-detection program can prevent a virus from infecting your computer.

Windows A graphical user interface (GUI) program from Microsoft. Windows makes the computer easier to interact with. Instead of making the user memorize commands and type them at a command prompt, Windows uses icons, pull-down menus, and dialog boxes with lists of commands that you can select with a mouse.

Windows 95 Microsoft's new and improved Windows program. It no longer requires DOS to run; Windows 95 is its own operating system. It's faster, sleeker, looks better, and runs better; you have to have it installed in order to use the Microsoft Office 95 programs.

Word A word-processing program made by Microsoft that you can use to create all kinds of text documents.

word processing A program designed especially for working with text and creating documents.

workbook A collection of Excel worksheets in one file.

worksheet A page in an Excel workbook in which you enter data.

Index

G

H

P-Q

383

W

X-Z